Thomas Wallace Knox

John

Or, Our Chinese Relations

Thomas Wallace Knox

John
Or, Our Chinese Relations

ISBN/EAN: 9783337169893

Printed in Europe, USA, Canada, Australia, Japan

Cover: Foto ©ninafisch / pixelio.de

More available books at **www.hansebooks.com**

AROUND THE TEA-TABLE.

BY
T. DE WITT TALMAGE,
Author of "*Crumbs Swept Up,*" "*Abominations of Modern Society,*"
"*Old Wells Dug Out,*" Etc.

PUBLISHED BY
THE CHRISTIAN HERALD,
Louis Klopsch, Proprietor,
BIBLE HOUSE, NEW YORK.

Copyright 1895.
By Louis Klopsch.

Press and Bindery of
HISTORICAL PUBLISHING CO.,
PHILADELPHIA.

PREFACE.

At breakfast we have no time to spare, for the duties of the day are clamoring for attention; at the noon-day dining hour some of the family are absent; but at six o'clock in the evening we all come to the tea-table for chit-chat and the recital of adventures. We take our friends in with us—the more friends, the merrier. You may imagine that the following chapters are things said or conversations indulged in, or papers read, or paragraphs, made up from that interview. We now open the doors very wide and invite all to come in and be seated around the tea-table.

T. DeW. T.

Brooklyn, N. Y.

CONTENTS.

CHAP.		PAGE
I.	The table-cloth is spread	17
II.	Mr. Givemfits and Dr. Butterfield	23
III.	A growler soothed	27
IV.	Carlo and the freezer	31
V.	Old games repeated	37
VI.	The full-blooded cow	41
VII.	The dregs in Leatherbacks' teacup	46
VIII.	The hot axle	50
IX.	Beefsteak for ministers	56
X.	Autobiography of an old pair of scissors	60
XI.	A lie, zoologically considered	65
XII.	A breath of English air	70
XIII.	The midnight lecture	74
XIV.	The sexton	79
XV.	The old cradle	84
XVI.	The horse's letter	89
XVII.	Kings of the kennel	94
XVIII.	The massacre of church music	99
XIX.	The battle of pew and pulpit	104
XX.	The devil's grist-mill	111
XXI.	The conductor's dream	116
XXII.	Push & Pull	121
XXIII.	Bostonians	125

CHAP.		PAGE
XXIV.	—Jonah vs. the whale	129
XXV.	—Something under the sofa	131
XXVI.	—The way to keep fresh	134
XXVII.	—Christmas bells	137
XXVIII.	—Poor preaching	139
XXIX.	—Shelves a man's index	142
XXX.	—Behavior at church	147
XXXI.	—Masculine and feminine	153
XXXII.	—Literary felony	156
XXXIII.	—Literary abstinence	159
XXXIV.	—Short or long pastorates	161
XXXV.	—An editor's chip basket	163
XXXVI.	—The manhood of service	166
XXXVII.	—Balky people	168
XXXVIII.	—Anonymous letters	170
XXXIX.	—Brawn or brain	174
XL.	—Warm-weather religion	181
XLI.	—Hiding eggs for Easter	185
XLII.	—Sink or swim	190
XLIII.	—Shells from the beach	194
XLIV.	—Catching the bay mare	198
XLV.	—Our first and last cigar	202
XLVI.	—Move, moving, moved	205
XLVII.	—The advantage of small libraries	210
XLVIII.	—Reformation in letter writing	215
XLIX.	—Royal marriages	217
L.	—Three visits	219
LI.	—Manahachtanienks	224
LII.	—A dip in the sea	226
LIII.	—Hard shell considerations	230

CHAP. PAGE
LIV.—Wiseman, Heavyasbricks and Quizzle 234
LV.—A layer of waffles 247
LVI.—Friday evening 263

SABBATH EVENINGS.

LVII.—The Sabbath evening tea-table . 271
LVIII.—The warm heart of Christ 273
LIX.—Sacrifice everything 277
LX.—The youngsters have left 280
LXI.—Family prayers 291
LXII.—A call to sailors 295
LXIII.—Jehoshaphat's shipping 298
LXIV.—All about mercy 303
LXV.—Under the camel's saddle . . . 308
LXVI.—Half-and-half churches 314
LXVII.—Thorns 317
LXVIII.—Who touched me? 320

AROUND THE TEA-TABLE.

CHAPTER I.

THE TABLE-CLOTH IS SPREAD.

Our theory has always been, "Eat lightly in the evening." While, therefore, morning and noon there is bountifulness, we do not have much on our tea-table but dishes and talk. The most of the world's work ought to be finished by six o'clock p. m. The children are home from school. The wife is done mending or shopping. The merchant has got through with drygoods or hardware. Let the ring of the tea-bell be sharp and musical. Walk into the room fragrant with Oolong or Young Hyson. Seat yourself at the tea-table wide enough apart to have room to take out your pocket-handkerchief if you want to cry at any pitiful story of the day, or to spread yourself in laughter if some one propound an irresistible conundrum.

The bottle rules the sensual world, but the teacup is queen in all the fair dominions. Once this leaf was very rare, and fifty dollars a pound; and when the East India Company made a present to the king of two pounds and two ounces, it was considered worth a mark in history. But now Uncle Sam and his wife every year pour thirty million pounds of it into their saucers. Twelve hundred years ago, a Chinese scholar by the name of Lo Yu wrote of tea, "It tempers the spirits and harmonizes the mind, dispels lassitude and relieves fatigue, awakens thought and prevents drowsiness, lightens and refreshes the body, and clears the perceptive faculties." Our own observation is that there is nothing that so loosens the hinge of the tongue, soothes the temper, exhilarates the diaphragm, kindles sociality and makes the future promising. Like one of the small glasses in the wall of Barnum's old museum, through which you could see cities and mountains bathed in sunshine, so, as you drink from the tea-cup, and get on toward the bottom so that it is sufficiently elevated, you can see almost anything glorious that you want to. We had a great-aunt who used to come from town with the pockets of her bombazine dress standing way out with nice things for the children, but she would come in looking black as a thunder cloud until she had got through with her first cup of tea, when she would empty her right pocket of sugar-plums, and having finished her second cup would empty the other pocket, and after she had taken an extra third cup, because she felt so very chilly, it took all the sitting-room and parlor and kitchen to contain her exhilaration.

Be not surprised if, after your friends are seated at the table, the style of the conversation depends very much on the kind of tea that the housewife pours for the guests. If it be genuine Young Hyson, the leaves of which are gathered early in the season, the talk will be fresh, and spirited, and sunshiny. If it be what the Chinese call Pearl tea, but our merchants have named Gunpowder, the conversation will be explosive, and somebody's reputation will be killed before you get through. If it be green tea, prepared by large infusion of Prussian blue and gypsum, or black tea mixed with pulverized black lead, you may expect there will be a poisonous effect in the conversation and the moral health damaged. The English Parliament found that there had come into that country two million pounds of what the merchants call "lie tea," and, as far as I can estimate, about the same amount has been imported into the United States; and when the housewife pours into the cups of her guests a decoction of this "lie tea," the group are sure to fall to talking about their neighbors, and misrepresenting everything they touch. One meeting of a "sewing society" up in Canada, where this tea was served, resulted in two law-suits for slander, four black eyes that were not originally of that color, the expulsion of the minister, and the abrupt removal from the top of the sexton's head of all capillary adornment.

But on our tea-table we will have first-rate Ningyong, or Pouchong, or Souchong, or Oolong, so that the conversation may be pure and healthy.

We propose from time to time to report some of the talk of our visitors at the tea-table. We do not entertain at tea many very great men. The fact is that great men at the tea-table for the most part are a bore. They are apt to be self-absorbed, or so profound I cannot understand them, or analytical of food, or nervous from having studied themselves half to death, or exhume a piece of brown bread from their coat-tail because they are dyspeptic, or make such solemn remarks about hydro-benzamide or sulphindigotic acid that the children get frightened and burst out crying, thinking something dreadful is going to happen. Learned Johnson, splashing his pompous wit over the table for Boswell to pick up, must have been a sublime nuisance. It was said of Goldsmith that "he wrote like an angel and talked like poor

Poll." There is more interest in the dining-room when we have ordinary people than when we have extraordinary.

There are men and women who occasionally meet at our tea-table whose portraits are worth taking. There are Dr. Butterfield, Mr. Givemfits, Dr. Heavyasbricks, Miss Smiley and Miss Stinger, who come to see us. We expect to invite them all to tea very soon; and as you will in future hear of their talk, it is better that I tell you now some of their characteristics.

Dr. Butterfield is one of our most welcome visitors at the tea-table. As his name indicates, he is both melting and beautiful. He always takes pleasant views of things. He likes his tea sweet; and after his cup is passed to him, he frequently hands it back, and says, "This is really delightful, but a little more sugar, if you please." He has a mellowing effect upon the whole company. After hearing him talk a little while, I find tears standing in my eyes without any sufficient reason. It is almost as good as a sermon to see him wipe his mouth with a napkin. I would not want him all alone to tea, because it would be making a meal of sweetmeats. But when he is present with others of different temperament, he is entertaining. He always reminds me of the dessert called floating island, beaten egg on custard. On all subjects—political, social and religious—he takes the smooth side. He is a minister, and preached a course of fifty-one sermons on heaven in one year, saying that he would preach on the last and fifty-second Sunday concerning a place of quite opposite character; but the audience assembling on that day, in August, he rose and said that it was too hot to preach, and so dismissed them immediately with a benediction. At the tea-table I never could persuade him to take any currant-jelly, for he always preferred strawberry-jam. He rejects acidity.

We generally place opposite him at the tea-table Mr. Givemfits. He is the very antipodes of Dr. Butterfield; and when the two talk, you get both sides of a subject. I have to laugh to hear them talk; and my little girl, at the controversial collisions, gets into such hysterics that we have to send her with her mouth full into the next room, to be pounded on the back to stop her from choking. My friend Givemfits is "down on" almost everything but tea, and I think one reason of his nervous, sharp, petulant way is that he takes too much of this beverage. He thinks the world is very soon coming to an end, and says, "The sooner the better, confound it!" He is a literary man, a newspaper writer, a book critic, and so on; but if he were a minister, he would preach a course of fifty-one sermons on "future punishment," proposing to preach the fifty-second and last Sabbath on "future rewards;" but the last Sabbath, coming in December, he would say to his audience, "Really, it is too cold to preach. We will close with the doxology and omit the benediction, as I must go down by the stove to warm."

He does not like women—thinks they are of no use in the world, save to set the tea a-drawing. Says there was no trouble in Paradise till a female came there, and that ever since Adam lost the rib woman has been to man a bad pain in the side. He thinks that Dr. Butterfield, who sits opposite him at the tea-table, is something of a hypocrite, and asks him all sorts of puzzling questions. The fact is, it is vinegar-cruet against sugar-bowl in perpetual controversy. I do not blame Givemfits as much as many do. His digestion is poor. The chills and fever enlarged his spleen. He has frequent attacks of neuralgia. Once a week he has the sick headache. His liver is out of order. He has twinges of rheumatism. Nothing he ever takes agrees with him but tea, and that doesn't. He has had a good deal of trial, and the thunder of trouble has soured the milk of human kindness. When he gets criticising Dr. Butterfield's sermons and books, I have sometimes to pretend that I hear somebody at the front door, so that I can go out in the hall and have an uproarious laugh without being indecorous. It is one of the great amusements of my life to have on opposite sides of my tea-table Dr. Butterfield and Mr. Givemfits.

But we have many others who come to our tea-table: Miss Smiley, who often runs in about six o'clock. All sweetness is Miss Smiley. She seems to like everybody, and everybody seems to like her. Also Miss Stinger, sharp as a hornet, prides herself on saying things that cut; dislikes men; cannot bear the sight of a pair of boots; loathes a shaving apparatus; thinks Eve would have shown better capacity for housekeeping if she had, the first time she used her broom, swept Adam out of Paradise. Besides these ladies, many good, bright, useful and sensible people of all kinds. In a few days we shall invite a group of them to tea, and you shall hear some of their discussions of men and books and things. We shall order a canister of the best Young Hyson, pull out the extension-table, hang on the kettle, stir the blaze, and with chamois and silver-powder scour up the tea-set that we never use save when we have company.

CHAPTER II.

MR. GIVEMFITS AND DR. BUTTERFIELD.

The tea-kettle never sang a sweeter song than on the evening I speak of. It evidently knew that company was coming. At the appointed time our two friends, Dr. Butterfield and Mr. Givemfits, arrived. As already intimated, they were opposite in temperament—the former mild, mellow, fat, good-natured and of fine digestion, always seeing the bright side of anything; the other, splenetic, harsh, and when he swallowed anything was not sure whether he would be the death of it, or it would be the death of him.

No sooner had they taken their places opposite each other at the table than conversation opened. As my wife was handing the tea over to Mr. Givemfits the latter broke out in a tirade against the weather. He said that this winter was the most unbearable that had ever been known in the almanacs. When it did not rain, it snowed; and when it was not mud, it was sleet. At this point he turned around and coughed violently, and said that in such atmosphere it was impossible to keep clear of colds. He thought he would go South. He would rather not live at all than live in such a climate as this. No chance here, save for doctors and undertakers, and even they have to take their own medicines and lie in their own coffins. At this Dr. Butterfield gave a good-natured laugh, and said, "I admit the inconveniences of the weather; but are you not aware that there has been a drought for three years in the country, and great suffering in the land for lack of rain? We need all this wet weather to make an equilibrium. What is discomfort to you is the wealth of the land. Besides that, I find that if I cannot get sunshine in the open air I can carry it in the crown of my hat. He who has a warm coat, and a full stove, and a comfortable house, ought not to spend much of his time in complaint."

Miss Smiley slid this moment into the conversation with a hearty "Ha! ha!" She said, "This last winter has been the happiest of my life. I never hear the winds gallop but I want to join them. The snow is only the winter in blossom. Instead of here and there on the pond, the whole country is covered with white lilies. I have seen gracefulness enough in the curve of a snowdrift to keep me in admiration for a week. Do you remember that morning after the storm of sleet, when every tree stood in mail of ice, with drawn sword of icicle? Besides, I think the winter drives us in, and drives us together. We have never had such a time at our house with checker-boards and dominoes, and blind-man's-buff, and the piano, as this winter. Father and mother said it seemed to them like getting married over again. Besides that, on nights when the storm was so great that the door-bell went to bed and slept soundly, Charles Dickens stepped in from Gad's Hill; and Henry W. Longfellow, without knocking, entered the sitting-room, his hair white as if he had walked through the snow with his hat off; and William H. Prescott, with his eyesight restored, happened in from Mexico, a cactus in his buttonhole; and Audubon set a cage of birds on the table—Baltimore oriole, chaffinch, starling and bobolink doing their prettiest; and Christopher North thumped his gun down on the hall floor, and hung his 'sporting jacket' on the hat-rack, and shook the carpet brown with Highland heather. As Walter Scott came in his dog scampered in after him, and put both paws up on the marble-top table; and Minnie asked the old man why he did not part his hair better, instead of letting it hang all over his forehead, and he apologized for it by the fact that he had been on a long tramp from Melrose Abbey to Kenilworth Castle. But I think as thrilling an evening as we had this winter was with a man who walked in with a prison-jacket, his shoes mouldy, and his cheek pallid for the want of the sunlight. He was so tired that he went immediately to sleep. He would not take the sofa, saying he was not used to that, but he stretched himself on the floor and put his head on an ottoman. At first he snored dreadfully, and it was evident he had a horrid dream; but after a while he got easier, and a smile came over his face, and he woke himself singing and shouting. I said, 'What is the matter with you, and what were you dreaming about?' 'Well,' he said, 'the bad dream I had was about the City of Destruction, and the happy dream was about the Celestial City;' and we all knew him right away, and shouted, 'Glorious old John Bunyan! How is Christiana?' So, you see," said Miss Smiley, "on stormy nights we really have a pleasanter time than when the moon and stars are reigning."

Miss Stinger had sat quietly looking into her tea-cup until this moment, when she clashed her spoon into the saucer, and said, "If there is anything I dislike, it is an attempt at poetry when you can't do it. I know some people who always try to show themselves in public; but when they are home, they never have their collar on straight, and in the morning look like a whirlwind breakfasting on a haystack. As for me, I am practical, and winter is winter, and sleet is sleet, and ice is ice, and a tea-cup is a tea-cup; and if you will pass mine up to the hostess to be resupplied, I will like it a great deal better than all this sentimentalism. No sweetening, if you please. I do not like things sweet. Do not put in any of your beautiful snow for sugar, nor stir it with an icicle."

This sudden jerk in the conversation snapped it off, and for a moment there was quiet. I knew not how to get conversation started again. Our usual way is to talk about the weather; but that subject had been already exhausted.

Suddenly I saw the color for the first time in years come into the face of Mr. Givemfits. The fact was that, in biting a hard crust of bread, he had struck a sore tooth which had been troubling him, and he broke out with the exclamation, "Dr. Butterfield, the physical and moral world is degenerating. Things get worse and worse. Look, for instance, at the tone of many of the newspapers; gossip, abuse, lies, blackmail, make up the chief part of them, and useful intelligence is the exception. The public have more interest in murders and steamboat explosions than in the items of mental and spiritual progress. Church and State are covered up with newspaper mud."

"Stop!" said Dr. Butterfield. "Don't you ever buy newspapers?"

CHAPTER III.

A GROWLER SOOTHED.

Givemfits said to Dr. Butterfield, "You asked me last evening if I ever bought newspapers. I reply, Yes, and write for them too.

"But I see their degeneracy. Once you could believe nearly all they said; now he is a fool who believes a tenth part of it. There is the New York 'Scandalmonger,' and the Philadelphia 'Prestidigitateur,' and the Boston 'Prolific,' which do nothing but hoodwink and confound the public mind. Ten dollars will get a favorable report of a meeting, or as much will get it caricatured. There is a secret spring behind almost every column. It depends on what the editor had for supper the night before whether he wants Foster hung or his sentence commuted. If the literary man had toast and tea, as weak as this before me, he sleeps soundly, and next day says in his columns that Foster ought not to be executed; he is a good fellow, and the clergymen who went to Albany to get him pardoned were engaged in a holy calling, and their congregations had better hold fast of them lest they go up like Elijah. But if the editor had a supper at eleven o'clock at night of scallops fried in poor lard, and a little too much bourbon, the next day he is headachy, and says Foster, the scalawag, ought to be hung, or beaten to death with his own carnook, and the ministers who went to Albany to get him pardoned might better have been taking tea with some of the old ladies. I have been behind the scenes and know all about it, and must admit that I have done some of the bad work myself. I have on my writing-stand thirty or forty books to discuss as a critic, and the column must be made up. Do you think I take time to read the thirty or forty books? No. I first take a dive into the index, a second dive into the preface, a third dive into the four hundredth page, the fourth dive into the seventieth page, and then seize my pen and do up the whole job in fifteen minutes. I make up my mind to like the book or not to like it, according as I admire or despise the author. But the leniency or severity of my article depends on whether the room is cold and my rheumatism that day is sharp or easy. Speaking of these things reminds me that the sermon which the Right Reverend Bishop Goodenough preached last Sunday, on 'Growth in Grace,' was taken down and brought to our office by a reporter who fell over the door-sill of the sanctum so drunk we had to help him up and fish in his pockets for the bishop's sermon on holiness of heart and life, which we were sure was somewhere about him."

"Tut! tut!" cried Dr. Butterfield. "I think, Mr. Givemfits, you are entirely mistaken. (The doctor all the while stirring the sugar in his cup.) I think the printing-press is a mighty agency for the world's betterment. If I were not a minister, I would be an editor. There are Bohemians in the newspaper profession, as in all others, but do not denounce the entire apostleship for the sake of one Judas. Reporters, as I know them, are clever fellows, worked almost to death, compelled to keep unseasonable hours, and have temptations to fight which few other occupations endure. Considering the blunders and indistinctness of the public speaker, I think they get things wonderfully accurate. The speaker murders the king's English, and is mad because the reporter cannot resuscitate the corpse. I once made a speech at an ice-cream festival amid great embarrassments, and hemmed, and hawed, and expectorated cotton from my dry mouth, and sweat like a Turkish bath, the adjectives, and the nouns, and verbs, and prepositions of my address keeping an Irish wake; but the next day, in the 'Johnstown Advocate,' my remarks read as gracefully as Addison's 'Spectator.' I knew a phonographer in Washington whose entire business it was to weed out from Congressmen's speeches the sins against Anglo-Saxon; but the work was too much for him, and he died of delirium tremens, from having drank too much of the wine of syntax, in his ravings imagining that 'interrogations' were crawling over him like snakes, and that 'interjections' were thrusting him through with daggers and 'periods' struck him like bullets, and his body seemed torn apart by disjunctive conjunctions. No, Mr. Givemfits, you are too hard. And as to the book-critics whom you condemn, they do more for the circulation of books than any other class, especially if they denounce and caricature, for then human nature will see the book at any price. After I had published my book on 'The Philosophy of Civilization,' it was so badgered by the critics and called so many hard names that my publishers could not print it fast enough to meet the demands of the curious. Besides, what would we do without the newspaper? With the iron rake of the telegraph it draws the whole world to our door every morning. The sermon that the minister preached to five hundred people on Sabbath the newspaper next day preaches to fifty thousand. It takes the verses which the poet chimed in his small room of ten feet by six, and rings them into the ears of the continent. The cylinder of the printing-press is to be one of the wheels of the Lord's chariot. The good newspapers will overcome the bad ones, and the honey-bees will outnumber the hornets. Instead of the three or four religious newspapers that once lived on gruel and pap, sitting down once a week on some good man's door-step to rest, thankful if not kicked off, now many of the denominations have stalwart journals that swing their scythe through the sins of the world, and are avant couriers of the Lord's coming."

As Dr. Butterfield concluded this sentence his face shone like a harvest moon. We had all dropped our knives, and were looking at him. The Young Hyson tea was having its mollifying effect on the whole company. Mr. Givemfits had made way with his fourth cup (they were small cups, the set we use for company), and he was entirely soothed and moderated in his opinions about everything, and actually clapped his hands at Dr. Butterfield's peroration. Even Miss Stinger was in a glow, for she had drank large quantities of the fragrant beverage while piping hot, and in her delight she took Givemfits' arm, and asked him if he ever meant to get married. Miss Smiley smiled. Then Dr. Butterfield lifted his cup, and proposed a toast which we all drank standing: "The mission of the printing-press! The salubrity of the climate! The prospects ahead! The wonders of Oolong and Young Hyson!"

CHAPTER IV.

CARLO AND THE FREEZER.

We had a jolly time at our tea-table this evening. We had not seen our old friend for ten years. When I heard his voice in the hall, it seemed like a snatch of "Auld Lang Syne." He came from Belleville, where was the first home we ever set up for ourselves. It was a stormy evening, and we did not expect company, but we soon made way for him at the table. Jennie was very willing to stand up at the corner; and after a fair napkin had been thrown over the place where she had dropped a speck of jelly, our friend and I began the rehearsal of other days. While I was alluding to a circumstance that occurred between me and one of my Belleville neighbors the children cried out with stentorian voice, "Tell us about Carlo and the freezer;" and they kicked the leg of the table, and beat with both hands, and clattered the knives on the plate, until I was compelled to shout, "Silence! You act like a band of Arabs! Frank, you had better swallow what you have in your mouth before you attempt to talk." Order having been gained, I began:

We sat in the country parsonage, on a cold winter day, looking out of our back window toward the house of a neighbor. She was a model of kindness, and a most convenient neighbor to have. It was a rule between us that when either house was in want of anything it should borrow of the other. The rule worked well for the parsonage, but rather badly for the neighbor, because on our side of the fence we had just begun to keep house, and needed to borrow everything, while we had nothing to lend, except a few sermons, which the neighbor never tried to borrow, from the fact that she had enough of them on Sundays. There is no danger that your neighbor will burn a hole in your new brass kettle if you have none to lend. It will excite no surprise to say that we had an interest in all that happened on the other side of the parsonage fence, and that any injury inflicted on so kind a woman would rouse our sympathy.

On the wintry morning of which we speak our neighbor had been making ice-cream; but there being some defect in the machinery, the cream had not sufficiently congealed, and so she set the can of the freezer containing the luxury on her back steps, expecting the cold air would completely harden it. What was our dismay to see that our dog Carlo, on whose early education we were expending great care, had taken upon himself the office of ice-cream inspector, and was actually busy with the freezer! We hoisted the window and shouted at him, but his mind was so absorbed in his undertaking he did not stop to listen. Carlo was a greyhound, thin, gaunt and long-nosed, and he was already making his way on down toward the bottom of the can. His eyes and all his head had disappeared in the depths of the freezer. Indeed, he was so far submerged that when he heard us, with quick and infuriate pace, coming up close behind him, he could not get his head out, and so started with the encumbrance on his head, in what direction he knew not. No dog was ever in a more embarrassing position—freezer to the right of him, freezer to the left of him, freezer on the top of him, freezer under him.

So, thoroughly blinded, he rushed against the fence then against the side of the house, then against a tree. He barked as though he thought he might explode the nuisance with loud sound, but the sound was confined in so strange a speaking-trumpet that he could not have known his own voice. His way seemed hedged up. Fright and anger and remorse and shame whirled him about without mercy.

A feeling of mirthfulness, which sometimes takes me on most inappropriate occasions, seized me, and I sat down on the ground, powerless at the moment when Carlo most needed help. If I only could have got near enough, I would have put my foot on the freezer, and, taking hold of the dog's tail, dislodged him instantly; but this I was not permitted to do. At this stage of the disaster my neighbor appeared with a look of consternation, her cap-strings flying in the cold wind. I tried to explain, but the aforesaid untimely hilarity hindered me. All I could do was to point at the flying freezer and the adjoining dog and ask her to call off her freezer, and, with assumed indignation, demand what she meant by trying to kill my greyhound.

The poor dog's every attempt at escape only wedged himself more thoroughly fast. But after a while, in time to save the dog, though not to save the ice-cream, my neighbor and myself effected a rescue. Edwin Landseer, the great painter of dogs and their friends, missed his best chance by not being there when the parishioner took hold of the freezer and the pastor seized the dog's tail, and, pulling mightily in opposite directions, they each got possession of their own property.

Carlo was cured of his love for luxuries, and the sight of the freezer on the back steps till the day of his death would send him howling away.

Carlo found, as many people have found, that it is easier to get into trouble than to get out.

Nothing could be more delicious than while he was eating his way in, but what must have been his feelings when he found it impossible to get out! While he was stealing the freezer the freezer stole him.

Lesson for dogs and men! "Come in!" says the gray spider to the house-fly; "I have entertained a great many flies. I have plenty of room, fine meals and a gay life. Walk on this suspension bridge. Give me your hand. Come in, my sweet lady fly. These walls are covered with silk, and the tapestry is gobelin. I am a wonderful creature. I have eight eyes, and of course can see your best interest. Philosophers have written volumes about my antennæ and cephalothorax." House-fly walks gently in. The web rocks like a cradle in the breeze. The house-fly feels honored to be the guest of such a big spider. We all have regard for big bugs. "But what is this?" cries the fly, pointing to a broken wing, "and this fragment of an insect's foot. There must have been a murder here! Let me go back!" "Ha! ha!" says the spider, "the gate is locked, the drawbridge is up. I only contracted to bring you in. I cannot afford to let you out. Take a drop of this poison, and it will quiet your nerves. I throw this hook of a fang over your neck to keep you from falling off." Word went back to the house-fly's family, and a choir of great green-bottled insects sang this psalm at the funeral:

"An unfortunate fly a-visiting went,
And in a gossamer web found himself pent."

The first five years of a dissipated life is comparatively easy, for it is all down hill; but when the man wakes up and finds his tongue wound with blasphemies, and his eyes swimming in rheum, and the antennæ of vice feeling along his nerves, and the spiderish poison eating through his very life, and, he resolves to return, he finds it hard traveling, for it is up hill, and the fortresses along the road open on him their batteries. We go into sin, hop, skip and jump; we come out of it creeping on all fours.

Let flies and dogs and men keep out of mischief. It is smooth all the way there, and rough all the way back. It is ice-cream for Carlo clear down to the bottom of the can, but afterward it is blinded eyes and sore neck and great fright. It is only eighteen inches to go into the freezer; it is three miles out. For Robert Burns it is rich wine and clapping hands and carnival all the way going to Edinburgh; but going back, it is worn-out body, and lost estate, and stinging conscience, and broken heart, and a drunkard's grave.

Better moderate our desires. Carlo had that morning as good a breakfast as any dog need to have. It was a law of the household that he should be well fed. Had he been satisfied with bread and meat, all would have been well. But he sauntered out for luxuries. He wanted ice-cream. He got it, but brought upon his head the perils and damages of which I have written. As long as we have reasonable wants we get on comfortably, but it is the struggle after luxuries that fills society with distress, and populates prisons, and sends hundreds of people stark mad. Dissatisfied with a plain house, and ordinary apparel, and respectable surroundings, they plunge their head into enterprises and speculations from which they have to sneak out in disgrace. Thousands of men have sacrificed honor and religion for luxuries, and died with the freezer about their ears.

Young Catchem has one horse, but wants six. Lives in a nice house on Thirtieth street, but wants one on Madison Square. Has one beautiful wife, but wants four. Owns a hundred thousand dollars of Erie stock, but wants a million.

Plunges his head into schemes of all sorts, eats his way to the bottom of the can till he cannot extricate himself, and constables, and sheriffs, and indignant society, which would have said nothing had he been successful, go to pounding him because he cannot get his head out.

Our poor old Carlo is dead now. We all cried when we found that he would never frisk again at our coming, nor put up his paw against us. But he lived long enough to preach the sermon about caution and contentment of which I have been the stenographer.

CHAPTER V.

OLD GAMES REPEATED.

We tarried longer in the dining-room this evening than usual, and the children, losing their interest in what we were saying got to playing all about us in a very boisterous way, but we said nothing, for it is the evening hour, and I think it keeps one fresh to have these things going on around us. Indeed, we never get over being boys and girls. The good, healthy man sixty years of age is only a boy with added experience. A woman is only an old girl. Summer is but an older spring. August is May in its teens. We shall be useful in proportion as we keep young in our feelings. There is no use for fossils except in museums and on the shelf. I like young old folks.

Indeed, we all keep doing over what we did in childhood. You thought that long ago you got through with "blind-man's-buff," and "hide-and-seek," and "puss in the corner," and "tick-tack-to," and "leap-frog," but all our lives are passed in playing those old games over again.

You say, "What a racket those children make in the other room! When Squire Jones' boys come over to spend the evening with our children, it seems as if they would tear the house down." "Father, be patient!" the wife says; "we once played 'blind-man's-buff' ourselves." Sure enough, father is playing it now, if he only knew it. Much of our time in life we go about blindfolded, stumbling over mistakes, trying to catch things that we miss, while people stand round the ring and titter, and break out with half-suppressed laughter, and push us ahead, and twitch the corner of our eye-bandage. After a while we vehemently clutch something with both hands, and announce to the world our capture; the blindfold is taken from our eyes, and, amid the shouts of the surrounding spectators, we find we have, after all, caught the wrong thing. What is that but "blind-man's buff" over again?

You say, "Jenny and Harry, go to bed. It seems so silly for you to sit there making two parallel lines perpendicular, and two parallel lines horizontal, and filling up the blanks with crosses and o's, and then crying out 'tick-tack-to.'" My dear man, you are doing every day in business just what your children are doing in the nursery. You find it hard to get things into a line. You have started out for worldly success. You get one or two things fixed but that is not what you want. After a while you have had two fine successes. You say, "If I can have a third success, I will come out ahead." But somebody is busy on the same slate, trying to hinder you getting the game. You mark; he marks. I think you will win. To the first and second success which you have already gained you add the third, for which you have long been seeking. The game is yours, and you clap your hands, and hunch your opponent in the side, and shout,

  "Tick-tack-to,
  Three in a row."

The funniest play that I ever joined in at school, and one that sets me a-laughing now as I think of it so I can hardly write, is "leap-frog." It is unartistic and homely. It is so humiliating to the boy who bends himself over and puts his hands down on his knees, and it is so perilous to the boy who, placing his hands on the stooped shoulders, attempts to fly over. But I always preferred the risk of the one who attempted the leap rather than the humiliation of the one who consented to be vaulted over. It was often the case that we both failed in our part and we went down together. For this Jack Snyder carried a grudge against me and would not speak, because he said I pushed him down a-purpose. But I hope he has forgiven me by this time, for he has been out as a missionary. Indeed, if Jack will come this way, I will right the wrong of olden time by stooping down in my study and letting him spring over me as my children do.

Almost every autumn I see that old-time schoolboy feat repeated. Mr. So-and-so says, "You make me governor and I will see that you get to be senator. Make me mayor and I will see that you become assessor. Get me the office of street-sweeper and you shall have one of the brooms. You stoop down and let me jump over you, and then I will stoop down and let you jump over me. Elect me deacon and you shall be trustee. You write a good thing about me and I will write a good thing about you." The day of election in Church or State arrives. A man once very upright in his principles and policy begins to bend. You cannot understand it. He goes down lower and lower, until he gets his hands away down on his knees. Then a spry politician or ecclesiastic comes up behind him, puts his hand on the bowed strategist and springs clear over into some great position. Good thing to have so good a man in a prominent place. But after a while he himself begins to bend. Everybody says, "What is the matter now? It cannot be possible that he is going down too." Oh yes! Turn-about is fair play. Jack Snyder holds it against me to this day, because, after he had stooped down to let me leap over him, I would not stoop down to let him leap over me. One half the strange things in Church and State may be accounted for by the fact that, ever since Adam bowed down so low as to let the race, putting its hands on him, fly over into ruin, there has been a universal and perpetual tendency to political and ecclesiastical "leap-frog." In one sense, life is a great "game of ball." We all choose sides and gather into denominational and political parties. We take our places on the ball ground. Some are to pitch; they are the radicals. Some are to catch; they are the conservatives. Some are to strike; they are those fond of polemics and battle. Some are to run; they are the candidates. There are four hunks—youth, manhood, old age and death. Some one takes the bat, lifts it and strikes for the prize and misses it, while the man who was behind catches it and goes in. This man takes his turn at the bat, sees the flying ball of success, takes good aim and strikes it high, amid the clapping of all the spectators. We all have a chance at the ball. Some of us run to all the four hunks, from youth to manhood, from manhood to old age, from old age to death. At the first hunk we bound with uncontrollable mirth; coming to the second, we run with a slower but stronger tread; coming to the third, our step is feeble; coming to the fourth, our breath entirely gives out. We throw down the bat on the black hunk of death, and in the evening catchers and pitchers go home to find the family gathered and the food prepared. So may we all find the candles lighted, and the table set, and the old folks at home.

CHAPTER VI.

THE FULL-BLOODED COW.

We never had any one drop in about six o'clock p. m. whom we were more glad to see than Fielding, the Orange County farmer. In the first place, he always had a good appetite, and it did not make much difference what we had to eat. He would not nibble about the end of a piece of bread, undecided as to whether he had better take it, nor sit sipping his tea as though the doctor had ordered him to take only ten drops at a time, mixed with a little sugar and hot water. Perpetual contact with fresh air and the fields and the mountains gave him a healthy body, while the religion that he learned in the little church down by the mill-dam kept him in healthy spirits. Fielding keeps a great drove of cattle and has an overflowing dairy. As we handed him the cheese he said, "I really believe this is of my own making." "Fielding," I inquired, how does your dairy thrive, and have you any new stock on your farm? Come give us a little touch of the country." He gave me a mischievous look and said, "I will not tell you a word until you let me know all about that full-blooded cow, of which I have heard something. You need not try to hide that story any longer." So we yielded to his coaxing. It was about like this:

The man had not been able to pay his debts. The mortgage on the farm had been foreclosed. Day of sale had come. The sheriff stood on a box reading the terms of vendue. All payments to be made in six months. The auctioneer took his place. The old man and his wife and the children all cried as the piano, and the chairs, and the pictures, and the carpets, and the bedsteads went at half their worth. When the piano went, it seemed to the old people as if the sheriff were selling all the fingers that had ever played on it; and when the carpets were struck off, I think father and mother thought of the little feet that had tramped it; and when the bedstead was sold, it brought to mind the bright, curly heads that had slept on it long before the dark days had come, and father had put his name on the back of a note, signing his own death warrant. The next thing to being buried alive is to have the sheriff sell you out when you have been honest and have tried always to do right. There are so many envious ones to chuckle at your fall, and come in to buy your carriage, blessing the Lord that the time has come for you to walk and for them to ride.

But to us the auction reached its climax of interest when we went to the barn. We were spending our summers in the country, and must have a cow. There were ten or fifteen sukies to be sold. There were reds, and piebalds, and duns, and browns, and brindles, short horns, long horns, crumpled horns and no horns. But we marked for our own a cow that was said to be full-blooded, whether Alderney, or Durham, or Galloway, or Ayrshire, I will not tell lest some cattle fancier feel insulted by what I say; and if there is any grace that I pride myself on, it is prudence and a determination always to say smooth things. "How much is bid for this magnificent, full-blooded cow?" cried the auctioneer. "Seventy-five dollars," shouted some one. I made it eighty. He made it ninety. Somebody else quickly made it a hundred. After the bids had risen to one hundred and twenty-five dollars, I got animated, and resolved that I would have that cow if it took my last cent. "One hundred and forty dollars," shouted my opponent. The auctioneer said it was the finest cow he had ever sold; and not knowing much about vendues, of course I believed him. It was a good deal of money for a minister to pay, but then I could get the whole matter off my hands by giving "a note." In utter defiance of everything I cried out, "One hundred and fifty dollars!" "Going at that," said the auctioneer. "Going at that! once! twice! three times! gone! Mr. Talmage has it." It was one of the proudest moments of our life. There she stood, tall, immense in the girth, horns branching graceful as a tree branch, full-uddered, silk-coated, pensive-eyed.

We hired two boys to drive her home while we rode in a carriage. No sooner had we started than the cow showed what turned out to be one of her peculiarities, great speed of hoof. She left the boys, outran my horse, jumped the fence, frightened nearly to death a group of school-children, and by the time we got home we all felt as if we had all day been out on a fox-chase.

We never had any peace with that cow. She knew more tricks than a juggler. She could let down any bars, open any gate, outrun any dog and ruin the patience of any minister. We had her a year, and yet she never got over wanting to go to the vendue. Once started out of the yard, she was bound to see the sheriff. We coaxed her with carrots, and apples, and cabbage, and sweetest stalks, and the richest beverage of slops, but without avail.

As a milker she was a failure. "Mike," who lived just back of our place, would come in at nights from his "Kerry cow," a scraggly runt that lived on the commons, with his pail so full he had to carry it cautiously lest it spill over. But after our full-blooded had been in clover to her eyes all day, Bridget would go out to the barnyard, and tug and pull for a supply enough to make two or three custards. I said, "Bridget, you don't know how to milk. Let me try." I sat down by the cow, tried the full force of dynamics, but just at the moment when my success was about to be demonstrated, a sudden thought took her somewhere between the horns, and she started for the vendue, with one stroke of her back foot upsetting the small treasure I had accumulated, and leaving me a mere wreck of what I once was.

She had, among other bad things, a morbid appetite. Notwithstanding we gave her the richest herbaceous diet, she ate everything she could put her mouth on. She was fond of horse blankets and articles of human clothing. I found her one day at the clothes line, nearly choked to death, for she had swallowed one leg of something and seemed dissatisfied that she could not get down the other. The most perfect nuisance that I ever had about my place was that full-blooded.

Having read in our agricultural journals of cows that were slaughtered yielding fourteen hundred pounds neat weight, we concluded to sell her to the butcher. We set a high price upon her and got it—that is, we took a note for it, which is the same thing. My bargain with the butcher was the only successful chapter in my bovine experiences. The only taking-off in the whole transaction was that the butcher ran away, leaving me nothing but a specimen of poor chirography, and I already had enough of that among my manuscripts.

My friend, never depend on high-breeds. Some of the most useless of cattle had ancestors spoken of in the "Commentaries of Cæsar." That Alderney whose grandfather used to graze on a lord's park in England may not be worth the grass she eats.

Do not depend too much on the high-sounding name of Durham or Devon. As with animals, so with men. Only one President ever had a President for a son. Let every cow make her own name, and every man achieve his own position. It is no great credit to a fool that he had a wise grandfather. Many an Ayrshire and Hereford has had the hollow-horn and the foot-rot. Both man and animal are valuable in proportion as they are useful. "Mike's" cow beat my full-blooded.

CHAPTER VII.

THE DREGS IN LEATHERBACKS' TEA-CUP.

We have an earlier tea this evening than usual, for we have a literary friend who comes about this time of the week, and he must go home to retire about eight o'clock. His nervous system is so weak that he must get three or four hours sleep before midnight; otherwise he is next day so cross and censorious he scalps every author he can lay his hand on. As he put his hand on the table with an indelible blot of ink on his thumb and two fingers, which blot he had not been able to wash off, I said, "Well, my old friend Leatherbacks, what books have you been reading to-day?"

He replied, "I have been reading 'Men and Things.' Some books touch only the head and make us think; other books touch only the heart and make us feel; here and there one touches us under the fifth rib and makes us laugh; but the book on 'Men and Things,' by the Rev. Dr. C. S. Henry, touched me all over. I have felt better ever since. I have not seen the author but once since the old university days, when he lectured us and pruned us and advised us and did us more good than almost any other instructor we ever had. Oh, those were grand days! No better than the present, for life grows brighter to me all the time; but we shall not forget the quaint, strong, brusque professor who so unceremoniously smashed things which he did not like, and shook the class with merriment or indignation. The widest awake professorial room in the land was Dr. Henry's, in the New York

University. But the participators in those scenes are all scattered. I know the whereabouts of but three or four. So we meet for a little while on earth, and then we separate. There must be a better place somewhere ahead of us.

"I have also been looking over a book that overhauls the theology and moral character of Abraham Lincoln. This is the only kind of slander that is safe. I have read all the stuff for the last three years published about Abraham Lincoln's unfair courtships and blank infidelity. The protracted discussion has made only one impression upon me, and that is this: How safe it is to slander a dead man! You may say what you will in print about him, he brings no rebutting evidence. I have heard that ghosts do a great many things, but I never heard of one as printing a book or editing a newspaper to vindicate himself. Look out how you vilify a living man, for he may respond with pen, or tongue, or cowhide; but only get a man thoroughly dead (that is, so certified by the coroner) and have a good, heavy tombstone put on the top of him, and then you may say what you will with impunity.

"But I have read somewhere in an old book that there is a day coming when all wrongs will be righted; and I should not wonder if then the dead were vindicated, and all the swine who have uprooted graveyards should, like their ancestors of Gadara, run down a steep place into the sea and get choked. The fact that there are now alive men so debauched of mind and soul that they rejoice in mauling the reputation of those who spent their lives in illustrious achievement for God and their country, and then died as martyrs for their principles, makes me believe in eternal damnation."

With this last sentence my friend Leatherbacks gave a violent gesture that upset his cup and left the table-cloth sopping wet.

"By the way," said he, "have you heard that Odger is coming?"

"What!" said I. He continued without looking up, for he was at that moment running his knife, not over-sharp, through a lamb-chop made out of old sheep. (Wife, we will have to change our butcher!) He continued with a severity perhaps partly caused by the obstinacy of the meat: "I see in the 'Pall-Mall Budget' the startling intelligence that Mr. Odger is coming to the United States on a lecturing expedition. Our American newspapers do not seem, as yet, to have got hold of this news, but the tidings will soon fly, and great excitement may be expected to follow."

Some unwise person might ask the foolish question, "Who is Odger?" I hope, however, that such inquiry will not be made, for I would be compelled to say that I do not know. Whether he is a clergyman or a reformer, or an author, or all these in one, we cannot say. Suffice it he is a foreigner, and that is enough to make us all go wild. A foreigner does not need more than half as much brain or heart to do twice as well as an American, either at preaching or lecturing. There is for many Americans a bewitchment in a foreign brogue. I do not know but that he may have dined with the queen, or have a few drops of lordly blood distributed through his arteries.

I notice, however, that much of this charm has been broken. I used to think that all English lords were talented, till I heard one of them make the only poor speech that was made at the opening meeting of the Evangelical Alliance. Our lecturing committees would not pay very large prices next year for Mr. Bradlaugh and Edmund Yates. Indeed, we expect that the time will soon come when the same kind of balances will weigh Englishmen, Scotchmen, Irishmen, Frenchmen and Americans.

If a man can do anything well, he will be acceptable without reference to whether he was born by the Clyde, the Thames, the Seine, or the Hudson. But until those scales be lifted it is sufficient to announce the joyful tidings that "Odger is coming."

CHAPTER VIII.

THE HOT AXLE.

The express train was flying from Cork to Queenstown. It was going like sixty—that is, about sixty miles an hour. No sight of an Irish village to arrest our speed, no sign of break-down, and yet the train halted. We looked out of the window, saw the brakemen and a crowd of passengers gathering around the locomotive and a dense smoke arising. What was the matter? A hot axle!

We were on the lightning train for Cleveland. We had no time to spare. If we stopped for a half hour we should be greeted by the anathema of a lecturing committee. We felt a sort of presentiment that we should be too late, when to confirm it the whistle blew, and the brakes fell, and the cry all along the train was, "What is the matter?" Answer: "A hot axle!" The wheels had been making too many revolutions in a minute. The car was on fire. It was a very difficult thing to put it out; water, sand and swabs were tried, and caused long detention and a smoke that threatened flame down to the end of the journey.

We thought then, and think now, this is what is the matter with people everywhere. In this swift, "express," American life, we go too fast for our endurance. We think ourselves getting on splendidly, when in the midst of our successes we come to a dead halt. What is the matter? Nerves or muscles or brains give out. We have made too many revolutions in an hour. A hot axle!

Men make the mistake of working according to their opportunities, and not according to their capacity of endurance. "Can I run this train from Springfield to Boston at the rate of fifty miles an hour?" says an engineer. Yes. "Then I will run it reckless of consequences." Can I be a merchant, and the president of a bank, and a director in a life insurance company, and a school commissioner, and help edit a paper, and supervise the politics of our ward, and run for Congress? "I can!" the man says to himself. The store drives him; the school drives him; politics drive him. He takes all the scoldings and frets and exasperations of each position. Some day at the height of the business season he does not come to the store; from the most important meetings of the bank directors he is absent. In the excitements of the political canvass he fails to be at the place appointed. What is the matter? His health has broken down. The train halts long before it gets to the station. A hot axle!

Literary men have great opportunities opening in this day. If they take all that open, they are dead men, or worse, living men who ought to be dead. The pen runs so easy when you have good ink, and smooth paper, and an easy desk to write on, and the consciousness of an audience of one, two or three hundred thousand readers. There are the religious newspapers through which you preach, and the musical journals through which you may sing, and the agricultural periodicals through which you can plough, and family newspapers in which you may romp with the whole household around the evening stand. There are critiques to be written, and reviews to be indulged in, and poems to be chimed, and novels to be constructed. When out of a man's pen he can shake recreation, and friendship, and usefulness, and bread, he is apt to keep it shaking. So great are the invitations to literary work that the professional men of the day are overcome. They sit faint and fagged out on the verge of newspapers and books. Each one does the work of three, and these men sit up late nights, and choke down chunks of meat without mastication, and scold their wives through irritability, and maul innocent authors, and run the physical machinery with a liver miserably given out. The driving shaft has gone fifty times a second. They stop at no station. The steam-chest is hot and swollen. The brain and the digestion begin to smoke. Stop, ye flying quills! "Down brakes!" A hot axle!

Some of the worst tempered people of the day are religious people, from the fact that they have no rest. Added to the necessary work of the world, they superintend two Sunday-schools, listen to two sermons, and every night have meetings of charitable and Christian institutions. They look after the beggars, hold conventions, speak at meetings, wait on ministers, serve as committeemen, take all the hypercriticisms that inevitably come to earnest workers, rush up and down the world and develop their hearts at the expense of all the other functions. They are the best men on earth, and Satan knows it, and is trying to kill them as fast as possible. They know not that it is as much a duty to take care of their health as to go to the sacrament. It is as much a sin to commit suicide with the sword of truth as with a pistol.

Our earthly life is a treasure to be guarded. It is an outrageous thing to die when we ought to live. There is no use in firing up a Cunarder to such a speed that the boiler bursts mid-Atlantic, when at a more moderate rate it might have reached the docks at Liverpool. It is a sin to try to do the work of thirty years in five years.

A Rocky Mountain locomotive engineer told us that at certain places they change locomotives and let the machine rest, as a locomotive always kept in full heat soon got out of order. Our advice to all overworked good people is, "Slow up!" Slacken your speed as you come to the crossings. All your faculties for work at this rate will be consumed. You are on fire now—see the premonitory smoke. A hot axle!

Some of our young people have read till they are crazed of learned blacksmiths who at the forge conquered thirty languages, and of shoemakers who, pounding sole-leather, got to be philosophers, and of milliners who, while their customers were at the glass trying on their spring hats, wrote a volume of first-rate poems. The fact is no blacksmith ought to be troubled with more than five languages; and instead of shoemakers becoming philosophers, we would like to turn our surplus of philosophers into shoemakers; and the supply of poetry is so much greater than the demand that we wish milliners would stick to their business. Extraordinary examples of work and endurance may do as much harm as good. Because Napoleon slept only three hours a night, hundreds of students have tried the experiment; but instead of Austerlitz and Saragossa, there came of it only a sick headache and a botch of a recitation. We are told of how many books a man can read in the five spare minutes before breakfast, and the ten minutes at noon, but I wish some one could tell us how much rest a man can get in fifteen minutes after dinner, or how much health in an hour's horseback ride, or how much fun in a Saturday afternoon of cricket. He who has such an idea of the value of time that he takes none of it for rest wastes all his time.

Most Americans do not take time for sufficient sleep. We account for our own extraordinary health by the fact that we are fanatics on the subject of sleep. We differ from our friend Napoleon Bonaparte in one respect: we want nine hours' sleep, and we take it—eight hours at night and one hour in the day. If we miss our allowance one week, as we often do, we make it up the next week or the next month. We have sometimes been twenty-one hours in arrearages. We formerly kept a memorandum of the hours for sleep lost. We pursued those hours till we caught them. If at the beginning of our summer vacation we are many hours behind in slumber, we go down to the sea-shore or among the mountains and sleep a month. If the world abuses us at any time, we go and take an extra sleep; and when we wake up, all the world is smiling on us. If we come to a knotty point in our discourse, we take a sleep; and when we open our eyes, the opaque has become transparent. We split every day in two by a nap in the afternoon. Going to take that somniferous interstice, we say to the servants, "Do not call me for anything. If the house takes fire, first get the children out and my private papers; and when the roof begins to fall in call me." Through such fanaticism we have thus far escaped the hot axle.

Somebody ought to be congratulated—I do not know who, and so I will shake hands all around—on the fact that the health of the country seems improving. Whether Dio Lewis, with his gymnastic clubs, has pounded to death American sickness, or whether the coming here of many English ladies with their magnificent pedestrian habits, or whether the medicines in the apothecary shops through much adulteration have lost their force, or whether the multiplication of bathtubs has induced to cleanliness people who were never washed but once, and that just after their arrival on this planet, I cannot say. But sure I am that I never saw so many bright, healthy-faced people as of late.

Our maidens have lost the languor they once cultivated, and walk the street with stout step, and swing the croquet mallet with a force that sends the ball through two arches, cracking the opposing ball with great emphasis. Our daughters are not ashamed to culture flower beds, and while they plant the rose in the ground a corresponding rose blooms in their own cheek.

But we need another proclamation of emancipation. The human locomotive goes too fast. Cylinder, driving-boxes, rock-shaft, truck and valve-gear need to "slow up." Oh! that some strong hand would unloose the burdens from our over-tasked American life, that there might be fewer bent shoulders, and pale cheeks, and exhausted lungs, and quenched eyes, the law, and medicine, and theology less frequently stopped in their glorious progress, because of the hot axle!

CHAPTER IX.

BEEFSTEAK FOR MINISTERS.

There have been lately several elaborate articles remarking upon what they call the lack of force and fire in the clergy. The world wonders that, with such a rousing theme as the gospel, and with such a grand work as saving souls, the ministry should ever be nerveless. Some ascribe it to lack of piety, and some to timidity of temperament. We believe that in a great number of cases it is from the lack of nourishing food. Many of the clerical brotherhood are on low diet. After jackets and sacks have been provided for the eight or ten children of the parsonage, the father and mother must watch the table with severest economy. Coming in suddenly upon the dinner-hour of the country clergyman, the housewife apologizes for what she calls "a picked-up" dinner, when, alas! it is nearly always picked up.

Congregations sometimes mourn over dull preaching when themselves are to blame. Give your minister more beefsteak and he will have more fire. Next to the divine unction, the minister needs blood; and he cannot make that out of tough leather. One reason why the apostles preached so powerfully was that they had healthy food. Fish was cheap along Galilee, and this, with unbolted bread, gave them plenty of phosphorus for brain food. These early ministers were never invited out to late suppers, with chicken salad and doughnuts. Nobody ever embroidered slippers for the big foot of Simon Peter, the fisherman preacher. Tea parties, with hot waffles, at ten o'clock at night, make namby-pamby ministers; but good hours and substantial diet, that furnish nitrates for the muscles, and phosphates for the brain, and carbonates for the whole frame, prepare a man for effective work. When the water is low, the mill-wheel goes slow: but a full race, and how fast the grists are ground! In a man the arteries are the mill-race and the brain the wheel, and the practical work of life is the grist ground. The reason our soldiers failed in some of the battles was because their stomachs had for several days been innocent of everything but "hard tack." See that your minister has a full haversack. Feed him on gruel during the week and on Sunday he will give you gruel. What is called the "parson's nose" in a turkey or fowl is an allegory setting forth that in many communities the minister comes out behind.

Eight hundred or a thousand dollars for a minister is only a slow way of killing him, and is the worst style of homicide. Why do not the trustees and elders take a mallet or an axe, and with one blow put him out of his misery? The damage begins in the college boarding house. The theological student has generally small means, and he must go to a cheap boarding house. A frail piece of sausage trying to swim across a river of gravy on the breakfast plate, but drowned at last, "the linked sweetness long drawn out" of flies in the molasses cup, the gristle of a tough ox, and measly biscuit, and buckwheat cakes tough as the cook's apron, and old peas in which the bugs lost their life before they had time to escape from the saucepan, and stale cucumbers cut up into small slices of cholera morbus,—are the provender out of which we are trying at Princeton and Yale and New Brunswick to make sons of thunder. Sons of mush! From such depletion we step gasping into the pulpit, and look so heavenly pale that the mothers in Israel are afraid we will evaporate before we get through our first sermon.

Many of our best young men in preparation for the ministry are going through this martyrdom. The strongest mind in our theological class perished, the doctors said afterward from lack of food. The only time he could afford a doctor was for his post-mortem examination.

I give the financial condition of many of our young theological students when I say:

Income	$250 00
Outgo:	
Board at $3 per week (cheap place) . .	156 00
Clothing (shoddy)	100 00
Books (no morocco)	25 00
Traveling expenses	20 00
Total	$301 00

Here you see a deficit of fifty-one dollars. As there are no "stealings" in a theological seminary, he makes up the balance by selling books or teaching school. He comes into life cowed down, with a patch on both knees and several other places, and a hat that has been "done over" four or five times, and so weak that the first sharp wind that whistles round the corner blows him into glory. The inertness you complain of in the ministry starts early. Do you suppose that if Paul had spent seven years in a cheap boarding house, and the years after in a poorly-supplied parsonage, he would have made Felix tremble? No! The first glance of the Roman procurator would have made him apologize for intrusion.

Do not think that all your eight-hundred-dollar minister needs is a Christmas present of an elegantly-bound copy of "Calvin's Institutes." He is sound already on the doctrine of election, and it is a poor consolation if in this way you remind him that he has been foreordained to starve to death. Keep your minister on artichokes and purslain, and he will be fit to preach nothing but funeral sermons from the text "All flesh is grass." While feeling most of all our need of the life that comes from above, let us not ignore the fact that many of the clergy to-day need more gymnastics, more fresh air, more nutritious food. Prayer cannot do the work of beefsteak. You cannot keep a hot fire in the furnace with poor fuel and the damper turned.

CHAPTER X.

AUTOBIOGRAPHY OF AN OLD PAIR OF SCISSORS.

I was born in Sheffield, England, at the close of the last century, and was, like all those who study Brown's Shorter Catechism, made out of dust. My father was killed at Herculaneum at the time of the accident there, and buried with other scissors and knives and hooks and swords. On my mother's side I am descended from a pair of shears that came to England during the Roman invasion. My cousin hung to the belt of a duchess. My uncle belonged to Hampton Court, and used to trim the king's hair. I came to the United States while the grandfathers of the present generation of children were boys.

When I was young I was a gay fellow—indeed, what might have been called "a perfect blade." I look old and rusty hanging here on the nail, but take me down, and though my voice is a little squeaky with old age, I can tell you a pretty tale. I am sharper than I look. Old scissors know more than you think. They say I am a little garrulous, and perhaps I may tell things I ought not.

I helped your grandmother prepare for her wedding. I cut out and fitted all the apparel of that happy day. I hear her scold the young folks now for being so dressy, but I can tell you she was once that way herself. Did not I, sixty years ago, lie on the shelf and laugh as I saw her stand by the half hour before the glass, giving an extra twist to her curl and an additional dash of white powder on her hair—now fretted because the powder was too thick, now fretted because it was too thin? She was as proud in cambric and calico and nankeen as Harriet is to-day in white tulle and organdy. I remember how careful she was when she ran me along the edges of the new dress. With me she clipped and notched and gored and trimmed, and day and night I went click! click! click! and it seemed as if she would never let me rest from cutting.

I split the rags for the first carpet on the old homestead, and what a merry time we had when the neighbors came to "the quilting!" I lay on the coverlet that was stretched across the quilting-frame and heard all the gossip of 1799. Reputations were ripped and torn just as they are now. Fashions were chattered about, the coal-scuttle bonnet of some offensive neighbor (who was not invited to the quilting) was criticised, and the suspicion started that she laced too tight; and an old man who happened to have the best farm in the county was overhauled for the size of his knee-buckles, and the exorbitant ruffles on his shirt, and the costly silk lace to his hat. I lay so still that no one supposed I was listening. I trembled on the coverlet with rage and wished that I could clip the end of their tattling tongues, but found no chance for revenge, till, in the hand of a careless neighbor, I notched and nearly spoiled the patch-work.

Yes, I am a pair of old scissors. I cut out many a profile of old-time faces, and the white dimity bed curtains. I lay on the stand when your grandparents were courting—for that had to be done then as well as now—and it was the same story of chairs wide apart, and chairs coming nearer, and arm over the back of the chair, and late hours, and four or five gettings up to go with the determination to stay, protracted interviews on the front steps, blushes and kisses. Your great-grandmother, out of patience at the lateness of the hour, shouted over the banister to your immediate grandmother, "Mary! come to bed!" Because the old people sit in the corner looking so very grave, do not suppose their eyes were never roguish, nor their lips ruby, nor their hair flaxen, nor their feet spry, nor that they always retired at half-past eight o'clock at night. After a while, I, the scissors, was laid on the shelf, and finally thrown into a box among nails and screws and files. Years of darkness and disgrace for a scissors so highly born as I. But one day I was hauled out. A bell tinkled in the street. An Italian scissors-grinder wanted a job. I was put upon the stone, and the grinder put his foot upon the treadle, and the bands pulled, and the wheel sped, and the fire flew, and it seemed as if, in the heat and pressure and agony, I should die. I was ground, and rubbed, and oiled, and polished, till I glittered in the sun; and one day, when young Harriet was preparing for the season, I plunged into the fray. I almost lost my senses among the ribbons, and flew up and down among the flounces, and went mad amongst the basques. I move round as gay as when I was young; and modern scissors, with their stumpy ends, and loose pivots, and weak blades, and glaring bows, and course shanks, are stupid beside an old family piece like me. You would be surprised how spry I am flying around the sewing-room, cutting corsage into heart-shape, and slitting a place for button holes, and making double-breasted jackets, and hollowing scallops, and putting the last touches on velvet arabesques and Worth overskirts. I feel almost as well at eighty years of age as at ten, and I lie down to sleep at night amid all the fineries of the wardrobe, on olive-green cashmere, and beside pannier puffs, and pillowed on feathers of ostrich.

Oh! what a gay life the scissors live! I may lie on gayest lady's lap, and little children like me better than almost anything else to play with. The trembling octogenarian takes me by the hand, and the rollicking four-year-old puts on me his dimpled fingers. Mine are the children's curls and the bride's veil. I am welcomed to the Christmas tree, and the sewing-machine, and the editor's table. I have cut my way through the ages. Beside pen, and sword, and needle, I dare to stand anywhere, indispensable to the race, the world-renowned scissors!

But I had a sad mission once. The bell tolled in the New England village because a soul had passed. I sat up all the night cutting the pattern for a shroud. Oh, it was gloomy work. There was wailing in the house, but I could not stop to mourn. I had often made the swaddling-clothes for a child, but that was the only time I fashioned a robe for the grave. To fit it around the little neck, and make the sleeves just long enough for the quiet arms—it hurt me more than the tilt hammers that smote me in Sheffield, than the files of the scissors-grinder at the door. I heard heart-strings snap as I went through the linen, and in the white pleats to be folded over the still heart I saw the snow banked on a grave. Give me, the old scissors, fifty bridal dresses to make rather than one shroud to prepare.

I never recovered from the chill of those dismal days, but at the end of life I can look back and feel that I have done my work well. Other scissors have frayed and unraveled the garments they touched, but I have always made a clean path through the linen or the damask I was called to divide. Others screeched complainingly at their toil; I smoothly worked my jaws. Many of the fingers that wrought with me have ceased to open and shut, and my own time will soon come to die, and I shall be buried in a grave of rust amid cast-off tenpenny nails and horse-shoes. But I have stayed long enough to testify, first, that these days are no worse than the old ones, the granddaughter now no more proud than the grandmother was; secondly, that we all need to be hammered and ground in order to take off the rust; and thirdly, that an old scissors, as well as an old man, may be scoured up and made practically useful.

CHAPTER XI.

A LIE, ZOOLOGICALLY CONSIDERED.

We stand agape in the British Museum, looking at the monstrous skeletons of the mastodon, megatherium and iguanodon, and conclude that all the great animals thirty feet long and eleven feet high are extinct.

Now, while we do not want to frighten children or disturb nervous people, we have to say that the other day we caught a glimpse of a monster beside which the lizards of the saurian era were short, and the elephants of the mammalian period were insignificant. We saw it in full spring, and on the track of its prey. Children would call the creature "a fib;" rough persons would term it "a whopper;" polite folks would say it was "a fabrication;" but plain and unscientific people would style it "a lie." Naturalists might assign it to the species "Tigris regalis," or "Felis pardus."

We do not think that anatomical and zoological justice has been done to the lie. It is to be found in all zones. Livingstone saw it in Central Africa; Dr. Kane found it on an iceberg, beside a polar bear; Agassiz discovered it in Brazil. It thrives about as well in one clime as another, with perhaps a little preference for the temperate zone. It lives on berries, or bananas, or corn, grapes, or artichokes; drinks water, or alcohol, or tea. It eats up a great many children, and would have destroyed the boy who afterward became the father of his country had he not driven it back with his hatchet. (See the last two hundred Sunday-school addresses.)

The first peculiarity of this Tigris regalis or Felis pardus, commonly called a lie, is its

LONGEVITY.

If it once get born, it lives on almost interminably. Sometimes it has followed a man for ten, twenty or forty years, and has been as healthy in its last leap as in the first. It has run at every president from General Washington to General Grant, and helped kill Horace Greeley. It has barked at every good man since Adam, and every good woman since Eve, and every good boy since Abel, and every good cow since Pharaoh's lean kine. Malarias do not poison it, nor fires burn it, nor winters freeze it. Just now it is after your neighbor; to-morrow it will be after you. It is the healthiest of all monsters. Its tooth knocks out the "tooth of time." Its hair never turns white with age, nor does it limp with decrepitude. It is distinguished for its longevity.

THE LENGTH OF ITS LEGS.

It keeps up with the express train, and is present at the opening and the shutting of the mailbags. It takes a morning run from New York to San Francisco or over to London before breakfast. It can go a thousand miles at a jump. It would despise seven-league boots as tedious. A telegraph pole is just knee-high to this monster, and from that you can judge its speed of locomotion. It never gets out of wind, carries a bag of reputations made up in cold hash, so that it does not have to stop for victuals. It goes so fast that sometimes five million people have seen it the same morning.

KEENNESS OF NOSTRIL.

It can smell a moral imperfection fifty miles away. The crow has no faculty compared with this for finding carrion. It has scented something a hundred miles off, and before night "treed" its game. It has a great genius for smelling. It can find more than is actually there. When it begins to snuff the air, you had better look out. It has great length and breadth and depth and height of nose.

ACUTENESS OF EAR.

The rabbit has no such power to listen as this creature we speak of. It hears all the sounds that come from five thousand keyholes. It catches a whisper from the other side the room, and can understand the scratch of a pen. It has one ear open toward the east and the other toward the west, and hears everything in both directions. All the tittle-tattle of the world pours into those ears like vinegar through a funnel. They are always up and open, and to them a meeting of the sewing society is a jubilee and a political campaign is heaven.

SIZE OF THROAT.

The snake has hard work to choke down a toad, and the crocodile has a mighty struggle to take in the calf; but the monster of which I speak can swallow anything. It has a throat bigger than the whale that took down the minister who declined the call to Nineveh, and has swallowed whole presbyteries and conferences of clergymen. A Brobdingnagian goes down as easily as a Liliputian. The largest story about business dishonor, or female frailty, or political deception, slips through with the ease of a homœopathic pellet. Its throat is sufficient for anything round, or square, or angular, or octagonal.

Nothing in all the earth is too big for its mastication and digestion save the truth, and that will stick in its gullet.

IT IS GREGARIOUS.

It goes in a flock with others of its kind. If one takes after a man or woman, there are at least ten in its company. As soon as anything bad is charged against a man, there are many others who know things just as deleterious. Lies about himself, lies about his wife, lies about his children, lies about his associates, lies about his house, lies about his barn, lies about his store—swarms of them, broods of them, herds of them. Kill one of them, and there will be twelve alive to act as its pall-bearers, another to preach its funeral sermon, and still another to write its obituary.

These monsters beat all the extinct species. They are white, spotted and black. They have a sleek hide, a sharp claw and a sting in their tail. They prowl through every street of the city, craunch in the restaurants, sleep in the hall of Congress, and in grandest parlor have one paw under the piano, another under the sofa, one by the mantel and the other on the door-sill.

Now, many people spend half their time in hunting lies. You see a man rushing anxiously about to correct a newspaper paragraph, or a husband, with fist clenched, on the way to pound some one who has told a false thing about his wife. There is a woman on the next street who heard, last Monday, a falsehood about her husband, and has had her hat and shawl on ever since in the effort to correct wrong impressions. Our object in this zoological sketch of a lie is to persuade you of the folly of such a hunting excursion. If these monsters have such long legs, and go a hundred miles at a jump, you might as well give up the chase. If they have such keenness of nostril, they can smell you across the State, and get out of your way. If they have such long ears, they can hear the hunter's first step in the woods. If they have such great throats, they can swallow you at a gape. If they are gregarious, while you shoot one, forty will run upon you like mad buffaloes, and trample you to death. Arrows bound back from their thick hide; and as for gunpowder, they use it regularly for pinches of snuff. After a shower of bullets has struck their side, they lift their hind foot to scratch the place, supposing a black fly has been biting. Henry the Eighth, in a hawking party, on foot, attempted to leap a ditch in Hertfordshire, and with his immense avoirdupois weight went splashing into the mud and slime, and was hauled out by his footman half dead. And that is the fate of men who spend their time hunting for lies. Better go to your work, and let the lies run. Their bloody muzzles have tough work with a man usefully busy. You cannot so easily overcome them with sharp retort as with adze and yardstick. All the howlings of Californian wolves at night do not stop the sun from kindling victorious morn on the Sierra Nevadas, and all the ravenings of defamation and revenge cannot hinder the resplendent dawn of heaven on a righteous soul.

But they who spend their time in trying to lasso and decapitate a lie will come back worsted, as did the English cockneys from a fox chase described in the poem entitled "Pills to Purge Melancholy:"

"And when they had done their sport, they came to London, where they dwell,
Their faces all so torn and scratched their wives scarce knew them well;
For 'twas a very great mercy so many 'scaped alive,
For of twenty saddles carried out, they brought again but five."

CHAPTER XII.

A BREATH OF ENGLISH AIR.

My friend looked white as the wall, flung the "London Times" half across the room, kicked one slipper into the air and shouted, "Talmage, where on earth did you come from?" as this summer I stepped into his English home. "Just come over the ferry to dine with you," I responded. After some explanation about the health of my family, which demanded a sea voyage, and thus necessitated my coming, we planned two or three excursions.

At eight o'clock in the morning we gathered in the parlor in the Red Horse Hotel, at Stratford-on-Avon. Two pictures of Washington Irving, the chair in which the father of American literature sat, and the table on which he wrote, immortalizing his visit to that hotel, adorn the room. From thence we sallied forth to see the clean, quaint village of Stratford. It was built just to have Shakspeare born in. We have not heard that there was any one else ever born there, before or since. If, by any strange possibility, it could be proved that the great dramatist was born anywhere else, it would ruin all the cab drivers, guides and hostelries of the place.

We went of course to the house where Shakspeare first appeared on the stage of life, and enacted the first act of his first play. Scene the first. Enter John Shakspeare, the father; Mrs. Shakspeare, the mother, and the old nurse, with young William.

A very plain house it is. Like the lark, which soars highest, but builds its nest lowest, so with genius; it has humble beginnings. I think ten thousand dollars would be a large appraisement for all the houses where the great poets were born. But all the world comes to this lowly dwelling. Walter Scott was glad to scratch his name on the window, and you may see it now. Charles Dickens, Edmund Kean, Albert Smith, Mark Lemon and Tennyson, so very sparing of their autographs, have left their signatures on the wall. There are the jambs of the old fire-place where the poet warmed himself and combed wool, and began to think for all time. Here is the chair in which he sat while presiding at the club, forming habits of drink which killed him at the last, his own life ending in a tragedy as terrible as any he ever wrote. Exeunt wine-bibbers, topers, grogshop keepers, Drayton, Ben Jonson and William Shakspeare. Here also is the letter which Richard Quyney sent to Shakspeare, asking to borrow thirty pounds. I hope he did not loan it; for if he did, it was a dead loss.

We went to the church where the poet is buried. It dates back seven hundred years, but has been often restored. It has many pictures, and is the sleeping place of many distinguished dead; but one tomb within the chancel absorbs all the attention of the stranger. For hundreds of years the world has looked upon the unadorned stone lying flat over the dust of William Shakspeare, and read the epitaph written by himself:

"Good friend, for Jesus' sake forbeare
To dig the dust enclosed here;
Bleste be ye man yt spares these stones,
And curst be he that moves my bones."

Under such anathema the body has slept securely. A sexton once looked in at the bones, but did not dare to touch them, lest his "quietus" should be made with a bare bodkin.

From the church door we mounted our carriage; and crossing the Avon on a bridge which the lord mayor of London built four hundred years ago, we start on one of the most memorable rides of our life. The country looked fresh and luxuriant from recent rains. The close-trimmed hedges, the sleek cattle, the snug cottages, the straggling villages with their historic inns, the castle from whose park Shakspeare stole the deer, the gate called "Shakspeare's stile," curious in the fact that it looks like ordinary bars of fence, but as you attempt to climb over, the whole thing gives way, and lets you fall flat, righting itself as soon as it is unburdened of you; the rabbits darting along the hedges, undisturbed, because it is unlawful, save for licensed hunters, to shoot, and then not on private property; the perfect weather, the blue sky, the exhilarating breeze, the glorious elms and oaks by the way,—make it a day that will live when most other days are dead.

At two o'clock we came in sight of Kenilworth Castle. Oh, this is the place to stir the blood. It is the king of ruins. Warwick is nothing, Melrose is nothing, compared with it. A thousand great facts look out through the broken windows. Earls and kings and queens sit along the shattered sides of the banqueting halls. The stairs are worn deep with the feet that have clambered them for eight hundred years. As a loving daughter arranges the dress of an old man, so every season throws a thick mantle of ivy over the mouldering wall. The roof that caught and echoed back the merriment of dead ages has perished. Time has struck his chisel into every inch of the structure. By the payment of only threepence you find access to places where only the titled were once permitted to walk. You go in, and are overwhelmed with the thoughts of past glory and present decay. These halls were prom-

enacted by Richard Cœur de Lion; in this chapel burned the tomb lights over the grave of Geoffrey de Clinton; in these dungeons kings groaned; in these doorways duchesses fainted. Scene of gold, and silver, and scroll work, and chiseled arch, and mosaic. Here were heard the carousals of the Round Table; from those very stables the caparisoned horses came prancing out for the tournament; through that gateway strong, weak, heroic, mean, splendid, Queen Elizabeth advanced to the castle, while the waters of the lake gleamed under torchlights, and the battlements were aflame with rockets; and cornet, and hautboy, and trumpet poured their music on the air; and goddesses glided out from the groves to meet her; and from turret to foundation Kenilworth trembled under a cannonade, and for seventeen days, at a cost of five thousand dollars a day, the festival was kept. Four hundred servants standing in costly livery; sham battles between knights on horseback; jugglers tumbling on the grass; thirteen bears baited for the amusement of the guests; three hundred and twenty hogsheads of beer consumed, till all Europe applauded, denounced and stood amazed.

Where is the glory now? What has become of the velvet? Who wears the jewels? Would Amy Robsart have so longed to get into the castle had she known its coming ruin? Where are those who were waited on, and those who waited? What has become of Elizabeth, the visitor, and Robert Dudley, the visited? Cromwell's men dashed upon the scene; they drained the lakes; they befouled the banquet hall; they dismantled the towers; they turned the castle into a tomb, on whose scarred and riven sides ambition and cruelty and lust may well read their doom. "So let all thine enemies perish, O Lord; but let them that love him be as the sun when he goeth forth in his might."

CHAPTER XIII.

THE MIDNIGHT LECTURE.

At eight o'clock precisely, on consecutive nights, we stepped on the rostrum at Chicago, Zanesville, Indianapolis, Detroit, Jacksonville, Cleveland and Buffalo. But it seemed that Dayton was to be a failure. We telegraphed from Indianapolis, "Missed connection. Cannot possibly meet engagement at Dayton." Telegram came back saying, "Take a locomotive and come on!" We could not get a locomotive. Another telegram arrived: "Mr. Gale, the superintendent of railroad, will send you in an extra train. Go immediately to the depot!" We gathered up our traps from the hotel floor and sofa, and hurled them at the satchel. They would not go in. We put a collar in our hat, and the shaving apparatus in our coat pocket; got on the satchel with both feet, and declared the thing should go shut if it split everything between Indianapolis and Dayton. Arriving at the depot, the train was ready. We had a locomotive and one car. There were six of us on the train—namely, the engineer and stoker on the locomotive; while following were the conductor, a brakeman at each end of the car, and the pastor of a heap of ashes on Schermerhorn street, Brooklyn. "When shall we get to Dayton?" we asked. "Half-past nine o'clock!" responded the conductor. "Absurd!" we said; "no audience will wait till half-past nine at night for a lecturer."

Away we flew. The car, having such a light load, frisked and kicked, and made merry of a journey that to us was becoming very grave. Going round a sharp curve at break-neck speed, we felt inclined to suggest to the conductor that it would make no especial difference if we did not get to Dayton till a quarter to ten. The night was cold, and the hard ground thundered and cracked. The bridges, instead of roaring, as is their wont, had no time to give any more than a grunt as we struck them and passed on. At times it was so rough we were in doubt as to whether we were on the track or taking a short cut across the field to get to our destination a little sooner. The flagmen would hastily open their windows and look at the screeching train. The whistle blew wildly, not so much to give the villages warning as to let them know that something terrible had gone through. Stopped to take in wood and water. A crusty old man crawled out of a depot, and said to the engineer, "Jim, what on earth is the matter?" "Don't know," said Jim; "that fellow in the car yonder is bound to get to Dayton, and we are putting things through." Brakes lifted, bell rung, and off again. Amid the rush and pitch of the train there was no chance to prepare our toilet, and no looking-glass, and it was quite certain that we would have to step from the train immediately into the lecturing hall. We were unfit to be seen. We were sure our hair was parted in five or six different places, and that the cinders had put our face in mourning, and that something must be done. What time we could spare from holding on to the bouncing seat we gave to our toilet, and the arrangements we made, though far from satisfactory, satisfied our conscience that we had done what we could. A button broke as we were fastening our collar—indeed, a button always does break when you are in a hurry and nobody to sew it on. "How long before we get there;?" we anxiously asked. "I have miscalculated," said the conductor; "we cannot get there till five minutes of ten o'clock." "My dear man," I cried, "you might as well turn round and go back; the audience will be gone long before ten o'clock." "No!" said the conductor; "at the last depot I got a telegram saying they are waiting patiently, and telling us to hurry on." The locomotive seemed to feel it was on the home stretch. At times, what with the whirling smoke and the showering sparks, and the din, and rush, and bang, it seemed as if we were on our last ride, and that the brakes would not fall till we stopped for ever.

At five minutes of ten o'clock we rolled into the Dayton depot, and before the train came to a halt we were in a carriage with the lecturing committee, going at the horse's full run toward the opera house. Without an instant in which to slacken our pulses, the chairman rushed in upon the stage, and introduced the lecturer of the evening. After in the quickest way shedding overcoat and shawl, we confronted the audience, and with our head yet swimming from the motion of the rail-train, we accosted the people—many of whom had been waiting since seven o'clock—with the words, "Long-suffering but patient ladies and gentlemen, you are the best-natured audience I ever saw." When we concluded what we had to say, it was about midnight, and hence the title of this little sketch.

We would have felt it more worthy of the railroad chase if it had been a sermon rather than a lecture. Why do not the Young Men's Christian Associations of the country intersperse religious discourses with the secular, the secular demanding an admission fee, the religious without money or price? If such associations would take as fine a hall, and pay as much for advertising, the audience to hear the sermon would be as large as the audience to hear the lecture. What consecrated minister would not rather tell the story of Christ and heaven free of charge than to get five hundred dollars for a secular address? Wake up, Young Men's Christian Associations, to your glorious opportunity. It would afford a pleasing change. Let Wendell Phillips give in the course his great lecture on "The Lost Arts;" and A. A. Willitts speak on "Sunshine," himself the best illustration of his subject; and Mr. Milburn, by "What a Blind Man Saw in England," almost prove that eyes are a superfluity; and W. H. H. Murray talk of the "Adirondacks," till you can hear the rifle crack and the fall of the antlers on the rock. But in the very midst of all this have a religious discourse that shall show that holiness is the lost art, and that Christ is the sunshine, and that the gospel helps a blind man to see, and that from Pisgah and Mount Zion there is a better prospect than from the top of fifty Adirondacks.

As for ourselves, save in rare and peculiar circumstances, good-bye to the lecturing platform, while we try for the rest of our life to imitate the minister who said, "This one thing I do!" There are exhilarations about lecturing that one finds it hard to break from, and many a minister who thought himself reformed of lecturing has, over-tempted, gone up to the American Library or Boston Lyceum Bureau, and drank down raw, a hundred lecturing engagements. Still, a man once in a while finds a new pair of spectacles to look through.

Between Indianapolis and Dayton, on that wild, swift ride, we found a moral which we close with—for the printer-boy with inky fingers is waiting for this paragraph—Never take the last train when you can help it. Much of the trouble in life is caused by the fact that people, in their engagements, wait til' the last minute. The seven-o'clock train will take them to the right place if everything goes straight, but in this world things are very apt to go crooked. So you had better take the train that starts an hour earlier. In everything we undertake let us leave a little margin. We tried, jokingly, to persuade Captain Berry, when off Cape Hatteras, to go down and get his breakfast, while we took his place and watched the course of the steamer. He intimated to us that we were running too near the bar to allow a greenhorn to manage matters just there. There is always danger in sailing near a coast, whether in ship or in plans and morals. Do not calculate too closely on possibilities. Better have room and time to spare. Do not take the last train. Not heeding this counsel makes bad work for this world and the next. There are many lines of communication between earth and heaven. Men say they can start at any time. After a while, in great excitement, they rush into the depot of mercy and find that the final opportunity has left, and, behold! it is the last train!

CHAPTER XIV.

THE SEXTON.

King David, it is evident, once thought something of becoming a church sexton, for he said, "I had rather be a doorkeeper," and so on. But he never carried out the plan, perhaps because he had not the qualification. It requires more talent in some respects to be sexton than to be king. A sexton, like a poet, is born. A church, in order to peace and success, needs the right kind of man at the prow, and the right kind at the stern—that is, a good minister and a good sexton. So far as we have observed, there are four kinds of janitors.

THE FIDGETY SEXTON.

He is never still. His being in any one place proves to him that he ought to be in some other. In the most intense part of the service, every ear alert to the truth, the minister at the very climax of his subject, the fidgety official starts up the aisle. The whole congregation instantly turn from the consideration of judgment and eternity to see what the sexton wants. The minister looks, the elders look, the people in the gallery get up to look. It is left in universal doubt as to why the sexton frisked about at just that moment. He must have seen a fly on the opposite side of the church wall that needed to be driven off before it spoiled the fresco, or he may have suspicion that a rat terrier is in one of the pews by the pulpit, from the fact that he saw two or three children laughing. Now, there is nothing more perplexing than a dog chase during religious services. At a prayer meeting once in my house, a snarling poodle came in, looked around, and then went and sat under the chair of its owner. We had no objection to its being there (dogs should not be shut out from all advantages), but the intruder would not keep quiet. A brother of dolorous whine was engaged in prayer, when poodle evidently thought that the time for response had come, and gave a loud yawn that had no tendency to solemnize the occasion. I resolved to endure it no longer. I started to extirpate the nuisance. I made a fearful pass of my hand in the direction of the dog, but missed him. A lady arose to give me a better chance at the vile pup, but I discovered that he had changed position. I felt by that time obstinately determined to eject him. He had got under a rocking chair, at a point beyond our reach, unless we got on our knees; and it being a prayer meeting, we felt no inappropriateness in taking that position. Of course the exercise had meanwhile been suspended, and the eyes of all were upon my undertaking. The elders wished me all success in this police duty, but the mischievous lads by the door were hoping for my failure. Knowing this I resolved that if the exercises were never resumed, I would consummate the work and eject the disturber. While in this mood I gave a lunge for the dog, not looking to my feet, and fell over a rocker; but there were sympathetic hands to help me up, and I kept on until by the back of the neck I grasped the grizzly-headed pup, as he commenced kicking, scratching, barking, yelping, howling, and carried him to the door in triumph, and, without any care as to where he landed, hurled him out into the darkness.

Give my love to the sexton, and tell him never to chase a dog in religious service. Better let it alone, though it should, like my friend's pollparrot, during prayer time, break out with the song, "I would not live alway!" But the fidgety sexton is ever on the chase; his boots are apt to be noisy and say as he goes up the aisle, "Creakety-crack! Here I come. Creakety-crack!" Why should he come in to call the doctor out of his pew when the case is not urgent? Cannot the patient wait twenty minutes, or is this the cheap way the doctor has of advertising? Dr. Camomile had but three cases in three months, and, strange coincidence, they all came to him at half-past eleven o'clock Sunday morning, while he was in church. If windows are to be lowered, or blinds closed, or register to be shut off, let it be before the sermon.

THE LAZY SEXTON.

He does not lead the stranger to the pew, but goes a little way on the aisle, and points, saying, "Out yonder!" You leave the photograph of your back in the dust of the seat you occupy; the air is in an atmospheric hash of what was left over last Sunday. Lack of oxygen will dull the best sermon, and clip the wings of gladdest song, and stupefy an audience. People go out from the poisoned air of our churches to die of pneumonia. What a sin, when there is so much fresh air, to let people perish for lack of it! The churches are the worst ventilated buildings on the continent. No amount of grace can make stale air sacred. "The prince of the power of the air" wants nothing but poisoned air for the churches. After audiences have assembled, and their cheeks are flushed, and their respiration has become painful, it is too late to change it. Open a window or door now, and you ventilate only the top of that man's bald head, and the back of the neck of that delicate woman; and you send off hundreds of people coughing and sneezing. One reason why the Sabbaths are so wide apart is that every church building may have six days of atmospheric purification. The best man's breath once ejected is not worth keeping. Our congregations are dying of asphyxia. In the name of all the best interests of the church, I indict one-half the sextons.

THE GOOD SEXTON.

He is the minister's blessing, the church's joy, a harbinger of the millennium. People come to church to have him help them up the aisle. He wears slippers. He stands or sits at the end of the church during an impressive discourse, and feels that, though he did not furnish the ideas, he at least furnished the wind necessary in preaching it. He has a quick nostril to detect unconsecrated odors, and puts the man who eats garlic on the back seat in the corner. He does not regulate the heat by a broken thermometer, minus the mercury. He has the window blinds arranged just right—the light not too glaring so as to show the freckles, nor too dark so as to cast a gloom, but a subdued light that makes the plainest face attractive. He rings the bell merrily for Christmas festival, and tolls it sadly for the departed. He has real pity for the bereaved in whose house he goes for the purpose of burying their dead—not giving by cold, professional manner the impression that his sympathy for the troubled is overpowered by the joy that he has in selling another coffin. He forgets not his own soul; and though his place is to stand at the door of the ark, it is surely inside of it. After a while, a Sabbath comes when everything is wrong in church: the air is impure, the furnaces fail in their work, and the eyes of the people are blinded with an unpleasant glare. Everybody asks, "Where is our old sexton?" Alas! he will never come again. He has gone to join Obed-edom and Berechiah, the doorkeepers of the ancient ark. He will never again take the dusting whisk from the closet under the church stairs, for it is now with him "Dust to dust." The bell he so often rang takes up its saddest tolling for him who used to pull it, and the minister goes into his disordered and unswept pulpit, and finds the Bible upside down as he takes it up to read his text in Psalms, 84th chapter and 10th verse: "I had rather be a doorkeeper in the house of my God than to dwell in the tents of wickedness."

CHAPTER XV.

THE OLD CRADLE.

The historic and old-time cradle is dead, and buried in the rubbish of the garret. A baby of five months, filled with modern notions, would spurn to be rocked in the awkward and rustic thing. The baby spits the "Alexandra feeding-bottle" out of its mouth, and protests against the old-fashioned cradle, giving emphasis to its utterances by throwing down a rattle that cost seven dollars, and kicking off a shoe imported at fabulous expense, and upsetting the "baby-basket," with all its treasures of ivory hair brushes and "Meen Fun." Not with voice, but by violence of gesture and kicks and squirms, it says: "What! You going to put me in that old cradle? Where is the nurse? My patience! What does mother mean? Get me a 'patented self-rocker!'"

The parents yield. In comes the new-fangled crib. The machine is wound up, the baby put in, the crib set in motion, and mother goes off to make a first-rate speech at the "Woman's Rights Convention!"

Conundrum: Why is a maternal elocutionist of this sort like a mother of old time, who trained four sons for the holy ministry, and through them was the means of reforming and saving a thousand souls, and through that thousand of saving ten thousand more? You answer: "No resemblance at all!" You are right. Guessed the conundrum the first time. Go up to the head of the class!

Now, the "patented self-rockers," no doubt, have their proper use; but go up with me into the garret of your old homestead, and exhume the cradle that you, a good while ago, slept in. The rockers are somewhat rough, as though a farmer's plane had fashioned them, and the sides just high enough for a child to learn to walk by. What a homely thing, take it all in all! You say: Stop your depreciation! We were all rocked in that. For about fifteen years that cradle was going much of the time. When the older child was taken out, a smaller child was put in. The crackle of the rockers is pleasant yet in my ears. There I took my first lessons in music as mother sang to me. Have heard what you would call far better singing since then, but none that so thoroughly touched me. She never got five hundred dollars per night for singing three songs at the Academy, with two or three encores grudgefully thrown in; but without pay she sometimes sang all night, and came out whenever encored, though she had only two little ears for an audience. It was a low, subdued tone that sings to me yet across thirty-five years.

You see the edge of that rocker worn quite deep? That is where her foot was placed while she sat with her knitting or sewing, on summer afternoons, while the bees hummed at the door and the shout of the boy at the oxen was heard afield. From the way the rocker is worn, I think that sometimes the foot must have been very tired and the ankle very sore; but I do not think she stopped for that. When such a cradle as that got a-going, it kept on for years.

Scarlet-fever came in the door, and we all had it; and oh, how the cradle did go! We contended as to who should lie in it, for sickness, you know, makes babies of us all. But after a while we surrendered it to Charlie. He was too old to lie in it, but he seemed so very, very sick; and with him in the cradle it was "Rock!" "Rock!" "Rock!" But one day, just as long ago as you can remember, the cradle stopped. When a child is asleep, there is no need of rocking. Charlie was asleep. He was sound asleep. Nothing would wake him. He needed taking up. Mother was too weak to do it. The neighbors came in to do that, and put a flower, fresh out of the garden-dew, between the two still hands. The fever had gone out of the cheek, and left it white, very white—the rose exchanged for the lily. There was one less to contend for the cradle. It soon started again, and with a voice not quite so firm as before, but more tender, the old song came back: "Bye! bye! bye!" which meant more to you than "Il Trovatore," rendered by opera troupe in the presence of an American audience, all leaning forward and nodding to show how well they understood Italian.

There was a wooden canopy at the head of the old cradle that somehow got loose and was taken off. But your infantile mind was most impressed with the face which much of the time hovered over you. Other women sometimes looked in at the child, and said: "That child's hair will be red!" or, "What a peculiar chin!" or, "Do you think that child will live to grow up?" and although you were not old enough to understand their talk, by instinct you knew it was something disagreeable, and began to cry till the dear, sweet, familiar face again hovered and the rainbow arched the sky. Oh, we never get away from the benediction of such a face! It looks at us through storm and night. It smiles all to pieces the world's frown. After thirty-five years of rough tumbling on the world's couch, it puts us in the cradle again, and hushes us as with the very lullaby of heaven.

Let the old cradle rest in the garret. It has earned its quiet. The hands that shook up its pillow have quit work. The foot that kept the rocker in motion is through with its journey. The face that hovered has been veiled from mortal sight. Cradle of blessed memories! Cradle that soothed so many little griefs! Cradle that kindled so many hopes! Cradle that rested so many fatigues! Sleep now thyself, after so many years of putting others to sleep!

One of the great wants of the age is the right kind of a cradle and the right kind of a foot to rock it. We are opposed to the usurpation of "patented self-rockers." When I hear a boy calling his grandfather "old daddy," and see the youngster whacking his mother across the face because she will not let him have ice-cream and lemonade in the same stomach, and at some refusal holding his breath till he gets black in the face, so that to save the child from fits the mother is compelled to give him another dumpling, and he afterward goes out into the world stubborn, willful, selfish and intractable,—I say that boy was brought up in a "patented self-rocker." The old-time mother would have put him down in the old-fashioned cradle, and sung to him,

"Hush, my dear, lie still and slumber,
Holy angels guard thy bed;"

and if that did not take the spunk out of him would have laid him in an inverted position across her lap, with his face downward, and with a rousing spank made him more susceptible to the music.

When a mother, who ought to be most interested in training her children for usefulness and heaven, gives her chief time to fixing up her back hair, and is worried to death because the curls she bought are not of the same shade as the sparsely-settled locks of her own raising; and culturing the dromedarian hump of dry-goods on her back till, as she comes into church, a good old elder bursts into laughter behind his pocket-handkerchief, making the merriment sound as much like a sneeze as possible; her waking moments employed with discussions about polonaise, and vert-de-gris velvets, and ecru percale, and fringed guipure, and poufs, and sashes, and rose-de-chêne silks, and scalloped flounces; her happiness in being admired at balls and parties and receptions,—you may know that she has thrown off the care of her children, that they are looking after themselves, that they are being brought up by machinery instead of loving hands—in a word, that there is in her home a "patented self-rocker!"

So far as possible, let all women dress beautifully: so God dresses the meadows and the mountains. Let them wear pearls and diamonds if they can afford it: God has hung round the neck of his world strings of diamonds, and braided the black locks of the storm with bright ribbons of rainbow. Especially before and right after breakfast, ere they expect to be seen of the world, let them look neat and attractive for the family's sake. One of the most hideous sights is a slovenly woman at the breakfast table. Let woman adorn herself. Let her speak on platforms so far as she may have time and ability to do so. But let not mothers imagine that there is any new way of successfully training children, or of escaping the old-time self-denial and continuous painstaking.

Let this be the commencement of the law suit:

OLD CRADLE
versus
PATENTED SELF-ROCKER.

Attorneys for plaintiff—all the cherished memories of the past.

Attorneys for the defendant—all the humbugs of the present.

For jury—the good sense of all Christendom.

Crier, open the court and let the jury be empaneled.

CHAPTER XVI.

A HORSE'S LETTER.

[TRANSLATED FOR THE TEA-TABLE.]

                Brooklyn Livery Stables,
                        January 20, 1874.

My dear Gentlemen and Ladies: I am aware that this is the first time a horse has ever taken upon himself to address any member of the human family. True, a second cousin of our household once addressed Balaam, but his voice for public speaking was so poor that he got unmercifully whacked, and never tried it again. We have endured in silence all the outrages of many thousands of years, but feel it now time to make remonstrance. Recent attentions have made us aware of our worth. During the epizoötic epidemic we had at our stables innumerable calls from doctors and judges and clergymen. Everybody asked about our health. Groomsmen bathed our throats, and sat up with us nights, and furnished us pocket-handkerchiefs. For the first time in years we had quiet Sundays. We overheard a conversation that made us think that the commerce and the fashion of the world waited the news from the stable. Telegraphs announced our condition across the land and under the sea, and we came to believe that this world was originally made for the horse, and man for his groom.

But things are going back again to where they were. Yesterday I was driven fifteen miles, jerked in the mouth, struck on the back, watered when I was too warm; and instead of the six quarts of oats that my driver ordered for me, I got two. Last week I was driven to a wedding, and I heard music and quick feet and laughter that made the chandeliers rattle, while I stood unblanketed in the cold. Sometimes the doctor hires me, and I stand at twenty doors waiting for invalids to rehearse all their pains. Then the minister hires me, and I have to stay till Mrs. Tittle-Tattle has time to tell the dominie all the disagreeable things of the parish.

The other night, after our owner had gone home and the hostlers were asleep, we held an indignation meeting in our livery stable. "Old Sorrel" presided, and there was a long line of vice-presidents and secretaries, mottled bays and dappled grays and chestnuts, and Shetland and Arabian ponies. "Charley," one of the old inhabitants of the stable, began a speech, amid great stamping on the part of the audience. But he soon broke down for lack of wind. For five years he had been suffering with the "heaves." Then "Pompey," a venerable nag, took his place; and though he had nothing to say, he held out his spavined leg, which dramatic posture excited the utmost enthusiasm of the audience. "Fanny Shetland," the property of a lady, tried to damage the meeting by saying that horses had no wrongs. She said, "Just look at my embroidered blanket. I never go out when the weather is bad. Everybody who comes near pats me on the shoulder. What can be more beautiful than going out on a sunshiny afternoon to make an excursion through the park, amid the clatter of the hoofs of the stallions? I walk, or pace, or canter, or gallop, as I choose. Think of the beautiful life we live, with the prospect, after our easy work is done, of going up and joining Elijah's horses of fire."

Next, I took the floor, and said that I was

born in a warm, snug Pennsylvania barn; was, on my father's side, descended from Bucephalus; on my mother's side, from a steed that Queen Elizabeth rode in a steeple chase. My youth was passed in clover pastures and under trusses of sweet-smelling hay. I flung my heels in glee at the farmer when he came to catch me. But on a dark day I was over-driven, and my joints stiffened, and my fortunes went down, and my whole family was sold. My brother, with head down and sprung in the knees, pulls the street car. My sister makes her living on the tow path, hearing the canal boys swear. My aunt died of the epizoötic. My uncle—blind, and afflicted with the bots, the ringbone and the spring-halt—wanders about the commons, trying to persuade somebody to shoot him. And here I stand, old and sick, to cry out against the wrongs of horses—the saddles that gall, the spurs that prick, the snaffles that pinch, the loads that kill.

At this a vicious-looking nag, with mane half pulled out, and a "watch-eye," and feet "interfering," and a tail from which had been subtracted enough hair to make six "waterfalls," squealed out the suggestion that it was time for a rebellion, and she moved that we take the field, and that all those who could kick should kick, and that all those who could bite should bite, and that all those who could bolt should bolt, and that all those who could run away should run away, and that thus we fill the land with broken wagons and smashed heads, and teach our oppressors that the day of retribution has come, and that our down-trodden race will no more be trifled with.

When this resolution was put to vote, not one said "Aye," but all cried "Nay, nay," and for the space of half an hour kept on neighing.

Instead of this harsh measure, it was voted that, by the hand of Henry Bergh, president of the Society for the Prevention of Cruelty to Animals, I should write this letter of remonstrance.

My dear gentlemen and ladies, remember that we, like yourselves, have moods, and cannot always be frisky and cheerful. You do not slap your grandmother in the face because this morning she does not feel as well as usual; why, then do you slash us? Before you pound us, ask whether we have been up late the night before, or had our meals at irregular hours, or whether our spirits have been depressed by being kicked by a drunken hostler. We have only about ten or twelve years in which to enjoy ourselves, and then we go out to be shot into nothingness. Take care of us while you may. Job's horse was "clothed with thunder," but all we ask is a plain blanket. When we are sick, put us in a "horse-pital." Do not strike us when we stumble or scare. Suppose you were in the harness and I were in the wagon, I had the whip and you the traces, what an ardent advocate you would be for kindness to the irrational creation! Do not let the blacksmith drive the nail into the quick when he shoes me, or burn my fetlocks with a hot file. Do not mistake the "dead-eye" that nature put on my foreleg for a wart to be exterminated. Do not cut off my tail short in fly-time. Keep the north wind out of our stables. Care for us at some other time than during the epizoötics, so that we may see your kindness is not selfish.

My dear friends, our interests are mutual. I am a silent partner in your business. Under my sound hoof is the diamond of national prosperity. Beyond my nostril the world's progress may not go. With thrift, and wealth, and comfort, I daily race neck and neck. Be kind to me if you want me to be useful to you. And near be the day when the red horse of war shall be hocked and impotent, and the pale horse of death shall be hurled back on his haunches, but the white horse of peace, and joy, and triumph shall pass on, its rider with face like the sun, all nations following!

Your most obedient servant,
CHARLEY BUCEPHALUS.

CHAPTER XVII.

KINGS OF THE KENNEL.

I said, when I lost Carlo, that I would never own another dog. We all sat around, like big children, crying about it; and what made the grief worse, we had no sympathizers. Our neighbors were glad of it, for he had not always done the fair thing with them. One of them had lost a chicken when it was stuffed and all ready for the pan, and suspicions were upon Carlo.

I was the only counsel for the defendant; and while I had to acknowledge that the circumstantial evidence was against him, I proved his general character for integrity, and showed that the common and criminal law were on our side, Coke and Blackstone in our favor, and a long list of authorities and decisions: II. Revised Statutes, New York, 132, § 27; also, Watch vs. Towser, Crompton and Meeson, p. 375; also, State of New Jersey vs. Sicem Blanchard.

When I made these citations, my neighbor and his wife, who were judges and jurors in the case, looked confounded; and so I followed up the advantage I had gained with the law maxim, "Non minus ex dolo quam ex culpa quisque hac lege tenetur," which I found afterward was the wrong Latin, but it had its desired effect, so that the jury did not agree, and Carlo escaped with his life; and on the way home he went spinning round like a top, and punctuating his glee with a semicolon made by both paws on my new clothes.

Yet, notwithstanding all his predicaments and frailties, at his decease we resolved, in our trouble, that we would never own another dog. But this, like many another resolution of our life, has been broken; and here is Nick, the Newfoundland, lying sprawled on the mat. He has a jaw set with strength; an eye mild, but indicative of the fact that he does not want too many familiarities from strangers; a nostril large enough to snuff a wild duck across the meadows; knows how to shake hands, and can talk with head, and ear, and tail; and, save an unreasonable antipathy to cats, is perfect, and always goes with me on my walk out of town.

He knows more than a great many people. Never do we take a walk but the poodles, and the rat-terriers, and the grizzly curs with stringy hair and damp nose, get after him. They tumble off the front door step and out of the kennels, and assault him front and rear. I have several times said to him (not loud enough for Presbytery to hear), "Nick, why do you stand all this? Go at them!" He never takes my advice. He lets them bark and snap, and passes on unprovokedly without sniff or growl. He seems to say, "They are not worth minding. Let them bark. It pleases them and don't hurt me. I started out for a six-mile tramp, and I cannot be diverted. Newfoundlanders like me have a mission. My father pulled three drowning men to the beach, and my uncle on my mother's side saved a child from the snow. If you have anything brave, or good, or great for me to do, just clap your hand and point out the work, and I will do it, but I cannot waste my time on rat-terriers."

If Nick had put that in doggerel, I think it would have read well. It was wise enough to become the dogma of a school. Men and women are more easily diverted from the straight course than is Nick. No useful people escape being barked at. Mythology represents Cerberus a monster dog at the mouth of hell, but he has had a long line of puppies. They start out at editors, teachers, philanthropists and Christians. If these men go right on their way, they perform their mission and get their reward, but one-half of them stop and make attempt to silence the literary, political and ecclesiastical curs that snap at them.

Many an author has got a drop of printers' ink spattered in his eye, and collapsed. The critic who had lobsters for supper the night before, and whose wife in the morning had parted his hair on the wrong side, snarled at the new book, and the time that the author might have spent in new work he squanders in gunning for critics. You might better have gone straight ahead, Nick! You will come to be estimated for exactly what you are worth. If a fool, no amount of newspaper or magazine puffery can set you up; and if you are useful, no amount of newspaper or magazine detraction can keep you down. For every position there are twenty aspirants; only one man can get it; forthwith the other nineteen are on the offensive. People are silly enough to think that they can build themselves up with the bricks they pull out of your wall. Pass on and leave them. What a waste of powder for a hunter to go into the woods to shoot black flies, or for a man of great work to notice infinitesimal assault! My Newfoundland would scorn to be seen making a drive at a black-and-tan terrier.

But one day, on my walk with Nick, we had an awful time. We were coming in at great speed, much of the time on a brisk run, my mind full of white clover tops and the balm that exudes from the woods in full leafage, when, passing the commons, we saw a dog fight in which there mingled a Newfoundland as large as Nick, a blood-hound and a pointer. They had been interlocked for some time in terrific combat.

They had gnashed upon and torn each other until there was getting to be a great scarcity of ears, and eyes and tails.

Nick's head was up, but I advised him that he had better keep out of that canine misunderstanding. But he gave one look, as much as to say, "Here at last is an occasion worthy of me," and at that dashed into the fray. There had been no order in the fight before, but as Nick entered they all pitched at him. They took him fore, and aft, and midships. It was a greater undertaking than he had anticipated. He shook, and bit, and hauled, and howled. He wanted to get out of the fight, but found that more difficult than to get in.

Now, if there is anything I like, it is fair play. I said, "Count me in!" and with stick and other missiles I came in like Blucher at nightfall. Nick saw me and plucked up courage, and we gave it to them right and left, till our opponents went scampering down the hill, and I laid down the weapons of conflict and resumed my profession as a minister, and gave the mortified dog some good advice on keeping out of scrapes, which homily had its proper effect, for with head down and penitent look, he jogged back with me to the city.

Lesson for dogs and men: Keep out of fights. If you see a church contest, or a company of unsanctified females overhauling each other's good name until there is nothing left of them but a broken hoop skirt and one curl of back hair, you had better stand clear. Once go in, and your own character will be an invitation to their muzzles. Nick's long, clean ear was a temptation to all the teeth. You will have enough battles of your own, without getting a loan of conflicts at twenty per cent a month.

Every time since the unfortunate struggle I

have described, when Nick and I take a country walk and pass a dog fight, he comes close up by my side, and looks me in the eye with one long wipe of the tongue over his chops, as much as to say, "Easier to get into a fight than to get out of it. Better jog along our own way;" and then I preach him a short sermon from Proverbs xxvi. 17: "He that passeth by, and meddleth with strife belonging not to him, is like one that taketh a dog by the ears."

CHAPTER XVIII.

THE MASSACRE OF CHURCH MUSIC.

There has been an effort made for the last twenty years to kill congregational singing. The attempt has been tolerably successful; but it seems to me that some rules might be given by which the work could be done more quickly, and completely. What is the use of having it lingering on in this uncertain way? Why not put it out of its misery? If you are going to kill a snake, kill it thoroughly, and do not let it keep on wagging its tail till sundown. Congregational singing is a nuisance, anyhow, to many of the people. It interferes with their comfort. It offends their taste. It disposes their nose to flexibility in the upward direction. It is too democratic in its tendency. Down with congregational singing, and let us have no more of it.

The first rule for killing it is to have only such tunes as the people cannot sing!

In some churches it is the custom for choirs at each service to sing one tune which the people know. It is very generous of the choir to do that. The people ought to be very thankful for the donation. They do not deserve it. They are all "miserable offenders" (I heard them say so), and, if permitted once in a service to sing, ought to think themselves highly favored. But I oppose this singing of even the one tune that the people understand. It spoils them. It gets them hankering after more. Total abstinence is the only safety; for if you allow them to imbibe at all, they will after a while get in the habit of drinking too much of it, and the first thing you know they will be going around drunk on sacred psalmody.

Beside that, if you let them sing one tune at a service, they will be putting their oar into the other tunes and bothering the choir. There is nothing more annoying to the choir than, at some moment when they have drawn out a note to exquisite fineness, thin as a split hair, to have some blundering elder to come in with a "Praise ye the Lord!" Total abstinence, I say! Let all the churches take the pledge even against the milder musical beverages; for they who tamper with champagne cider soon get to Hock and old Burgundy.

Now, if all the tunes are new, there will be no temptation to the people. They will not keep humming along, hoping they will find some bars down where they can break into the clover pasture. They will take the tune as an inextricable conundrum, and give it up. Besides that, Pisgah, Ortonville and Brattle Street are old fashioned. They did very well in their day. Our fathers were simple-minded people, and the tunes fitted them. But our fathers are gone, and they ought to have taken their baggage with them. It is a nuisance to have those old tunes floating around the church, and sometime, just as we have got the music as fine as an opera, to have a revival of religion come, and some new-born soul break out in "Rock of Ages, Cleft for Me!" till the organist stamps the pedal with indignation, and the leader of the tune gets red in the face and swears. Certainly anything that makes a man swear is wrong—ergo, congregational singing is wrong. "Quod erat demonstrandum;" which, being translated, means "Plain as the nose on a man's face."

What right have people to sing who know nothing about rhythmics, melodics, dynamics? The old tunes ought to be ashamed of themselves when compared with our modern beauties. Let Dundee, and Portuguese Hymn, and Silver Street hide their heads beside what we heard not long ago in a church—just where I shall not tell. The minister read the hymn beautifully. The organ began, and the choir sang, as near as I could understand, as follows:

  Oo—aw—gee—bah
   Ah—me—la—he
  O—pah—sah—dah
  Wo—haw—gee-e-e-e.

My wife, seated beside me, did not like the music. But I said: "What beautiful sentiment! My dear, it is a pastoral. You might have known that from 'Wo-haw-gee!' You have had your taste ruined by attending the Brooklyn Tabernacle." The choir repeated the last line of the hymn four times. Then the prima donna leaped on to the first line, and slipped, and fell on to the second, and that broke and let her through into the third. The other voices came in to pick her up, and got into a grand wrangle, and the bass and the soprano had it for about ten seconds; but the soprano beat (women always do), and the bass rolled down into the cellar, and the soprano went up into the garret, but the latter kept on squalling as though the bass, in leaving her, had wickedly torn out all her back hair. I felt anxious about the soprano, and looked back to see if she had fainted; but found her reclining in the arms of a young man who looked strong enough to take care of her.

Now, I admit that we cannot all have such things in our churches. It costs like sixty. In the Church of the Holy Bankak it costs one hundred dollars to have sung that communion piece:

"Ye wretched, hungry, starving poor!"

But let us come as near to it as we can. The tune "Pisgah" has been standing long enough on "Jordan's stormy banks." Let it pass over and get out of the wet weather. Good-bye, "Antioch," "Harwell" and "Boylston." Good-bye till we meet in glory.

But if the prescription of new tunes does not end congregational singing, I have another suggestion. Get an irreligious choir, and put them in a high balcony back of the congregation. I know choirs who are made up chiefly of religious people, or those, at least, respectful for sacred things. That will never do, if you want to kill the music. The theatrical troupe are not busy elsewhere on Sabbath, and you can get them at half price to sing the praises of the Lord. Meet them in the green room at the close of the "Black Crook" and secure them. They will come to church with opera-glasses, which will bring the minister so near to them they can, from their high perch, look clear down his throat and see his sermon before it is delivered. They will make excellent poetry on Deacon Goodsoul as he carries around the missionary box. They will write dear little notes to Gonzaldo, asking him how his cold is and how he likes gum-drops. Without interfering with the worship below, they can discuss the comparative fashionableness of the "basque" and the "polonaise," the one lady vowing she thinks the first style is "horrid," and the other saying she would rather die than be seen in the latter; all this while the chorister is gone out during sermon to refresh himself with a mint-julep, hastening back in time to sing the last hymn. How much like heaven it will be when, at the close of a solemn service, we are favored with snatches from Verdi's "Trovatore,"

Meyerbeer's "Huguenots" and Bellini's "Sonnambula," from such artists as

Mademoiselle Squintelle,
Prima Donna Soprano, from Grand Opera House, Paris.
Signor Bombastani,
Basso Buffo, from Royal Italian Opera.
Carl Schneiderine.,
First Baritone, of His Majesty's Theatre, Berlin.

If after three months of taking these two prescriptions the congregational singing is not thoroughly dead, send me a letter directed to my name, with the title of O. F. M. (Old Fogy in Music), and I will, on the receipt thereof, write another prescription, which I am sure will kill it dead as a door nail, and that is the deadest thing in all history.

CHAPTER XIX.

THE BATTLE OF PEW AND PULPIT.

Two more sermons unloaded, and Monday morning I went sauntering down town, ready for almost anything. I met several of my clerical friends going to a ministers' meeting. I do not often go there, for I have found that some of the clerical meetings are gridirons where they roast clergymen who do not do things just as we do them. I like a Presbyterian gridiron no better than a Methodist one, and prefer to either of them an old-fashioned spit, such as I saw this summer in Oxford, England, where the rabbit is kept turning round before a slow fire, in blessed state of itinerancy, the rabbit thinking he is merely taking a ride, while he is actually roasting.

As on the Monday morning I spoke of I was passing down the street, I heard high words in a church. What could it be? Was it the minister, and the sexton, and the trustees fighting? I went in to see, when, lo! I found that the Pew and the Pulpit were bantering each other at a great rate, and seemed determined to tell each one the other's faults. I stood still as a mouse that I might hear all that was said, and my presence not be noticed.

The Pew was speaking as I went in, and said to the Pulpit, in anything but a reverential tone: "Why don't you speak out on other days as well as you do to-day? The fact is, I never knew a Pulpit that could not be heard when it was thoroughly mad. But when you give out the hymn on Sabbaths, I cannot tell whether it is the seventieth or the hundredth. When you read the chapter, you are half through with it before I know whether it is Exodus or Deuteronomy. Why do you begin your sermon in so low a key? If the introduction is not worth hearing, it is not worth delivering. Are you explaining the text? If so, the Lord's meaning is as important as anything you will have in your sermon. Throw back your shoulders, open your mouth! Make your voice strike against the opposite wall! Pray not only for a clean heart, but for stout lungs. I have nearly worn out my ears trying to catch your utterances. When a captain on a battlefield gives an order, the company all hear; and if you want to be an officer in the Lord's army, do not mumble your words. The elocution of Christ's sermon is described when we are told he opened his mouth and taught them—that is, spoke distinctly, as those cannot who keep their lips half closed. Do you think it a sign of modesty to speak so low? I think the most presuming thing on earth for a Pulpit to do is to demand that an audience sit quiet when they cannot hear, simply looking. The handsomest minister I ever saw is not worth looking at for an hour and a half at a stretch. The truth is that I have often been so provoked with your inarticulate speech that I would have got up and left the church, had it not been for the fact that I am nailed fast, and my appearance on the outside on a Sabbath-day, walking up and down, would have brought around me a crowd of unsanctified boys to gaze at me, a poor church pew on its travels."

The Pulpit responded in anything but a pious tone: "The reason you do not hear is that your mind on Sundays is full of everything but the gospel. You work so hard during the week that you rob the Lord of his twenty-four hours. The man who works on Sunday as well as the rest of the week is no worse than you who abstain on that day, because your excessive devotion to business during the week kills your Sunday; and a dead Sunday is no Sunday at all. You throw yourself into church as much as to say, 'Here, Lord, I am too tired to work any more for myself; you can have the use of me while I am resting!' Besides that, O Pew! you have a miserable habit. Even when you can hear my voice on the Sabbath and are wide awake, you have a way of putting your head down or shutting your eyes, and looking as if your soul had vacated the premises for six weeks. You are one of those hearers who think it is pious to look dull; and you think that the Pew on the other side the aisle is an old sinner because he hunches the Pew behind him, and smiles when the truth hits the mark. If you want me to speak out, it is your duty not only to be wide awake, but to look so. Give us the benefit of your two eyes. There is one of the elders whose eyes I have never caught while speaking, save once, and that was when I was preaching from Psalm cxiii. 12, 'They compassed me about like bees,' and by a strange coincidence a bumble-bee got into church, and I had my attention divided between my text and the annoying insect, which flew about like an illustration I could not catch. A dull Pew is often responsible for a dull Pulpit. Do not put your head down on the back of the seat in front, pretending you are very much affected with the sermon, for we all know you are napping.''

The Pew: "If you want me to be alert, give me something fresh and startling. Your sermons all sound alike. It don't make any difference where you throw the net, you never fish up anything but moss-bunkers. You are always talking about stale things. Why don't you give us a touch of learned discussion, such as the people hear every Sunday in the church of Reverend Doctor Heavyasbricks, when, with one eye on heaven and the other on the old man in the gallery, he speaks of the Tridentine theory of original sin, and Patristic Soteriology, Mediæval Trinitarianism, and Antiochian Anthropology? Why do you not give us some uncommon words, and instead of 'looking back upon your subject,' sometimes 'recapitulate,' and instead of talking about a man's 'peculiarities,' mention his 'idiot-sin-crasies,' and describe the hair as the capillary adornment; and instead of speaking of a thing as tied together, say it was 'inosculated.'"

The Pulpit: "You keep me so poor I cannot buy the books necessary to keep me fresh. After the babies are clothed, and the table is provided for, and the wardrobe supplied, my purse is empty, and you know the best carpenter cannot make good shingles without tools. Better pay up your back salary instead of sitting there howling at me. You eased your conscience by subscribing for the support of the gospel, but the Lord makes no record of what a man subscribes; he waits to see whether he pays. The poor widow with the two mites is applauded in Scripture because she paid cash down. I have always noticed that you Pews make a big noise about Pulpit deficiencies, just in proportion to the little you do. The fifty cents you pay is only premium on your policy of five dollars' worth of grumbling. O critical Pew! you had better scour the brass number on your own door before you begin to polish the silver knob on mine."

The Pew: "I think it is time for you to go away. I am glad that conference is coming. I shall see the bishop, and have you removed to some other part of the Lord's vineyard. You are too plain a Pulpit for such an elegant Pew.

Just look at your big hands and feet. We want a spiritual guide whose fingers taper to a fine point, and one who could wear, if need be, a lady's shoe. Get out, with your great paws and clodhoppers! We want in this church a Pulpit that will talk about heaven, and make no allusion to the other place. I have a highly educated nose, and can stand the smell of garlic and assafœtida better than brimstone. We want an oleaginous minister, commonly called oily. We want him distinguished for his unctuosity. We want an ecclesiastical scent-bag, or, as you might call him, a heavenly nosegay, perfect in every respect, his ordinary sneeze as good as a doxology. If he cry during some emotional part of his discourse, let it not be an old-fashioned cry, with big hands or coat sleeve sopping up the tears, but let there be just two elegant tears, one from each eye, rolling down parallel into a pocket-handkerchief richly embroidered by the sewing society, and inscribed with the names of all the young ladies' Bible class. If he kneel before sermon, let it not be a coming down like a soul in want, but on one knee, so artistically done that the foot shall show the twelve-dollar patent leather shoe, while the aforesaid pocket-handkerchief is just peeping from the coat pocket, to see if the ladies who made it are all there—the whole scene a religious tableau. We want a Pulpit that will not get us into a tearing-down revival, where the people go shouting and twisting about, regardless of carpets and fine effects, but a revival that shall be born in a band-box, and wrapped in ruffles, and lie on a church rug, so still that nobody will know it is there. If we could have such a Pulpit as that, all my fellow-Pews would join me, and we would give it a handsome support; yes, we would pay him; if we got just what we want, we could afford to give, in case he were thoroughly eloquent, Demosthenic and bewitching—I am quite certain we could, although I should not want myself to be held responsible; yes, he should have eight hundred dollars a year, and that is seven hundred and sixty dollars more than Milton got for his 'Paradise Lost,' about which one of his learned contemporaries wrote: 'The old blind schoolmaster, John Milton, hath published a tedious poem on the fall of man; if its length be not considered a merit, it has no other.' Nothing spoils ministers like too big a salary. Jeshurun waxed fat and kicked; if it had not been for the wax and the fat, he would not have kicked. Sirloin steaks and mince pies are too rich for ministers. Put these men down on catfish and flounders, as were the fishermen apostles. Too much oats makes horses frisky, and a minister high-fed is sure to get his foot over the shaft. If we want to keep our pulpits spiritual, we must keep them poor. Blessed are the poor!''

"Stop! stop!" cried the Pulpit; and it seemed to rise higher than before, and to tremble from head to foot with excitement, and the banisters to twist as if to fly in indignation at the Pew, and the plush on the book-board to look red as fire; and seeing there was going to be a collision between Pulpit and Pew, I ran up the aisle and got between them (they were wide enough apart to allow me to get in), and I cried, "Silence! This is great talk for a church. Pulpits ought not to scold, and Pews ought not to grumble. As far as I can see, you are both to blame. Better shake hands and pray for a better spirit. It wants more than a bishop to settle this difficulty. The Lord Almighty alone can make Pulpit and Pew what they ought to be. You both need to be baptized over again!" Then, taking up a silver bowl that stood on the communion table, half full of the water yesterday used at a babe's christening, I stood between the belligerents, and sprinkled Pew and Pulpit with a Christian baptism, in the name of the Father, and the Son, and the Holy Ghost. And when I got through, I could not tell whether Pew or Pulpit said Amen the louder.

CHAPTER XX.

THE DEVIL'S GRIST-MILL.

The above name has been given to one of the geysers of California, that group of boiling springs, now famous. Indeed, the whole region has been baptized with Satanic nomenclature.

The guide showed us what he called the "Devil's Mush-pot," the "Devil's Pulpit," the "Devil's Machine Shop," and, hearing a shrill whistle in the distance, we were informed it was the "Devil's Tea-kettle." Seeing some black water rushing from a fountain, from which the people of the neighborhood and tourists dip up genuine ink, we were told it was the "Devil's Ink-stand." Indeed, you are prepared for this on the Pacific Railroad, as your guide book points you to the "Devil's Gate," and the "Devil's Slide," and the "Devil's Peak."

We protest against this surrender of all the geysers to the arch demon. All the writers talk of the place as infernal. We do not believe this place so near to hell as to heaven. We doubt if Satan ever comes here. He knows enough of hot climates, by experience, to fly from the hiss of these subterranean furnaces. Standing amid the roaring, thundering, stupendous wonder of two hundred spouting water springs, we felt like crying out, "Great and marvelous are thy works, Lord God almighty!"

Let all the chemists and geologists of the world come and see the footstep of God in crystals of alum and sulphur and salt. Here is the chemist's shop of the continent. Enough black indelible ink rushes out of this well, with terrific plash, to supply all the scribes of the world. There are infinite fortunes for those who will delve for the borax, nitric and sulphuric acid, soda, magnesia and other valuables. Enough sulphur here to purify the blood of the race, or in gunpowder to kill it; enough salt to savor all the vegetables of the world. Its acid water, which waits only for a little sugar to make it delicious lemonade, may yet be found in all the drug stores of the country. The water in one place roars like a steamboat discharging its steam. Your boots curl with the heat as you stand on the hot rocks, looking. Almost anywhere a thrust of your cane will evoke a gush of steam. Our thermometer, plunged into one spring, answered one hundred and seventy-five degrees of heat. Thrust in the "Witch's Caldron," it asserted two hundred and fifteen degrees. "The Ink-stand" declared itself two hundred degrees. An artificial whistle placed at the mouth of one of these geysers may be heard miles away. You get a hot bath without paying for it. The guide warns you off the crust in certain places, lest you at the same moment be drowned and boiled. Here an egg cooks hard in three minutes.

The whole scene is unique and incomparable. The Yosemite makes us think of the Alps; San Francisco reminds us of Chicago; Foss, the stage driver, hurling his passengers down the mountain at breakneck speed, suggests the driver of an Alpine diligence; Hutchings' mountain horse, that stumbled and fell flat upon us, suggested our mule-back experiences in Tête Noir Pass of Switzerland; but the geysers remind us of nothing that we ever saw, or ever expect to see. They have a voice, a bubble, a smoke, a death-rattle, peculiar to themselves. No photographist can picture them, no words describe them, no fancy sketch them.

You may visit them by either of two routes; but do not take the advice of Foss, the celebrated stage driver. You ought to go by one route, and return the other; yet Foss has made thousands of travelers believe that the only safe and interesting way to return is the way they go—namely, by his route. They who take his counsel miss some of the grandest scenery on the continent. Any stage driver who by his misrepresentations would shut a tourist out of the entrancing beauties of the "Russian Valley" ought to be thrashed with his own raw-hide. We heard Foss bamboozling a group of travelers with the idea that on the other route the roads were dangerous, the horses poor, the accommodations wretched and the scenery worthless. We came up in time to combat the statement with our own happy experiences of the Russian Valley, and to save his passengers from the oft-repeated imposition.

And thus I have suggested the chief annoyance of California travel. The rivalries of travel are so great that it is almost impossible to get accurate information. The stage drivers, guides and hotel proprietors, for the most part, are financially interested in different routes. Going to Yosemite Valley by the "Calaveras route," from the office in San Francisco where you buy your ticket to the end of your journey, everybody assures you that J. M. Hutchings, one of the hotel keepers of Yosemite, is a scholar, a poet, a gentleman and a Christian, and that to him all the world is indebted for the opening of the valley. But if you go in by the "Mariposa route," then from the office where you get your ticket, along by all the way stations and through the mountain passes, you are assured that Mr. Liedig, the hotel keeper of Yosemite, is the poet and Christian, and that J. M. Hutchings aforesaid is a nobody, a blower, a dead beat, the chief impediment to the interests of Yosemite—or, to use a generic term, a scalawag.

The fact is that no one can afford in California to take the same route twice, for each one has a glory of its own. If a traveler have but one day for the Louvre Gallery, he cannot afford to spend it all in one corridor; and as California is one great picture gallery, filled with the masterpieces of Him who paints with sunshine and dew and fire, and sculptures with chisel of hurricane and thunderbolt, we cannot afford to pass more than once before any canvas or marble.

But whatever route you choose for the "Hot Springs," and whatever pack of stage driver yarns you accept, know this—that in all this matchless California, with climate of perpetual summer, the sky cloudless and the wind blowing six months from the genial west; the open field a safe threshing floor for the grandest wheat harvests of the world; nectarines and pomegranates and pears in abundance that perish for lack of enough hands to pick; by a product in one year of six million five hundred thousand gallons of wine proving itself the vineyard of this hemisphere; African callas, and wild verbenas, and groves of oleander and nutmeg; the hills red with five thousand cattle in a herd, and white with a hundred and fifty thousand sheep in a flock; the neighboring islands covered with wild birds' eggs, that enrich the markets, or sounding with the constant "yoi-hoi," "yoi-hoi," of the sea-lions that tumble over them; a State that might be called the "Central Park" of the world; the gulches of gold pouring more than fifty million of dollars a year into the national lap; lofty lakes, like Tahoe, set crystalline in the crown of the mountain; waterfalls so weird that you do not wonder that the Indians think that whosoever points his finger at them must die, and in one place the water plunging from a height more than sixteen times greater than Niagara,—even in such a country of marvels as this, there is nothing that makes you ask more questions, or bow in profounder awe, or come away with more interesting reminiscences than the world renowned California geysers.

There is a bang at your bed-room door at five o'clock in the morning, rousing you to go up and explore them; and after spending an hour or two in wandering among them, you come back to the breakfast prepared by the model landlord of California, jolly, obliging, intelligent, reasonable. As you mount the stage for departure you give him a warm shake of the hand, and suggest that it would be a grand thing if some one with a vein of poetry in his mind and the faith of God in his heart would come round some day, and passing among the geysers with a sprinkle of hot steam, would baptize them with a Christian name.

Let us ascribe to Satan nothing that is grand, or creative, or wise. He could not make one of these grains of alum. He could not blow up one of these bubbles on the spring. He does some things that seem smart; but taking him all in all, he is the biggest fool in the universe.

If the devil wants to boil his "Tea-kettle," or stir his "Mush-pot," or whirl his "Grist-mill," let him do it in his own territory. Meanwhile, let the water and the fire and the vapor, at the lift of David's orchestral baton, praise the Lord!

CHAPTER XXI.

THE CONDUCTOR'S DREAM.

He had been on the train all day, had met all kinds of people, received all sorts of treatment, punctured all kinds of tickets, shouted "All out!" and "All aboard!" till throat, and head, and hand, and foot were weary. It would be a long while before we would get to another depot, and so he sagged down in the corner of the car to sleep. He was in the most uncomfortable position possible. The wind blew in his neck, his arm was hung over the back of the seat, he had one foot under him, and his knee pressing hard against a brass hinge. In that twisted and convoluted position he fell asleep, and soon began to dream.

It seemed to him, in his sleep, that the car was full of disagreeables. Here was a man who persisted in having a window up, while the rain and sleet drove in. There was a man who occupied the whole seat, and let the ladies stand. Here sat a man smoking three poor cigars at once, and expectorating into the beaver hat of the gentleman in front. Yonder was a burglar on his way to jail, and opposite a murderer going to the gallows. He thought that pickpockets took his watch and ruffians refused to pay their fare. A woman traveling alone shot at him a volley of questions: "Say, conductor, how long before we will get to the Junction?" "Are you sure we have not passed it?" "Do you always stop there?" "What time is it?" Madam, do keep quiet! "None of your impudence!" "How far from here to the Junction?" "Do you think that other train will wait?" "Do you think we will get there in time?" "Say, conductor, how many miles yet?" "Are you looking out?" "Now, you won't let me go past, will you?" "Here! conductor, here! Help me out with my carpet bag, and band-box, and shawl, and umbrella, and this bundle of sausage and head-cheese." What was worse, the train got going one hundred and fifty miles an hour, and pulling the connecting rope, it broke, and the cars got off the track, and leaped on again, and the stove changed places with the wood box, and things seemed going to terrible split and unmitigated smash. The cities flew past. The brakes were powerless. The whistle grew into a fiend's shriek. Then the train began to slow up, and sheeted ghosts swung lanterns along the track, and the cars rolled into a white depot, which turned out to be a great marble tomb; and looking back to see his passengers, they were all stark dead, frozen in upright horror to the car backs.

Hearing by the man's snore, and seeing by his painful look, he was having an awful dream, we tapped him on the shoulder and said, "Conductor! Turn over that seat, and take my shawl, and stretch yourself out, and have a comfortable nap." "Thank you, sir," he said, and immediately sprawled himself out in the easiest way possible. He began his slumbers just as an express train glides gracefully out of Pittsburg depot; then went at it more earnestly, lifted all the brakes, put on all the steam, and in five minutes was under splendid headway. He began a second dream, but it was the opposite of the first. He thought that he had just stepped on the platform of his car, and a lady handed him a bouquet fresh from the hot house. A long line of railroad presidents and superintendents had come to the depot to see him off, and tipped their hats as he glided out into the open air. The car was an improvement on Pullman's best. Three golden goblets stood at the end, and every time he turned the spigot of the water cask, it foamed soda-water—vanilla if you turned it one way, strawberry if you turned it the other. The spittoon was solid silver, and had never been used but once, when a child threw into it an orange peeling. The car was filled with lords and duchesses, who rose and bowed as he passed through to collect the fare. They all insisted on paying twice as much as was demanded, telling him to give half to the company and keep the rest for himself. Stopped a few minutes at Jolly Town, Gleeville and Velvet Junction, making connection with the Grand Trunk and Pan-Handle route for Paradise. But when the train halted there was no jolt, and when it started there was no jerk. The track was always clear, no freight train in the way, no snow bank to be shoveled—train always on time. Banks of roses on either side, bridges with piers of bronze, and flagmen clad in cloth-of-gold. The train went three hundred miles the hour, but without any risk, for all the passengers were insured against accident in a company that was willing to pay four times the price of what any neck was worth. The steam whistle breathed as sweetly as any church choir chanting its opening piece. Nobody asked the conductor to see his time-table, for the only dread any passenger had was that of coming to the end of its journey.

As night came on the self-adjusting couches spread themselves on either side; patent boot-jacks rolled up and took your boots off; unseen fingers tucked the damask covers all about you, and the porter took your pocket-book to keep till morning, returning it then with twice what you had in it at nightfall. After a while the train slackens to one hundred and seventy-five miles an hour, and the conductor, in his dream, announces that they are coming near the terminus. More brakes are dropped and they are running but ninety miles the hour; and some one, looking out of the window, says, "How slow we go!" "Yes," says the conductor, "we are holding up." Now they have almost stopped, going at only seventy miles the hour. The long line of depot lamps are flashing along the track. On the platform of the station are the lovers who are waiting for their betrothed, and parents who have come down to greet their children, returned with a fortune, and wives who have not been able to eat or drink since their spouses went away three weeks before. As the cushioned train flashes into the depot and stops, wedding bells peal, and the gong of many banquets sounds, and white arms are flung about necks, reckless of mistake, and innumerable percussions of affection echo through the depot, so crisp and loud that they wake the conductor, who thought that the boisterous smack was on his own cheek, but finds that he is nothing but a bachelor railroad man, with a lantern, at midnight getting out into a snow bank.

Application: Get an easy position when you sleep, if you have any choice between angels and gorgons. At midnight, seizing a chair, I ran into the next room, resolving to kill, at the first stroke, the ruffian who was murdering a member of my household. But there was no ruffian. The sweet girl had, during the day, been reading of St. Bartholomew's massacre, and was now lying on her back, dreaming it all over again. When dreams find anyone lying flat on the back, they cry out, "Here is a flat surface on which to skate and play ball," and from scalp to toe they sport themselves. The hardest nag in all the world to ride is the nightmare. Many think that sleep is lost time. But the style of your work will be mightily affected by the style of your slumber. Sound Asleep is sister of Wide Awake. Adam was the only man who ever lost a rib by napping too soundly; but when he woke up, he found that, instead of the twelve ribs with which he started, he really had nigh two dozen. By this I prove that sleep is not subtraction, but addition. This very night may that angel put balm on both your eyelids five minutes after you touch the pillow!

CHAPTER XXII.

PUSH & PULL.

We have long been acquainted with a business firm whose praises have never been sung. I doubt whether their names are ever mentioned on Exchange. They seem to be doing more business and have more branch houses than the Stewarts or Lippincotts. You see their names almost everywhere on the door. It is the firm of Push & Pull. They generally have one of their partners' names on outside of the door, and the other on the inside: "Push" on the outside and "Pull" on the inside. I have found their business-houses in New York, Brooklyn, Philadelphia, Boston, London and Edinburgh. It is under my eye, whether I go to buy a hat, a shawl, or a paper of pins, or watch, or ream of foolscap. They are in all kinds of business; and from the way they branch out, and put up new stores, and multiply their signboards on the outside and inside of doors, I conclude that the largest business firm on earth to-day is Push & Pull.

When these gentlemen join the church, they make things go along vigorously. The roof stops leaking; a new carpet blooms on the church floor; the fresco is retouched; the high pulpit is lowered till it comes into the same climate with the pew; strangers are courteously seated; the salary of the minister is paid before he gets hopelessly in debt to butcher and baker; and all is right, financially and spiritually, because Push & Pull have connected themselves with the enterprise.

A new parsonage is to be built, but the movement does not get started. Eight or ten men of slow circulation of blood and stagnant liver put their hands on the undertaking, but it will not budge. The proposed improvement is about to fail when Push comes up behind it and gives it a shove, and Pull goes in front and lays into the traces; and, lo! the enterprise advances, the goal is reached! And all the people who had talked about the improvement, but done nothing toward it, invite the strangers who come to town to go up and see "our" parsonage.

Push & Pull are wide-awake men. They never stand round with their hands in their pockets, as though feeling for money that they cannot find. They have made up their minds that there is a work for them to do; and without wasting any time in reverie, they go to work and do it. They start a "life insurance company." Push is the president, and Pull the secretary. Before you know it, all the people are running in to have their lungs sounded, and to tell how many times they have had the rheumatism; how old they are; whether they ever had fits; and at what age their father and mother expired; and putting all the family secrets on paper, and paying Push & Pull two hundred dollars to read it. When this firm starts a clothing house, they make a great stir in the city. They advertise in such strong and emphatic way that the people are haunted with the matter, and dream about it, and go round the block to avoid that store door, lest they be persuaded in and induced to buy something they cannot afford. But some time the man forgets himself, and finds he is in front of the new clothing store, and, at the first glance of goods in the show window, is tempted to enter. Push comes up behind him, and Pull comes up before him, and the man is convinced of the shabbiness of his present appearance—that his hat will not do, that his coat and vest and all the rest of his clothes, clean down to his shoes, are unfit; and before one week is past, a boy runs up the steps of this customer with a pasteboard box marked, "From the clothing establishment of Push & Pull. C. O. D."

These men can do anything they set their hands to—publish a newspaper, lay out a street, build a house, control a railroad, manage a church, revolutionize a city. In fact, any two industrious, honorable, enterprising men can accomplish wonders. One does the outdoor work of the store, and the other the indoor work. One leads, the other follows; but both working in one direction, all obstacles are leveled before them.

I wish that more of our young men could graduate from the store of Push & Pull. We have tens of thousands of young men doing nothing. There must be work somewhere if they will only do it. They stand round, with soap locks and scented pocket-handkerchiefs, tipping their hats to the ladies; while, instead of waiting for business to come to them, they ought to go to work and make a business. Here is the ladder of life. The most of those who start at the top of the ladder spend their life in coming down, while those who start at the bottom may go up. Those who are born with a gold spoon in their mouth soon lose the spoon. The two school bullies that used to flourish their silk pocket-handkerchiefs in my face, and with their ivory-handled, four-bladed knives punch holes through my kite—one of them is in the penitentiary, and the other ought to be.

Young man, the road of life is up hill, and our load heavy. Better take off your kid gloves, and patent leathers, and white vest, and ask Push, with his stout shoulder, and Pull, with his strong grip, to help you. Energy, pluck, courage, obstinate determination are to be cultured. Eat strong meat, drop pastries, stop reading sickly novelettes, pray at both ends of the day and in the middle, look a man in the eye when you talk to him, and if you want to be a giant keep your head out of the lap of indulgences that would put a pair of shears through your locks.

If you cannot get the right kind of business partner, marry a good, honest wife. Fine cheeks and handsome curls are very well, but let them be mere incidentals. Let our young men select practical women; there are a few of them left. With such a one you can get on with almost all heavy loads of life. You will be Pull, and she Push; and if you do not get the house built and the fortune established, send me word, and I will tear this article up in such small pieces that no one will ever be able to find it.

Life is earnest work, and cannot be done with the tips of the fingers. We want more crowbars and fewer gold toothpicks. The obstacles before you cannot be looked out of countenance by a quizzing glass. Let sloth and softliness go to the wall, but three cheers for Push & Pull, and all their branch business houses!

CHAPTER XXIII.

BOSTONIANS.

We ran up to the Boston anniversaries to cast our vote with those good people who are in that city on the side of the right. We like to go to the modern Athens two or three times a year. Among other advantages, Boston always soothes our nerves. It has a quieting effect upon us. The people there are better satisfied than any people we know of. Judging from a few restless spirits who get on some of the erratic platforms of that city, and who fret and fume about things in general, the world has concluded that Boston is at unrest. But you may notice that the most of the restless people who go there are imported speakers, whom Boston hires to come once a year and do for her all the necessary fretting.

The genuine Bostonian is satisfied. He rises moderately early, goes to business without any especial haste, dresses comfortably, talks deliberately, lunches freely, and goes home to his family at plausible hours. He would like to have the world made better, but is not going to make himself sick in trying to cure the moral ailments of others.

The genuine Bostonian is, for the most part, pleased with himself, has confidence that the big elm will last another hundred years, keeps his patriotism fresh by an occasional walk near the meat market under Faneuil Hall, and reads the "Atlantic Monthly." We believe there is less fidgeting in Boston than in any city of the country. We think that the average of human life must be longer there than in most cities.

Dyspepsia is a rarity; for when a mutton chop is swallowed of a Bostonian it gives up, knowing that there is no need of fighting against such inexorable digestion.

The ladies of Boston have more color in their cheeks than those of many cities, and walk as though they would live to get round the next corner. It is not so fashionable to be delicate. They are robust in mind and always ready for an argument. State what you consider an indisputable proposition, and they will say: "Yes, but then—" They are not afraid to attack the theology of a minister, or the jurisprudence of a lawyer, or the pharmacy of a doctor. If you do not look out, the Boston woman will throw off her shawl and upset your logic in a public meeting.

We like the men and women of Boston. They have opinions about everything—some of them adverse to your own, but even in that case so well expressed that, in admiration for the rhetoric, you excuse the divergence of sentiment. We never found a half-and-half character in Boston. The people do not wait till they see which way the smoke of their neighbors' chimneys blows before they make up their own minds.

The most conspicuous book on the parlor table of the hotels of other cities is a book of engravings or a copy of the Bible. In some of the Boston hotels, the prominent book on the parlor table is "Webster's Unabridged Dictionary." You may be left in doubt about the Bostonian's character, but need not doubt his capacity to parse a sentence, or spell without any resemblance of blunder the word "idiosyncrasy."

Boston, having made up its mind, sticks to it. Many years ago it decided that the religious societies ought to hold a public anniversary in June, and it never wavers. New York is tired of these annual demonstrations, and goes elsewhere; but in the early part of every June, Boston puts its umbrella under its arm and starts for Tremont Temple, or Music Hall, determined to find an anniversary, and finds it. You see on the stage the same spectacles that shone on the speakers ten years ago, and the same bald heads, for the solid men of Boston got in the way of wearing their hair thin in front a quarter of a century ago, and all the solid men of Boston will, for the next century, wear their hair thin in front.

There are fewer dandies in Boston than in most cities. Clothes, as a general thing, do not make fun of the people they sit on. The humps on the ladies' backs are not within two feet of being as high as in some of the other cities, and a dromedary could look at them without thinking itself caricatured. You see more of the outlandishness of fashion in one day on Broadway than in a week on any one street of Boston. Doubtless, Boston is just as proud as New York, but her pride is that of brains, and those, from the necessities of the case, are hidden.

Go out on the fashionable drive of Boston, and you find that the horses are round limbed, and look as well satisfied as their owners. A restless man always has a thin horse. He does not give the creature time to eat, wears out on him so many whip lashes, and keeps jerking perpetually at the reins. Boston horses are, for the most part, fat, feel their oats, and know that the eyes of the world are upon them. You see, we think it no dishonor to a minister to admire good horses, provided he does not trade too often, and impose a case of glanders and bots on his unsophisticated neighbor. We think that, as a minister is set up for an example to his flock, he ought to have the best horse in the congregation.

A minister is no more sacred when riding behind a spavined and ringboned nag than when whirling along after a horse that can swallow a mile in 2.30.

The anniversary week in Boston closed by a display of flowers and fruits in Horticultural Hall. It was appropriate that philanthropists and Christians, hot from discussions of moral and religious topics, should go in and take a bath of rose leaves and geraniums. Indeed, I think the sweetest anniversary of the week was that of these flowers. A large rhododendron presided. Azaleas and verbenas took part in the meeting. The Chinese honeysuckle and clematis joined in the doxology. A magnolia pronounced the benediction. And we went home praying for the time when the lily of the valley shall be planted in every heart, and the desert shall blossom as the rose.

CHAPTER XXIV.

JONAH VERSUS THE WHALE.

Unbelievers have often told us that the story of the prophet swallowed by a great fish was an absurdity. They say that, so long in the stomach of the monster, the minister would have been digested. We have no difficulty in this matter. Jonah was a most unwilling guest of the whale. He wanted to get out. However much he may have liked fish, he did not want it three times a day and all the time. So he kept up a fidget, and a struggle, and a turning over, and he gave the whale no time to assimilate him. The man knew that if he was ever to get out he must be in perpetual motion. We know men that are so lethargic they would have given the matter up, and lain down so quietly that in a few hours they would have gone into flukes and fish bones, blow-holes and blubber.

Now we see men all around us who have been swallowed by monstrous misfortunes. Some of them sit down on a piece of whalebone and give up. They say: "No use! I will never get back my money, or restore my good name, or recover my health." They float out to sea and are never again heard of. Others, the moment they go down the throat of some great trouble, begin immediately to plan for egress. They make rapid estimate of the length of the vertebrate, and come to the conclusion how far they are in. They dig up enough spermaceti out of the darkness to make a light, and keep turning this way and that, till the first you know they are out. Determination to get well has much to do with recovered invalidism. Firm will to defeat bankruptcy decides financial deliverance. Never surrender to misfortune or discouragement. You can, if you are spry enough, make it as uncomfortable for the whale as the whale can make it uncomfortable for you. There will be some place where you can brace your foot against his ribs, and some long upper tooth around which you may take hold, and he will be as glad to get rid of you for tenant as you are to get rid of him for landlord. There is a way, if you are determined to find it. All our sympathies are with the plaintiff in the suit of Jonah versus Leviathan.

CHAPTER XXV.

SOMETHING UNDER THE SOFA.

Not more than twenty-five miles from New York city, and not more than two years ago, there stood a church in which occurred a novelty. We promised not to tell; but as we omit all names, we think ourselves warranted in writing the sketch. The sacred edifice had stood more than a hundred years, until the doors were rickety, and often stood open during the secular week. The window glass in many places had been broken out. The shingles were off and the snow drifted in, and the congregation during a shower frequently sat under the droppings of the sanctuary. All of which would have been a matter for sympathy, had it not been for the fact that the people of the neighborhood were nearly all wealthy, and lived in large and comfortable farm houses, making the appearance of their church a fit subject for satire.

The pulpit was giving way with the general wreck, was unpainted, and the upholstery on book-board and sofa seemed calling out with Jew's voice, "Any old clo'? Any old clo'?" One Sabbath, the minister felt some uneasiness under the sofa while the congregation were singing, and could not imagine the cause; but found out the next day that a maternal cat had made her nest there with her group of offspring, who had entered upon mortal life amid these honorable surroundings.

Highly-favored kittens! If they do not turn out well, it will not be the fault of their mother, who took them so early under good influences.

In the temple of old the swallow found a nest for herself where she might lay her young; but this is the first time we ever knew of the conference of such honors on the Felis domestica. It could not have been anything mercenary that took the old cat into the pulpit, for "poor as a church mouse" has become proverbial. Nothing but lofty aspirations could have taken her there, and a desire that her young should have advantages of high birth. If in the "Historical Society" there are mummied cats two thousand years old, much more will post-mortem honors be due this ecclesiastical Pussy.

We see many churches in city as well as town that need rehabilitation and reconstruction. People of a neighborhood have no right to live in houses better constructed than their church. Better touch up the fresco, and put on a new roof, and tear out the old pews which ignore the shape of a man's back, and supersede the smoky lamps by clarified kerosene or cheap gas brackets. Lower you high pulpit that your preacher may come down from the Mont Blanc of his isolation and solitariness into the same climate of sympathy with his audience. Tear away the old sofa, ragged and spring-broken, on which the pastors of forty years have been obliged to sit, and see whether there are any cats in your antediluvian pulpit.

Would it not be well for us all to look under our church sofas and see if there be anything lurking there that we do not suspect? A cat, in all languages, has been the symbol of deceit and spitefulness, and she is more fit for an ash barrel than a pulpit. Since we heard that story of feline nativity, whenever we see a minister of religion, on some question of Christian reform, skulking behind a barrier, and crawling away into some half-and-half position on the subject of temperance or oppression, and daring not to speak out, instead of making his pulpit a height from which to hurl the truth against the enemies of God, turning it into a cowardly hiding place, we say, "Another cat in the pulpit."

Whenever we see a professed minister of religion lacking in frankness of soul, deceitful in his friendship, shaking hands heartily when you meet him, but in private taking every possible opportunity of giving you a long, deep scratch, or in public newspapers giving you a sly dig with the claw of his pen, we say: "Another cat in the pulpit!"

Once a year let all our churches be cleaned with soap, and sand, and mop, and scrubbing brush, and the sexton not forget to give one turn of his broom under the pastor's chair. Would that with one bold and emphatic "scat!" we could drive the last specimen of deceitfulness and skulking from the American pulpit!

CHAPTER XXVI.

THE WAY TO KEEP FRESH.

How to get out of the old rut without twisting off the wheel, or snapping the shafts, or breaking the horse's leg, is a question not more appropriate to every teamster than to every Christian worker. Having once got out of the old rut, the next thing is to keep out. There is nothing more killing than ecclesiastical humdrum. Some persons do not like the Episcopal Church because they have the same prayers every Sabbath, but have we not for the last ten years been hearing the same prayers over and over again, the product of a self-manufactured liturgy that has not the thousandth part of the excellency of those petitions that we hear in the Episcopal Church?

In many of our churches sinners hear the same exhortations that they have been hearing for the last fifteen years, so that the impenitent man knows, the moment the exhorter clears his throat, just what is going to be said; and the hearer himself is able to recite the exhortation as we teach our children the multiplication table forward or backward. We could not understand the doleful strain of a certain brother's prayer till we found out that he composed it on a fast day during the yellow fever in 1821, and has been using it ever since.

There are laymen who do not like to hear a sermon preached the second time who yet give their pastors the same prayer every week at the devotional meeting—that is, fifty-two times the year, with occasional slices of it between meals.

If they made any spiritual advancement, they would have new wants to express and new thanksgivings to offer. But they have been for a decade of years stuck fast in the mud, and they splash the same thing on you every week. We need a universal church cleaning by which all canting and humdrum shall be scrubbed out.

If we would keep fresh, let us make occasional excursions into other circles than our own. Artists generally go with artists, farmers with farmers, mechanics with mechanics, clergymen with clergymen, Christian workers with Christian workers. But there is nothing that sooner freshens one up than to get in a new group, mingling with people whose thought and work run in different channels. For a change put the minister on the hay rack and the farmer in the clergyman's study.

Let us read books not in our own line. After a man has been delving in nothing but theological works for three months, a few pages in the Patent-office Report will do him more good than Doctor Dick on "The Perseverance of the Saints." Better than this, as a diversion, is it to have some department of natural history or art to which you may turn, a case of shells or birds, or a season ticket to some picture gallery. If you do nothing but play on one string of the bass viol, you will wear it out and get no healthy tune. Better take the bow and sweep it clear across in one grand swirl, bringing all four strings and all eight stops into requisition.

Let us go much into the presence of the natural world if we can get at it. Especially if we live in great thoroughfares let us make occasional flight to the woods and the mountains. Even the trees in town seem artificial. They dare not speak where there are so many to listen, and the hyacinth and geranium in flower pots in the window seem to know they are on exhibition. If we would once in a while romp the fields, we would not have so many last year's rose leaves in our sermons, but those just plucked, dewy and redolent.

We cannot see the natural world through the books or the eyes of others. All this talk about "babbling brooks" is a stereotyped humbug. Brooks never "babble." To babble is to be unintelligent and imperfect of tongue. But when the brooks speak, they utter lessons of beauty that the dullest ear can understand. We have wandered from the Androscoggin in Maine to the Tombigbee in Alabama, and we never found a brook, that "babbled." The people babble who talk about them, not knowing what a brook is. We have heard about the nightingale and the morning lark till we tire of them. Catch for your next prayer meeting talk a chewink or a brown thresher. It is high time that we hoist our church windows, especially those over the pulpit, and let in some fresh air from the fields and mountains.

CHAPTER XXVII.

CHRISTMAS BELLS.

The sexton often goes into the tower on a sad errand. He gives a strong pull at the rope, and forth from the tower goes a dismal sound that makes the heart sink. But he can now go up the old stairs with a lithe step and pull quick and sharp, waking up all the echoes of cavern and hill with Christmas bells. The days of joy have come, days of reunion, days of congratulation. "Behold I bring you good tidings of great joy that shall be to all people."

First, let the bells ring at the birth of Jesus! Mary watching, the camels moaning, the shepherds rousing up, the angels hovering, all Bethlehem stirring. What a night! Out of its black wing is plucked the pen from which to write the brightest songs of earth and the richest doxologies of heaven. Let camel or ox stabled that night in Bethlehem, after the burden-bearing of the day, stand and look at Him who is to carry the burdens of the world. Put back the straw and hear the first cry of Him who is come to assuage the lamentation of all ages.

Christmas bells ring out the peace of nations! We want on our standards less of the lion and eagle and more of the dove. Let all the cannon be dismounted, and the war horses change their gorgeous caparisons for plough harness. Let us have fewer bullets and more bread. Life is too precious to dash it out against the brick casements. The first Peace Society was born in the clouds, and its resolution was passed unanimously by angelic voices, "Peace on earth, good-will to men."

Christmas bells ring in family reunions! The rail trains crowded with children coming home. The poultry, fed as never since they were born, stand wondering at the farmer's generosity. The markets are full of massacred barnyards. The great table will be spread and crowded with two, or three, or four generations. Plant the fork astride the breast bone, and with skillful twitch, that we could never learn, give to all the hungry lookers-on a specimen of holiday anatomy. Mary is disposed to soar, give her the wing. The boy is fond of music, give him the drum stick. The minister is dining with you, give him the parson's nose. May the joy reach from grandfather, who is so dreadful old he can hardly find the way to his plate, down to the baby in the high chair with one smart pull of the table cloth upsetting the gravy into the cranberry. Send from your table a liberal portion to the table of the poor, some of the white meat as well as the dark, not confining your generosity to gizzards and scraps. Do not, as in some families, keep a plate and chair for those who are dead and gone. Your holiday feast would be but poor fare for them; they are at a better banquet in the skies.

Let the whole land be full of chime and carol. Let bells, silver and brazen, take their sweetest voice, and all the towers of Christendom rain music.

We wish all our friends a merry Christmas. Let them hang up their stockings; and if Santa Claus has any room for us in his sleigh, we will get in and ride down their chimney, upsetting all over the hearth a thousand good wishes.

CHAPTER XXVIII.

POOR PREACHING.

There never was a time when in all denominations of Christians there was so much attractive sermonizing as to-day. Princeton, and Middletown, and Rochester, and New Brunswick, are sending into the ministry a large number of sharp, earnest, consecrated men. Stupidity, after being regularly ordained, is found to be no more acceptable to the people than before, and the title of Doctorate cannot any longer be substituted for brains. Perhaps, however, there may get to be a surfeit of fine discourses. Indeed, we have so many appliances for making bright and incisive preachers that we do not know but that after a while, when we want a sleepy discourse as an anodyne, we shall have to go to the ends of the earth to find one; and dull sermons may be at a premium, congregations of limited means not being able to afford them at all; and so we shall have to fall back on chloral or morphine.

Are we not, therefore, doing a humanitarian work when we give to congregations some rules by which, if they want it, they may always have poor preaching?

First. Keep your minister poor. There is nothing more ruinous than to pay a pastor too much salary. Let every board of trustees look over their books and see if they have erred in this direction; and if so, let them cut down the minister's wages. There are churches which pay their pastors eight hundred dollars per annum. What these good men do with so much money we cannot imagine. Our ministers must be taken in. If by occasional fasting for a day our Puritan fathers in New England became so good, what might we not expect of our ministers if we kept them in perpetual fast? No doubt their spiritual capacity would enlarge in proportion to their shrinkage at the waistcoat. The average salary of ministers in the United States is about six hundred dollars. Perhaps by some spiritual pile-driver we might send it down to five hundred dollars; and then the millennium, for the lion by that time would be so hungry he would let the lamb lie down inside of him. We would suggest a very economical plan: give your spiritual adviser a smaller income, and make it up by a donation visit. When everything else fails to keep him properly humble, that succeeds. We speak from experience. Fourteen years ago we had one, and it has been a means of grace to us ever since.

Secondly. For securing poor preaching, wait on your pastor with frequent committees. Let three men some morning tie their horses at the dominie's gate, and go in and tell him how to preach, and pray, and visit. Tell him all the disagreeable things said about him for six months, and what a great man his predecessor was, how much plainer his wife dressed, and how much better his children behaved. Pastoral committees are not like the small-pox—you can have them more than once; they are more like the mumps, which you may have first on one side and then on the other. If, after a man has had the advantage of being manipulated by three church committees, he has any pride or spirit left, better give him up as incorrigible.

Thirdly. To secure poor preaching, keep the minister on the trot. Scold him when he comes to see you because he did not come before, and tell him how often you were visited by the former pastor. Oh, that blessed predecessor! Strange they did not hold on to the angel when they had him. Keep your minister going. Expect him to respond to every whistle. Have him at all the tea parties and "the raisings." Stand him in the draught of the door at the funeral—a frequent way of declaring a pulpit vacant. Keep him busy all the week in out-door miscellaneous work; and if at the end of that time he cannot preach a weak discourse, send for us, and we will show him how to do it. Of course there are exceptions to all rules; but if the plan of treatment we have proposed be carried out, we do not see that any church in city or country need long be in want of poor preaching.

CHAPTER XXIX.

SHELVES A MAN'S INDEX.

In Chelsea, a suburb of London, and on a narrow street, with not even a house in front, but, instead thereof, a long range of brick wall, is the house of Thomas Carlyle. You go through a narrow hall and turn to the left, and are in the literary workshop where some of the strongest thunderbolts of the world have been forged. The two front windows have on them scant curtains of reddish calico, hung at the top of the lower sash, so as not to keep the sun from looking down, but to hinder the street from looking in.

The room has a lounge covered with the same material, and of construction such as you would find in the plainest house among the mountains. It looks as if it had been made by an author not accustomed to saw or hammer, and in the interstices of mental work. On the wall are a few wood-cuts in plain frames or pinned against the wall; also a photograph of Mr. Carlyle taken one day, as his family told us, when he had a violent toothache and could attend to nothing else. It is his favorite picture, though it gives him a face more than ordinarily severe and troubled.

In long shelves, unpainted and unsheltered by glass or door, is the library of the world-renowned thinker. The books are worn, as though he had bought them to read. Many of them are uncommon books, the titles of which we never saw before. American literature is almost ignored, while Germany monopolizes many of the spaces. We noticed the absence of theological works, save those of Thomas Chalmers, whose name and genius he well-nigh worshiped. The carpets are old and worn and faded—not because he cannot afford better, but because he would have his home a perpetual protest against the world's sham. It is a place not calculated to give inspiration to a writer. No easy chairs, no soft divans, no wealth of upholstery, but simply a place to work and stay. Never having heard a word about it, it was nevertheless just such a place as we expected.

We had there confirmed our former theory of a man's study as only a part of himself, or a piece of tight-fitting clothing. It is the shell of the tortoise, just made to fit the tortoise's back. Thomas Carlyle could have no other kind of a workshop. What would he do with a damask-covered table, or a gilded inkstand, or an upholstered window? Starting with the idea that the intellect is all and the body naught but an adjunct or appendage, he will show that the former can live and thrive without any approval of the latter. He will give the intellect all costly stimulus, and send the body supperless to bed. Thomas Carlyle taken as a premise, this shabby room is the inevitable conclusion. Behold the principle.

We have a poetic friend. The backs of his books are scrolled and transfigured. A vase of japonicas, even in mid-winter, adorns his writing desk. The hot-house is as important to him as the air. There are soft engravings on the wall. This study-chair was made out of the twisted roots of a banyan. A dog, sleek-skinned, lies on the mat, and gets up as you come in. There stand in vermilion all the poets from Homer to Tennyson. Here and there are chamois heads and pressed seaweed. He writes on gilt-edged paper with a gold pen and handle twisted with a serpent. His inkstand is a mystery of beauty which unskilled hands dare not touch, lest the ink spring at him from some of the open mouths, or sprinkle on him from the bronze wings, or with some unexpected squirt dash into his eyes the blackness of darkness.

We have a very precise friend. Everything is in severe order. Finding his door-knob in the dark, you could reason out the position of stove, and chair, and table; and placing an arrow at the back of the book on one end of the shelf, it would fly to the other end, equally grazing all the bindings. It is ten years since John Milton, or Robert Southey, or Sir William Hamilton have been out of their places, and that was when an ignoramus broke into the study. The volumes of the encyclopedias never change places. Manuscripts unblotted, and free from interlineation, and labeled. The spittoon knows its place in the corner, as if treated by tobacco chewers with oft indignity. You could go into that study with your eyes shut, turn around, and without feeling for the chair throw yourself back with perfect confidence that the furniture would catch you. No better does a hat fit his head, or shoe his foot, or the glove his hand, than the study fits his whole nature.

We have a facetious friend. You pick off the corner of his writing table "Noctes Ambrosianæ" or the London "Punch." His chair is wide, so that he can easily roll off on the floor when he wants a good time at laughing. His inkstand is a monkey, with the variations. His study-cap would upset a judge's risibilities. Scrap books with droll caricatures and facetiæ. An odd stove, exciting your wonder as to where the coal is put in or the poker thrust for a shaking. All the works of Douglass Jerrold, and Sydney Smith, and Sterne, the scalawag ecclesiastic. India-rubber faces capable of being squashed into anything.

Puzzles that you cannot untangle. The four walls covered with cuts and engravings sheared from weekly pictorials and recklessly taken from parlor table books. Prints that put men and women into hopeless satire.

We have a friend of many peculiarities. Entering his house, you find nothing in the place where you expected it. "Don Quixote," with all its windmills mixed up with "Dr. Dick on the Sacraments," "Mark Twain's "Jumping Frog," and "Charnock on the Attributes." Passing across the room, you stumble against the manuscript of his last lecture, or put your foot in a piece of pie that has fallen off the end of the writing table. You mistake his essay on the "Copernican System" for blotting paper. Many of his books are bereft of the binding; and in attempting to replace the covers, Hudibras gets the cover which belongs to "Barnes on the Acts of the Apostles." An earthquake in the room would be more apt to improve than to unsettle. There are marks where the inkstand became unstable and made a handwriting on the wall that even Daniel could not have interpreted. If, some fatal day, the wife or housekeeper come in, while the occupant is absent, to "clear up," a damage is done that requires weeks to repair. For many days the question is, "Where is my pen? Who has the concordance? What on earth has become of the dictionary? Where is the paper cutter?" Work is impeded, patience lost, engagements are broken, because it was not understood that the study is a part of the student's life, and that you might as well try to change the knuckles to the inside of the hand, or to set the eyes in the middle of the forehead, as to make the man of whom we speak keep his pen on the rack, or his books off the floor, or the blotting paper straight in the portfolio.

The study is a part of the mental development. Don't blame a man for the style of his literary apartments any more than you would for the color of his hair or the shape of his nose. If Hobbes carries his study with him, and his pen and his inkstand in the top of his cane, so let him carry them. If Lamartine can best compose while walking his park, paper and pencil in hand, so let him ramble. If Robert Hall thinks easiest when lying flat on his back, let him be prostrate. If Lamasius writes best surrounded by children, let loose on him the whole nursery. Don't criticise Charles Dickens because he threw all his study windows wide open and the shades up. It may fade the carpet, but it will pour sunshine into the hearts of a million readers. If Thomas Carlyle chose to call around an ink-spattered table Goethe, and Schiller, and Jean Paul Frederick Richter, and dissect the shams of the world with a plain goose-quill, so be it. The horns of an ox's head are not more certainly a part of the ox than Thomas Carlyle's study and all its appointments are a part of Thomas Carlyle.

The gazelle will have soft fur, and the lion a shaggy hide, and the sanctum sanctorum is the student's cuticle.

CHAPTER XXX.

BEHAVIOR AT CHURCH.

Around the door of country meeting-houses it has always been the custom for the people to gather before and after church for social intercourse and the shaking of hands. Perhaps because we, ourselves, were born in the country and had never got over it, the custom pleases us. In the cities we arrive the last moment before service and go away the first moment after. We act as though the church were a rail-car, into which we go when the time for starting arrives, and we get out again as soon as the depot of the Doxology is reached. We protest against this business way of doing things. Shake hands when the benediction is pronounced with those who sat before and those who sat behind you. Meet the people in the aisle, and give them Christian salutation. Postponement of the dining hour for fifteen minutes will damage neither you nor the dinner. That is the moment to say a comforting word to the man or woman in trouble. The sermon was preached to the people in general; it is your place to apply it to the individual heart.

The church aisle may be made the road to heaven. Many a man who was unaffected by what the minister said has been captured for God by the Christian word of an unpretending layman on the way out.

You may call it personal magnetism, or natural cordiality, but there are some Christians who have such an ardent way of shaking hands after meeting that it amounts to a benediction. Such greeting is not made with the left hand. The left hand is good for a great many things, for instance to hold a fork or twist a curl, but it was never made to shake hands with, unless you have lost the use of the right. Nor is it done by the tips of the fingers laid loosely in the palm of another. Nor is it done with a glove on. Gloves are good to keep out the cold and make one look well, but have them so they can easily be removed, as they should be, for they are non-conductors of Christian magnetism. Make bare the hand. Place it in the palm of your friend. Clench the fingers across the back part of the hand you grip. Then let all the animation of your heart rush to the shoulder, and from there to the elbow, and then through the fore arm and through the wrist, till your friend gets the whole charge of gospel electricity.

In Paul's time he told the Christians to greet each other with a holy kiss. We are glad the custom has been dropped, for there are many good people who would not want to kiss us, as we would not want to kiss them. Very attractive persons would find the supply greater than the demand. But let us have a substitute suited to our age and land. Let it be good, hearty, enthusiastic, Christian hand-shaking.

Governor Wiseman, our grave friend at tea, broke in upon us at this moment and said: I am not fond of indiscriminate hand-shaking, and so am not especially troubled by the lack of cordiality on the part of church-goers. But I am sometimes very much annoyed on Sabbaths with the habit of some good people in church. It may be foolish in me; but when the wind blows from the east, it takes but little to disturb me.

There are some of the best Christian people who do not know how to carry themselves in religious assemblage. They never laugh. They never applaud. They never hiss. Yet, notwithstanding, are disturbers of public worship.

There is, for instance, the coughing brigade. If any individual right ought to be maintained at all hazards, it is the right of coughing. There are times when you must cough. There is an irresistible tickling in the throat which demands audible demonstration. It is moved, seconded and unanimously carried that those who have irritated windpipes be heard. But there are ways with hand or handkerchief of breaking the repercussion. A smothered cough is dignified and acceptable if you have nothing better to offer. But how many audiences have had their peace sacrificed by unrestrained expulsion of air through the glottis! After a sudden change in the weather, there is a fearful charge made by the coughing brigade. They open their mouths wide, and make the arches ring with the racket. They begin with a faint "Ahem!" and gradually rise and fall through all the scale of dissonance, as much as to say: "Hear, all ye good people! I have a cold! I have a bad cold! I have an awful bad cold! Hear how it racks me, tears me, torments me. It seems as if my diaphragm must be split. I took this awful bad cold the other night. I added to it last Sunday. Hear how it goes off! There it is again. Oh dear me! If I only had 'Brown's troches,' or the syrup of squills, or a mustard plaster, or a woolen stocking turned wrong side out around my neck!" Brethren and sisters who took cold by sitting in the same draught join the clamor, and it is glottis to glottis, and laryngitis to laryngitis, and a chorus of scrapings and explosions which make the service hideous for a preacher of sensitive nerves.

We have seen people under the pulpit coughing with their mouth so far open we have been tempted to jump into it. There are some persons who have a convenient ecclesiastical cough. It does not trouble them ordinarily; but when in church you get them thoroughly cornered with some practical truth, they smother the end of the sentences with a favorite paroxysm. There is a man in our church who is apt to be taken with one of these fits just as the contribution box comes to him, and cannot seem to get his breath again till he hears the pennies rattling in the box behind him. Cough by all means, but put on the brakes when you come to the down grade, or send the racket through at least one fold of your pocket-handkerchief.

Governor Wiseman went on further to say that the habits of the pulpit sometimes annoyed him as much as the habits of the pew. The Governor said: I cannot bear the "preliminaries" of religious service.

By common consent the exercises in the churches going before the sermon are called "preliminaries." The dictionary says that a "preliminary" is that which precedes the main business. We do not think the sermon ought to be considered the main business. When a pastor at the beginning of the first prayer says "O God!" he has entered upon the most important duty of the service. We would not depreciate the sermon, but we plead for more attention to the "preliminaries." If a minister cannot get the attention of the people for prayer or Bible reading, it is his own fault. Much of the interest of a service depends upon how it is launched.

The "preliminaries" are, for the most part, the time in which people in church examine their neighbors' clothes. Milliners and tailors get the advantage of the first three-quarters of an hour. The "preliminaries" are the time to scrutinize the fresco, and look round to see who is there, and get yourself generally fixed.

This idea is fostered by home elocutionary professors who would have the minister take the earlier exercises of the occasion to get his voice in tune. You must not speak out at first. It is to be a private interview between you and heaven. The people will listen to the low grumble, and think it must be very good if they could only hear it. As for ourselves, we refuse to put down our head in public prayer until we find out whether or not we are going to be able to hear. Though you preach like an angel, you will not say anything more important than that letter of St. Paul to the Corinthians, or that Psalm of David which you have just now read to the backs of the heads of the congregation. Laymen and ministers, speak out! The opening exercises were not instituted to clear your voice, but to save souls. If need be, squeeze a lemon and eat "Brown's troches" for the sake of your voice before you go to church; but once there, make your first sentence resonant and mighty for God. An hour and a half is short time anyhow to get five hundred or five thousand people ready for heaven. It is thought classic and elegant to have a delicate utterance, and that loud tones are vulgar. But we never heard of people being converted by anything they could not hear. It is said that on the Mount of Olives Christ opened His mouth and taught them, by which we conclude He spake out distinctly. God has given most Christians plenty of lungs, but they are too lazy to use them. There are in the churches old people hard of hearing who, if the exercises be not clear and emphatic, get no advantage save that of looking at the blessed minister.

People say in apology for their inaudible tones: "It is not the thunder that kills, but the lightning." True enough; but I think that God thinks well of the thunder or He would not use so much of it. First of all, make the people hear the prayer and the chapter. If you want to hold up at all, let it be on the sermon and the notices. Let the pulpit and all the pews feel that there are no "preliminaries."

CHAPTER XXXI.

MASCULINE AND FEMININE.

There are men who suppose they have all the annoyances. They say it is the store that ruffles the disposition; but if they could only stay at home as do their wives, and sisters, and daughters, they would be, all the time, sweet and fair as a white pond lily. Let some of the masculine lecturers on placidity of temper try for one week the cares of the household and the family. Let the man sleep with a baby on one arm all night, and one ear open to the children with the whooping-cough in the adjoining apartment. Let him see the tray of crockery and the cook fall down stairs, and nothing saved but the pieces. Let the pump give out on a wash-day, and the stove pipe, when too hot for handling, get dislocated. Let the pudding come out of the stove stiff as a poker. Let the gossiping gabbler of next door come in and tell all the disagreeable things that neighbors have been saying. Let the lungs be worn out by staying indoors without fresh air, and the needle be threaded with nerves exhausted. After one week's household annoyances, he would conclude that Wall street is heaven and the clatter of the Stock Exchange rich as Beethoven's symphony.

We think Mary of Bethany a little to blame for not helping Martha get the dinner. If women sympathize with men in the troubles of store and field, let the men also sympathize with the women in the troubles of housekeeping. Many a housewife has died of her annoyances. A bar of soap may become a murderous weapon. The poor cooking stove has sometimes been the slow fire on which the wife has been roasted. In the day when Latimer and Ridley are honored before the universe as the martyrs of the fire, we do not think the Lord will forget the long line of wives, mothers, daughters and sisters who have been the martyrs of the kitchen.

Accompanying masculine criticism of woman's temper goes the popular criticism of woman's dress.

A convention has recently been held in Vineland, attended by the women who are opposed to extravagance in dress. They propose, not only by formal resolution, but by personal example, to teach the world lessons of economy by wearing less adornment and dragging fewer yards of silk.

We wish them all success, although we would have more confidence in the movement if so many of the delegates had not worn bloomer dress. Moses makes war upon that style of apparel in Deuteronomy xxii. 5: "The woman shall not wear that which pertaineth unto man." Nevertheless we favor every effort to stop the extravagant use of dry goods and millinery.

We have, however, no sympathy with the implication that women are worse than men in this respect. Men wear all they can without interfering with their locomotion, but man is such an awkward creature he cannot find any place on his body to hang a great many fineries. He could not get round in Wall street with eight or ten flounces, and a big-handled parasol, and a mountain of back hair. Men wear less than women, not because they are more moral, but because they cannot stand it. As it is, many of our young men are padded to a superlative degree, and have corns and bunions on every separate toe from wearing shoes too tight.

Neither have we any sympathy with the implication that the present is worse than the past in matters of dress. Compare the fashion plates of the seventeenth century with the fashion plates of the nineteenth, and you decide in favor of our day. The women of Isaiah's time beat anything now. Do we have the kangaroo fashion Isaiah speaks of—the daughters who walked with "stretched forth necks?" Talk of hoops! Isaiah speaks of women with "round tires like the moon." Do we have hot irons for curling our hair? Isaiah speaks of "wimples and crisping pins." Do we sometimes wear glasses astride our nose, not because we are near-sighted, but for beautification? Isaiah speaks of the "glasses, and the earrings, and the nose jewels." The dress of to-day is far more sensible than that of a hundred or a thousand years ago.

But the largest room in the world is room for improvement, and we would cheer on those who would attempt reformation either in male or female attire. Meanwhile, we rejoice that so many of the pearls, and emeralds, and amethysts, and diamonds of the world are coming in the possession of Christian women. Who knows but that the spirit of ancient consecration may some day come upon them, and it shall again be as it was in the time of Moses, that for the prosperity of the house of the Lord the women may bring their bracelets, and earrings, and tablets and jewels? The precious stones of earth will never have their proper place till they are set around the Pearl of Great Price.

CHAPTER XXXII.
LITERARY FELONY.

We have recently seen many elaborate discussions as to whether plagiarism is virtuous or criminal—in other words, whether writers may steal. If a minister can find a sermon better than any one he can make, why not preach it? If an author can find a paragraph for his book better than any he can himself manufacture, why not appropriate it?

That sounds well. But why not go further and ask, if a woman find a set of furs better than she has in her wardrobe, why not take them? If a man find that his neighbor has a cow full Alderney, while he has in his own yard only a scrawny runt, why not drive home the Alderney? Theft is taking anything that does not belong to you, whether it be sheep, oxen, hats, coats or literary material.

Without attempting to point out the line that divides the lawful appropriation of another's ideas from the appropriation of another's phraseology, we have only to say that a literary man always knows when he is stealing. Whether found out or not, the process is belittling, and a man is through it blasted for this world and damaged for the next one. The ass in the fable wanted to die because he was beaten so much, but after death they changed his hide into a drum-head, and thus he was beaten more than ever. So the plagiarist is so vile a cheat that there is not much chance for him, living or dead. A minister who hopes to do good with such burglary will no more be a successful ambassador to men than a foreign minister despatched by our government to-day would succeed if he presented himself at the court of St. James with the credentials that he stole from the archives of those illustrious ex-ministers, James Buchanan or Benjamin Franklin.

What every minister needs is a fresh message that day from the Lord. We would sell cheap all our parchments of licensure to preach. God gives his ministers a license every Sabbath and a new message. He sends none of us out so mentally poor that we have nothing to furnish but a cold hash of other people's sermons. Our haystack is large enough for all the sheep that come round it, and there is no need of our taking a single forkful from any other barrack. By all means use all the books you can get at, but devour them, chew them fine and digest them, till they become a part of the blood and bone of your own nature. There is no harm in delivering an oration or sermon belonging to some one else provided you so announce it. Quotation marks are cheap, and let us not be afraid to use them. Do you know why "quotation" marks are made up of four commas, two at the head of the paragraph adopted and two at the close of it? Those four commas mean that you should stop four times before you steal anything.

If there were no question of morals involved, plagiarism is nevertheless most perilous. There are a great many constables out for the arrest of such defrauders. That stolen paragraph that you think will never be recognized has been committed to memory by that old lady with green goggles in the front pew. That very same brilliant passage you have just pronounced was delivered by the clergyman who preached in that pulpit the Sabbath before: two thieves met in one hen-roost. All we know of Doctor Hayward of

Queen Elizabeth's time is that he purloined from Tacitus. Be dishonest once in this respect, and when you do really say something original and good the world will cry out, "Yes, very fine! I always did like Joseph Addison!"

Sermons are successful not according to the head involved in them, but according to the heart implied, and no one can feel aright while preaching a literary dishonesty. Let us be content to wear our own coat, though the nap on it is not quite as well looking, to ride on our own horse, though he do not gallop as gracefully and will "break up" when others are passing. There is a work for us all to do, and God gives us just the best tools to do it. What folly to be hankering after our neighbor's chalk line and gimlet!

CHAPTER XXXIII.

LITERARY ABSTINENCE.

It is as much an art not to read as to read. With what pains, and thumps, and whacks at school we first learned the way to put words together!

We did not mind so much being whipped by the schoolmaster for not knowing how to read our lesson, but to have to go out ourselves and cut the hickory switch with which the chastisement was to be inflicted seemed to us then, as it does now, a great injustice.

Notwithstanding all our hard work in learning to read we find it quite as hard now to learn how not to read. There are innumerable books and newspapers from which one had better abstain.

There are but very few newspapers which it is safe to read all through, though we know of one that it is best to peruse from beginning to end, but modesty forbids us stating which one that is. In this day readers need as never before to carry a sieve.

It requires some heroism to say you have not read such and such a book. Your friend gives you a stare which implies your literary inferiority. Do not, in order to answer the question affirmatively, wade through indiscriminate slush.

We have to say that three-fourths of the novels of the day are a mental depletion to those who read them. The man who makes wholesale denunciation of fiction pitches overboard "Pilgrim's Progress" and the parables of our Lord. But the fact is that some of the publishing houses that once were cautious about the moral tone of their books have become reckless about everything but the number of copies sold. It is all the same to them whether the package they send out be corn starch, jujube paste or hellebore. They wrap up fifty copies and mark them C. O. D. But if the expressman, according to that mark, should collect on delivery all the curses that shall come on the head of the publishing house which printed them, he would break down his wagon and kill his horses with the load. Let parents and guardians be especially watchful. Have a quarantine at your front door for all books and newspapers. Let the health doctor go abroad and see whether there is any sickness there before you let it come to wharfage.

Whether young or old, be cautious about what you read in the newspapers. You cannot day after day go through three columns of murder trial without being a worse man than when you began. While you are trying to find out whether Stokes was lying in wait for Fisk, Satan is lying in wait for you. Skip that half page of divorce case. Keep out of the mud. The Burdell and Sickles cases, through the unclean reading they afforded to millions of people long ago, led their thousands into abandoned lives and pitched them off the edge of a lost eternity. With so much healthful literature of all sorts, there is no excuse for bringing your minds in contact with evil. If there were a famine, there might be some reason for eating garbage, but the land is full of bread. When we may, with our families, sit around the clean warm fire-hearth of Christian knowledge, why go hunting in the ash barrels for cinders?

CHAPTER XXXIV.

SHORT OR LONG PASTORATES.

The question is being discussed in many journals, "How long ought a minister to stay in one place?" Clergymen and laymen and editors are wagging tongue and pen on the subject—a most practical question and easy to answer. Let a minister stay in a place till he gets done—that is, when he has nothing more to say or do.

Some ministers are such ardent students of the Bible and of men, they are after a twenty-five years' residence in a parish so full of things that ought to be said, that their resignation would be a calamity. Others get through in three months and ought to go; but it takes an earthquake to get them away. They must be moved on by committees, and pelted with resolutions, stuck through with the needles of the ladies' sewing society, and advised by neighboring ministers, and hauled up before presbyteries and consociations; and after they have killed the church and killed themselves, the pastoral relation is dissolved.

We knew of a man who got a unanimous call. He wore the finest pair of gaiters that ever went into that pulpit; and when he took up the Psalm book to give out the song, it was the perfection of gracefulness. His tongue was dipped in "balm of a thousand flowers," and it was like the roll of one of Beethoven's symphonies to hear him read the hardest Bible names, Jechonias, Zerubbabel and Tiglath-pileser. It was worth all the salary paid him to see the way he lifted his pocket-handkerchief to his eyelids.

But that brother, without knowing it, got through in six weeks. He had sold out his entire stock of goods, and ought to have shut up shop. Congregations enjoy flowers and well-folded pocket-handkerchiefs for occasional desserts, but do not like them for a regular meal. The most urbane elder was sent to the minister to intimate that the Lord was probably calling him to some other field, but the elder was baffled by the graciousness of his pastor, and unable to discharge his mission, and after he had for an hour hemmed and hawed, backed out.

Next, a woman with a very sharp tongue was sent to talk to the minister's wife. The war-cloud thickened, the pickets were driven in, and then a skirmish, and after a while all the batteries were opened, and each side said that the other side lied, and the minister dropped his pocket-handkerchief and showed his claws as long as those of Nebuchadnezzar after he had been three years eating grass like an ox. We admire long pastorates when it is agreeable to both parties, but we know ministers who boast they have been thirty years in one place, though all the world knows they have been there twenty-nine years too long. Their congregations are patiently waiting their removal to a higher latitude. Meanwhile, those churches are like a man with chronic rheumatism, very quiet—not because they admire rheumatism, but because there is no use kicking with a swollen foot, since it would hurt them more than the object assaulted.

If a pastorate can be maintained only through conflict or ecclesiastical tyranny, it might better be abandoned. There are many ministers who go away from their settlements before they ought, but we think there are quite as many who do not go soon enough. A husband might just as well try to keep his wife by choking her to death with a marriage ring as a minister to try to keep a church's love by ecclesiastical violence. Study the best time to quit.

CHAPTER XXXV.

AN EDITOR'S CHIP-BASKET.

On our way out the newspaper rooms we stumbled over the basket in which is deposited the literary material we cannot use. The basket upset and surprised us with its contents. On the top were some things that looked like fifteen or twenty poems. People outside have no idea of the amount of rhyme that comes to a printing office. The fact is that at some period in every one's life he writes "poetry." His existence depends upon it. We wrote ten or fifteen verses ourselves once. Had we not written them just then and there, we might not be here. They were in long metre, and "Old Hundred" would have fitted them grandly.

Many people are seized with the poetic spasm when they are sick, and their lines are apt to begin with.

"O mortality! how frail art thou!"

Others on Sabbath afternoons write Sabbath-school hymns, adding to the batch of infinite nonsense that the children are compelled to swallow. For others a beautiful curl is a corkscrew pulling out canto after canto. Nine-tenths of the rhyme that comes to a printing office cannot be used. You hear a rough tear of paper, and you look around to see the managing editor adding to the responsibilities of his chip-basket. What a way that is to treat incipient Tennysons and Longfellows!

Next to the poetic effusions tumble out treatises on "constitutional law" heavy enough to break the basket. We have noticed that after a man has got so dull he can get no one willing to hear him he takes to profound exposition. Out from the same chip-basket rolls a great pile of announcements that people want put among the editorials, so as to save the expense of the advertising column. They tell us the article they wish recommended will have a highly beneficial effect upon the Church and world. It is a religious churn, or a moral horse-rake, or a consecrated fly trap. They almost get us crying over their new kind of grindstone, and we put the letter down on the table while we get out our pocket-handkerchief, when our assistant takes hold the document and gives it a ruthless rip, and pitches it into the chip-basket.

Next in the pile of torn and upset things is the speech of some one on the momentous occasion of the presentation of a gold-headed cane, or silver pitcher, or brass kettle for making preserves. It was "unexpected," a "surprise" and "undeserved," and would "long be cherished." "Great applause, and not a dry eye in the house," etc., etc. But there is not much room in a paper for speeches. In this country everybody speaks.

An American is in his normal condition when he is making a speech. He is born with "fellow-citizens" in his mouth, and closes his earthly life by saying, "One word more, and I have done." Speeches being so common, newspaper readers do not want a large supply, and so many of these utterances, intended to be immortal, drop into oblivion through that inexhaustible reservoir, the editorial chip-basket.

But there is a hovering of pathos over this wreck of matter. Some of these wasted things were written for bread by intelligent wives with drunken husbands trying to support their families with the pen. Over that mutilated manuscript some weary man toiled until daybreak. How we wish we could have printed what they wrote! Alas for the necessity that disappoints the literary struggle of so many women and men, when it is ten dollars for that article or children gone supperless to bed!

Let no one enter the field of literature for the purpose of "making a living" unless as a very last resort. There are thousands of persons to-day starving to death with a steel pen in their hand. The story of Grub street and poets living on thin soup is being repeated all over this land, although the modern cases are not so conspicuous. Poverty is no more agreeable because classical and set in hexameters. The hungry author cannot breakfast on "odes to summer." On this cold day how many of the literati are shivering! Martyrs have perished in the fire, but more persons have perished for lack of fire. Let no editor through hypercriticism of contributed articles add to this educated suffering.

What is that we hear in the next room? It is the roar of a big fire as it consumes unavailable literary material—epics, sonnets, homilies, tractates, compilations, circulars, dissertations. Some of them were obscure, and make a great deal of smoke. Some of them were merry, and crackle. All of them have ended their mission and gone down, ashes to ashes and dust to dust.

CHAPTER XXXVI.

THE MANHOOD OF SERVICE.

At the Crawford House, White Mountains, we noticed, this summer, unusual intelligence and courtesy on the part of those who served the tables. We found out that many of them were students from the colleges and seminaries—young men and women who had taken this mode of replenishing their purses and getting the benefit of mountain air. We felt like applauding them. We have admiration for those who can be independent of the oppressive conventionalities of society. May not all of us practically adopt the Christian theory that any work is honorable that is useful? The slaves of an ignominious pride, how many kill themselves earning a living! We have tens of thousands of women in our cities, sitting in cold rooms, stabbing their life out with their needles, coughing their lungs into tubercles and suffering the horrors of the social inquisition, for whom there waits plenty of healthy, happy homes in the country, if they could only, like these sons and daughters of Dartmouth and Northampton, consent to serve. We wish some one would explain to us how a sewing machine is any more respectable than a churn, or a yard stick is better than a pitchfork. We want a new Declaration of Independence, signed by all the laboring classes. There is plenty of work for all kinds of people, if they were not too proud to do it. Though the country is covered with people who can find nothing to do, we would be willing to open a bureau to-morrow, warranting to give to all the unemployed of the land occupation, if they would only consent to do what might be assigned them. We believe anything is more honorable than idleness.

During very hard times two Italian artists called at our country home, asking if we did not want some sketching done, and they unrolled some elegant pictures, showing their fine capacity. We told them we had no desire for sketches, but we had a cistern to clean, and would pay them well for doing it. Off went their coats, and in a few hours the work was done and their wages awarded. How much more honorable for them to do what they could get to do rather than to wait for more adapted employment!

Why did not the girls of Northampton spend their summers embroidering slippers or hemming handkerchiefs, and thus keep at work unobserved and more popular? Because they were not fools. They said: "Let us go up and see Mount Adams, and the Profile, and Mount Washington. We shall have to work only five hours a day, and all the time we will be gathering health and inspiration." Young men, those are the girls to seek when you want a wife, rather than the wheezing victims of ruinous work chosen because it is more popular. About the last thing we would want to marry is a medicine-chest. Why did not the students of Dartmouth, during their vacation, teach school? First, because teaching is a science, and they did not want to do three months of damage to the children of the common school. Secondly, because they wanted freedom from books as man makes them, and opportunity to open the ponderous tome of boulder and strata as God printed them. Churches and scientific institutions, these will be the men to call—brawny and independent, rather than the bilious, short-breathed, nerveless graduates who, too proud to take healthful recreation, tumble, at commencement day, into the lap of society so many Greek roots.

CHAPTER XXXVII.

BALKY PEOPLE.

Passing along a country road quite recently, we found a man, a horse and wagon in trouble. The vehicle was slight and the road was good, but the horse refused to draw, and his driver was in a bad predicament. He had already destroyed his whip in applying inducements to progress in travel. He had pulled the horse's ears with a sharp string. He had backed him into the ditch. He had built a fire of straw underneath him, the only result a smashed dash-board. The chief effect of the violences and cruelties applied was to increase the divergency of feeling between the brute and his master. We said to the besweated and outraged actor in the scene that the best thing for him to do was to let his horse stand for a while unwhipped and uncoaxed, setting some one to watch him while he, the driver, went away to cool off. We learned that the plan worked admirably; that the cold air, and the appetite for oats, and the solitude of the road, favorable for contemplation, had made the horse move for adjournment to some other place and time; and when the driver came up, he had but to take up the reins, and the beast, erst so obstinate, dashed down the road at a perilous speed.

There is not as much difference between horses and men as you might suppose. The road between mind and equine instinct is short and soon traveled. The horse is sometimes superior to his rider. If anything is good and admirable in proportion as it answers the end of its being, then the horse that bends into its traces before a

Fourth avenue car is better than its blaspheming driver. He who cannot manage a horse cannot manage a man.

We know of pastors who have balky parishioners. When any important move is to take place, and all the other horses of the team are willing to draw, they lay themselves back in the harness.

First the pastor pats the obstreperous elder or deacon on the neck and tells him how much he thinks of him. This only makes him shake his mane and grind his bit. He will die first before he consents to such a movement. Next, he is pulled by the ear, with a good many sharp insinuations as to his motives for holding back. Fires of indignation are built under him for the purpose of consuming his balkiness. He is whipped with the scourge of public opinion, but this only makes him kick fiercely and lie harder in the breeching-straps. He is backed down into the ditch of scorn and contempt, but still is not willing to draw an ounce. O foolish minister, trying in that way to manage a balky parishioner! Let him alone. Go on and leave him there. Pay less attention to the horse that balks, and give more oats to those that pull. Leave him out in the cold. Some day you will come back and find him glad to start. At your first advance he will arch his neck, paw his hoof, bend into the bit, stiffen the traces and dash on. We have the same prescription for balky horses and men: for a little while let them alone.

CHAPTER XXXVIII.

ANONYMOUS LETTERS.

In boyhood days we were impressed with the fertility of a certain author whose name so often appeared in the spelling books and readers, styled Anon. He seemed to write more than Isaac Watts, or Shakespeare, or Blair. In the index, and scattered throughout all our books, was the name of Anon. He appeared in all styles of poetry and prose and dialogue. We wondered where he lived, what his age was, and how he looked. It was not until quite late in boyhood that we learned that Anon was an abbreviation for anonymous, and that he was sometimes the best saint and at other times the most extraordinary villain.

After centuries of correspondence old Anonymous is as fertile of thought and brain and stratagem as ever, and will probably keep on writing till the last fire burns up his pen and cracks to pieces his ink bottle. Anonymous letters sometimes have a mission of kindness and gratitude and good cheer. Genuine modesty may sometimes hide the name of an epistolary author or authoress. It may be a "God bless you" from some one who thinks herself hardly in a position to address you. It may be the discovery of a plot for your damage, in which the revelator does not care to take the responsibility of a witness. It may be any one of a thousand things that mean frankness and delicacy and honor and Christian principle. We have received anonymous letters which we have put away among our most sacred archives.

But we suppose every one chiefly associates the idea of anonymous communications with everything cowardly and base. There are in all neighborhoods perfidious, sneaking, dastardly, filthy, calumnious, vermin-infested wretches, spewed up from perdition, whose joy it is to write letters with fictitious signatures. Sometimes they take the shape of a valentine, the fourteenth of February being a great outlet for this obscene spawn. If your nose be long, or your limbs slender, or your waist thick around, they will be pictorially presented. Sometimes they take the form of a delicate threat that if you do not thus or so there will be a funeral at your house, yourself the chief object of interest. Sometimes they will be denunciatory of your friends. Once being called to preside at a meeting for the relief of the sewing women of Philadelphia, and having been called in the opening speech to say something about oppressive contractors, we received some twenty anonymous letters, the purport of which was that it would be unsafe for us to go out of doors after dark. Three months after moving to Brooklyn we preached a sermon reviewing one of the sins of the city, and anonymous letters came saying that we would not last six months in the city of churches.

Sometimes the anonymous crime takes the form of a newspaper article; and if the matter be pursued, the editor-in-chief puts it off on the managing editor, and the managing editor upon the book critic, and the book critic upon the reporter.

Whether Adam or Eve or the serpent was the most to be blamed for the disappearance of the fair apple of reputation is uncertain; the only thing you can be sure of is that the apple is gone. No honest man will ever write a thing for a newspaper, in editorial or any other column, that he would be ashamed to sign with the Christian name that his mother had him baptized with. They who go skulking about under the editorial "we," unwilling to acknowledge their identity, are more fit for Delaware whipping-posts than the position of public educators. It is high time that such hounds were muzzled.

Let every young man know that when he is tempted to pen anything which requires him to disguise his handwriting he is in fearful danger. You despoil your own nature by such procedure more than you can damage any one else. Bowie-knife and dagger are more honorable than an anonymous pen sharpened for defamation of character. Better try putting strychnine in the flour barrel. Better mix ratsbane in the jelly cake. That behavior would be more elegant and Christian.

After much observation we have fixed upon this plan: If any one writes us in defamation of another, we adopt the opposite theory. If the letter says that the assaulted one lies, we take it as eulogistic of his veracity; or that he is unchaste, we set him down as pure; or fraudulent, we are seized with a desire to make him our executor. We do so on logical and unmistakable grounds. A defamatory letter is from the devil or his satellites. The devil hates only the good. The devil hates Mr. A; ergo, Mr. A is good.

Much of the work of the day of judgment will be with the authors of anonymous letters. The majority of other crimes against society were found out, but these creatures so disguised their handwriting in the main text of the letter, or so willfully misspelled the direction on the envelope, and put it in such a distant post-office, and looked so innocent when you met them, that it shall be for the most part a dead secret till the books are opened; and when that is done, we do not think these abandoned souls will wait to have their condemnation read, but, ashamed to meet the announcement, will leap pell-mell into the pit, crying, "We wrote them."

If, since the world stood, there have been composed and sent off by mail or private postmen 1,600,378 anonymous letters derogatory of character, then 1,600,378 were vicious and damnable. If you are compelled to choose between writing a letter with false signature vitriolic of any man's integrity or any woman's honor on the one hand, and the writing a letter with a red-hot nail dipped in adder's poison on a sheet woven of leper scales, choose the latter. It were healthier, nobler, and could better endure the test of man's review and God's scrutiny.

CHAPTER XXXIX.

BRAWN OR BRAIN.

Governor Wiseman (our oracular friend who talked in the style of an oration) was with us this evening at the tea-table, and we were mentioning the fact that about thirty colleges last summer in the United States contested for the championship in boat-racing. About two hundred thousand young ladies could not sleep nights, so anxious were they to know whether Yale or Williams would be the winner. The newspapers gave three and four columns to the particulars, the telegraph wires thrilled the victory to all parts of the land. Some of the religious papers condemned the whole affair, enlarging upon the strained wrists, broken blood-vessels and barbaric animalism of men who ought to have been rowing their race with the Binomial Theorem for one oar and Kames' Elements of Criticism for the other.

For the most part, we sympathized with the boys, and confess that at our hotel we kept careful watch of the bulletin to see whose boat came in ahead. We are disposed to applaud anything that will give our young men muscular development. Students have such a tendency to lounge, and mope, and chew, and eat almond-nuts at midnight, and read novels after they go to bed, the candlestick set up on Webster's dictionary or the Bible, that we prize anything that makes them cautious about their health, as they must be if they would enter the list of contestants. How many of our country boys enter the freshman class of college in robust health, which lasts them about a twelvemonth; then in the sophomore they lose their liver; in the junior they lose their stomach; in the senior they lose their back bone; graduating skeletons, more fit for an anatomical museum than the bar or pulpit.

"Midnight oil," so much eulogized, is the poorest kind of kerosene. Where hard study kills one student, bad habits kill a hundred. Kirk White, while at Cambridge, wrote beautiful hymns; but if he had gone to bed at ten o'clock that night instead of three o'clock the next morning, he would have been of more service to the world and a healthier example to all collegians. Much of the learning of the day is morbid, and much of the religion bilious. We want, first of all, a clean heart, and next a strong stomach. Falling from grace is often chargeable to derangement of gastric juices. Oar and bat may become salutary weapons.

But, after all, there was something wrong about those summer boat-races. A student with a stout arm, and great girth, and full chest, and nothing else, is not at all admirable. Mind and body need to be driven tandem, the body for the wheel horse and the intellect the leader. We want what is now proposed in some directions—a grand collegiate literary race. Let the mental contest be on the same week with the muscular. Let Yale and Harvard and Williams and Princeton and Dartmouth see who has the champion among scholars. Let there be a Waterloo in belles-lettres and rhetoric and mathematics and philosophy. Let us see whether the students of Doctors McCosh, or Porter, or Campbell, or Smith are most worthy to wear the belt. About twelve o'clock at noon let the literary flotilla start prow and prow, oar-lock and oar-lock. Let Helicon empty its waters to swell the river of knowledge on which they row. Right foot on right rib of the boat, and left foot on the left rib—bend into it, my hearties, bend!—and our craft come out four lengths ahead.

Give the brain a chance as well as the arm. Do not let the animal eat up the soul. Let the body be the well-fashioned hulk, and the mind the white sails, all hoisted, everything, from flying jib to spanker, bearing on toward the harbor of glorious achievement. When that boat starts, we want to be on the bank to cheer, and after sundown help fill the air with sky-rockets.

"By the way," I said, "Governor Wiseman, do you not think that we need more out-door exercise, and that contact with the natural world would have a cheering tendency? Governor, do you ever have the blues?"

The governor, putting his knife across the plate and throwing his spectacles up on his forehead, replied:

Almost every nature, however sprightly, sometimes will drop into a minor key, or a subdued mood that in common parlance is recognized as "the blues." There may be no adverse causes at work, but somehow the bells of the soul stop ringing, and you feel like sitting quiet, and you strike off fifty per cent from all your worldly and spiritual prospects. The immediate cause may be a northeast wind, or a balky liver, or an enlarged spleen, or pickled oysters at twelve o'clock the night before.

In such depressed state no one can afford to sit for an hour. First of all let him get up and go out of doors. Fresh air, and the faces of cheerful men, and pleasant women, and frolicsome children, will in fifteen minutes kill moping. The first moment your friend strikes the keyboard of your soul it will ring music. A hen might as well try on populous Broadway to hatch out a feathery group as for a man to successfully brood over his ills in lively society. Do not go for relief among those who feel as badly as you do. Let not toothache, and rheumatism, and hypochondria go to see toothache, rheumatism and hypochondria. On one block in Brooklyn live a doctor, an undertaker and a clergyman. That is not the row for a nervous man to walk on, lest he soon need all three. Throw back all the shutters of your soul and let the sunlight of genial faces shine in.

Besides that, why sit ye here with the blues, ye favored sons and daughters of men? Shone upon by such stars, and breathed on by such air, and sung to by so many pleasant sounds, you ought not to be seen moping. Especially if light from the better world strikes its aurora through your night sky, ought you be cheerful. You can afford to have a rough luncheon by the way if it is soon to end amid the banqueters in white. Sailing toward such a blessed port, do not have your flag at half mast. Leave to those who take too much wine "the gloomy raven tapping at the chamber door, on the night's Plutonian shore," and give us the robin red-breast and the chaffinch. Let some one with a strong voice give out the long-metre doxology, and the whole world "Praise God, from whom all blessings flow."

"But do you not suppose, Governor Wiseman, that every man has his irritated days?"

Yes, yes, responded the governor. There are times when everything seems to go wrong. From seven o'clock a. m. till ten p. m. affairs are in a twist. You rise in the morning, and the room is cold, and a button is off, and the breakfast is tough, and the stove smokes, and the pipes burst, and you start down the street nettled from head to foot. All day long things are adverse. Insinuations, petty losses, meanness on the part of customers. The ink bottle upsets and spoils the carpet. Some one gives a wrong turn to the damper, and the gas escapes. An agent comes in determined to insure your life, when it is already insured for more than it is worth, and you are afraid some one will knock you on the head to get the price of your policy; but he sticks to you, showing you pictures of old Time and the hourglass, and Death's scythe and a skeleton, making it quite certain that you will die before your time unless you take out papers in his company. Besides this, you have a cold in your head, and a grain of dirt in your eye, and you are a walking uneasiness. The day is out of joint, and no surgeon can set it.

The probability is that if you would look at the weather-vane you would find that the wind is northeast, and you might remember that you have lost much sleep lately. It might happen to be that you are out of joint instead of the day. Be careful and not write many letters while you are in that irritated mood. You will pen some things that you will be sorry for afterward.

Let us remember that these spiked nettles of life are part of our discipline. Life would get nauseating if it were all honey. That table would be poorly set that had on it nothing but treacle. We need a little vinegar, mustard, pepper and horse-radish that brings the tears even when we do not feel pathetic. If this world were all smoothness, we would never be ready for emigration to a higher and better. Blustering March and weeping April prepare us for shining May. This world is a poor hitching post. Instead of tying fast on the cold mountains, we had better whip up and hasten on toward the warm inn where our good friends are looking out of the window, watching to see us come up.

Interrupting the governor at this point, we asked him if he did not think that rowing, ball playing and other athletic exercises might be made an antidote to the morbid religion that is sometimes manifest. The governor replied:

No doubt much of the Christian character of the day lacks in swarthiness and power. It is gentle enough, and active enough, and well meaning enough, but is wanting in moral muscle. It can sweetly sing at a prayer meeting, and smile graciously when it is the right time to smile, and makes an excellent nurse to pour out with steady hand a few drops of peppermint for a child that feels disturbances under the waistband, but has no qualification for the robust Christian work that is demanded.

One reason for this is the ineffable softness of much of what is called Christian literature. The attempt is to bring us up on tracts made up of thin exhortations and goodish maxims. A nerveless treatise on commerce or science in that style would be crumpled up by the first merchant and thrown into his waste-basket. Religious twaddle is of no more use than worldly twaddle. If a man has nothing to say, he had better keep his pen wiped and his tongue still. There needs an infusion of strong Anglo-Saxon into religious literature, and a brawnier manliness and more impatience with insipidity, though it be prayerful and sanctimonious. He who stands with irksome repetitions asking people to "Come to Jesus," while he gives no strong common-sense reason why they should come, drives back the souls of men. If, with all the thrilling realities of eternity at hand, a man has nothing to write which can gather up and master the thoughts and feelings of men, his writing and speaking are a slander on the religion which he wishes to eulogize.

Morbidity in religion might be partially cured by more out-door exercise. There are some duties we can perform better on our feet than on our knees. If we carry the grace of God with us down into every-day practical Christian work, we will get more spiritual strength in five minutes than by ten hours of kneeling. If Daniel had not served God save when three times a day he worshiped toward the temple, the lions would have surely eaten him up. The school of Christ is as much out-of-doors as in-doors. Hard, rough work for God will develop an athletic soul. Religion will not conquer either the admiration or the affections of men by effeminacy, but by strength. Because the heart is soft is no reason why the head should be soft. The spirit of genuine religion is a spirit of great power. When Christ rides in apocalyptic vision, it is not on a weak and stupid beast, but on a horse—emblem of majesty and strength: "And he went forth conquering and to conquer."

CHAPTER XL.

WARM-WEATHER RELIGION.

It takes more grace to be an earnest and useful Christian in summer than in any other season. The very destitute, through lack of fuel and thick clothing, may find the winter the trying season, but those comfortably circumstanced find summer the Thermopylæ that tests their Christian courage and endurance.

The spring is suggestive of God and heaven and a resurrection day. That eye must be blind that does not see God's footstep in the new grass, and hear His voice in the call of the swallow at the eaves. In the white blossoms of the orchards we find suggestion of those whose robes have been made white in the blood of the Lamb. A May morning is a door opening into heaven.

So autumn mothers a great many moral and religious suggestions. The season of corn husking, the gorgeous woods that are becoming the catafalque of the dead year, remind the dullest of his own fading and departure.

But summer fatigues and weakens, and no man keeps his soul in as desirable a frame unless by positive resolution and especial implorations. Pulpit and pew often get stupid together, and ardent devotion is adjourned until September.

But who can afford to lose two months out of each year, when the years are so short and so few? He who stops religious growth in July and August will require the next six months to get over it. Nay, he never recovers. At the season when the fields are most full of leafage and life let us not be lethargic and stupid.

Let us remember that iniquity does not cease in summer-time. She never takes a vacation. The devil never leaves town. The child of want, living up that dark alley, has not so much fresh air nor sees as many flowers as in winter-time. In cold weather the frost blossoms on her window pane, and the snow falls in wreaths in the alley. God pity the wretchedness that pants and sweats and festers and dies on the hot pavements and in the suffocating cellars of the town!

Let us remember that our exit from this world will more probably be in the summer than in any other season, and we cannot afford to die at a time when we are least alert and worshipful. At mid-summer the average of departures is larger than in cool weather. The sun-strokes, the dysenteries, the fevers, the choleras, have affinity for July and August. On the edge of summer Death stands whetting his scythe for a great harvest. We are most careful to have our doors locked, and our windows fastened, and our "burglar alarm" set at times when thieves are most busy, and at a season of the year when diseases are most active in their burglaries of life we need to be ready.

Our charge, therefore, is, make no adjournment of your religion till cool weather. Whether you stay in town, or seek the farm house, or the seashore, or the mountains, be faithful in prayer, in Bible reading and in attendance upon Christian ordinances. He who throws away two months of life wastes that for which many a dying sinner would have been willing to give all his possessions when he found that the harvest was past and the summer was ended.

The thermometer to-day has stood at a high mark. The heat has been fierce. As far as possible people have kept within doors or walked on the shady side of the street. But we can have but a faint idea of what the people suffer crossing a desert or in a tropical clime. The head faints, the tongue swells and deathly sickness comes upon the whole body when long exposed to the summer sun. I see a whole caravan pressing on through the hot sands. "Oh," say the camel-drivers, "for water and shade!" At last they see an elevation against the sky. They revive at the sight and push on. That which they saw proves to be a great rock, and camels and drivers throw themselves down under the long shadow. Isaiah, who lived and wrote in a scorching climate, draws his figure from what he had seen and felt when he represents God as the shadow of a great rock in a weary land.

Many people have found this world a desert-march. They go half consumed of trouble all their days. But glory be to God! we are not turned out on a desert to die. Here is the long, cool, certain, refreshing shadow of the Lord.

A tree, when in full leafage, drops a great deal of refreshment; but in a little while the sun strikes through, and you keep shifting your position, until, after a while, the sun is set at such a point that you have no shade at all. But go in the heart of some great rock, such as you see in Yosemite or the Alps, and there is everlasting shadow. There has been thick shade there for six thousand years, and will be for the next six thousand. So our divine Rock, once covering us, always covers us. The same yesterday, to-day and for ever! always good, always kind, always sympathetic! You often hold a sunshade over your head passing along the road or a street; but after a while your arm gets tired, and the very effort to create the shadow makes you weary. But the rock in the mountains, with fingers of everlasting stone, holds its own shadow. So God's sympathy needs no holding up from us. Though we are too weak from sickness or trouble to do anything but lie down, over us He stretches the shadow of His benediction.

It is our misfortune that we mistake God's shadow for the night. If a man come and stand between you and the sun, his shadow falls upon you. So God sometimes comes and stands between us and worldly successes, and His shadow falls upon us, and we wrongly think that it is night. As a father in a garden stoops down to kiss his child the shadow of his body falls upon it; and so many of the dark misfortunes of our life are not God going away from us, but our heavenly Father stooping down to give us the kiss of His infinite and everlasting love. It is the shadow of a sheltering Rock, and not of a devouring lion.

Instead of standing right out in the blistering noon-day sun of earthly trial and trouble, come under the Rock. You may drive into it the longest caravan of disasters. Room for the suffering, heated, sunstruck, dying, of all generations, in the shadow of the great Rock:

> "Rock of ages, cleft for me,
> Let me hide myself in Thee."

CHAPTER XLI.

HIDING EGGS FOR EASTER.

Those who were so unfortunate as to have been born and brought up in the city know nothing about that chapter in a boy's history of which I speak.

About a month before Easter there comes to the farmhouse a scarcity of eggs. The farmer's wife begins to abuse the weasels and the cats as the probable cause of the paucity. The feline tribe are assaulted with many a harsh "Scat!" on the suspicion of their fondness for omelets in the raw. Custards fail from the table. The Dominick hens are denounced as not worth their mush. Meanwhile, the boys stand round the corner in a broad grin at what is the discomfiture of the rest of the family.

The truth must be told that the boys, in anticipation of Easter, have, in some hole in the mow or some barrel in the wagon-house, been hiding eggs. If the youngsters understand their business, they will compromise the matter, and see that at least a small supply goes to the house every day. Too great greed on the part of the boy will discover the whole plot, and the charge will be made: "De Witt, I believe you are hiding the eggs!" Forthwith the boy is collared and compelled to disgorge his possessions.

Now, there is nothing more trying to a boy than, after great care in accumulating these shelly resources, to have to place them in a basket and bring them forth to the light two weeks before Easter. Boys, therefore, manage with skill and dexterity. At this season of the year you see them lurking much about the hayrick and the hay-loft. You see them crawling out from stacks of straw and walking away rapidly with their hands behind them. They look very innocent, for I have noticed that the look of innocence in boys is proportioned to the amount of mischief with which they are stuffed. They seem to be determined to risk their lives on mow-poles where the hay lies thin. They come out from under the stable floor in a despicable state of toilet, and cannot give any excuse for their depreciation of apparel. Hens flutter off the nest with an unusual squawk, for the boys cannot wait any longer for the slow process of laying, and hens have no business to stand in the way of Easter. The most tedious hours of my boyhood were spent in waiting for a hen to get off her nest. No use to scare her off, for then she will get mad, and just as like as not take the egg with her. Indeed, I think the boy is excusable for his haste if his brother has a dozen eggs and he has only eleven.

At this season of the year the hens are melancholy. They want to hatch, but how can they? They have the requisite disposition, and the capacity, and the feathers, and the nest, and everything but the eggs. With that deficit, they sometimes sit obstinately and defy the boy's approaches. Many a boy has felt the sharp bill of old Dominick strike the back of his hand, inflicting a wound that would have roused up the whole farmhouse to see what was the matter had it not been that the boy wanted to excite no suspicion as to the nature of his expedition. Immediately over the hen's head comes the boy's cap, and there is a scatteration of feathers all over the hay-mow, and the boy is victor.

But at last the evening before Easter comes. While the old people are on the piazza the children come in with the accumulated treasures of many weeks, and put down the baskets. Eggs large and small, white-shelled and brown, Cochin-Chinas and Brahmapooters. The character of the hens is vindicated. The cat may now lie in the sun without being kicked by false suspicions. The surprised exclamation of parents more than compensates the boys for the strategy of long concealment. The meanest thing in the world is for father and mother not to look surprised in such circumstances.

It sometimes happens that, in the agitation of bringing the eggs into the household harbor, the boy drops the hat or the basket, and the whole enterprise is shipwrecked. From our own experience, it is very difficult to pick up eggs after you have once dropped them. You have found the same experience in after life. Your hens laid a whole nestful of golden eggs on Wall street. You had gathered them up. You were bringing them in. You expected a world of congratulations, but just the day before the consummation, something adverse ran against you, and you dropped the basket, and the eggs broke. Wise man were you if, instead of sitting down to cry or attempting to gather up the spilled yolks, you built new nests and invited a new laying.

It is sometimes found on Easter morning that the eggs have been kept too long. The boy's intentions were good enough, but the enterprise had been too protracted, and the casting out of the dozen was sudden and precipitate. Indeed, that is the trouble with some older boys I wot of. They keep their money, or their brain, or their influence hidden till it rots. They are not willing to come forth day by day on a humble mission, doing what little good they may, but are keeping themselves hidden till some great Easter day of triumph, and then they will astonish the Church and the world; but they find that faculties too long hidden are faculties ruined. Better for an egg to have succeeded in making one plain cake for a poor man's table than to have failed in making a banquet for the House of Lords.

That was a glad time when on Easter morning the eggs went into the saucepan, and came out striped, and spotted, and blue, and yellow, and the entire digestive capacity of the children was tested. You have never had anything so good to eat since. You found the eggs. You hid them. They were your contribution to the table. Since then you have seen eggs scrambled, eggs poached, eggs in omelet, eggs boiled, eggs done on one side and eggs in a nog, but you shall never find anything like the flavor of that Easter morning in boyhood.

Alas for the boys in town! Easter comes to them on stilts, and they buy their eggs out of the store. There is no room for a boy to swing round. There is no good place in town to fly a kite, or trundle a hoop, or even shout without people's throwing up the window to see who is killed. The holidays are robbed of half their life because some wiseacre will persist in telling him who Santa Claus is, while yet he is hanging up his first pair of stockings. Here the boy pays half a dollar for a bottle of perfume as big as his finger, when out of town, for nothing but the trouble of breathing it, he may smell a country full of new-mown hay and wild honeysuckle. In a painted bath-tub he takes his Saturday bath careful lest he hit his head against the spigot, while in the meadow-brook the boys plunge in wild glee, and pluck up health and long life from the pebbly bottom. Oh, the joy in the spring day, when, after long teasing of mother to let you take off your shoes, you dash out on the cool grass barefoot, or down the road, the dust curling about the instep in warm enjoyment, and, henceforth, for months, there shall be no shoes to tie or blacken.

Let us send the boys out into the country every year for an airing. If their grandfather and grandmother be yet alive, they will give them a good time. They will learn in a little while the mysteries of the hay-mow, how to drive oxen and how to keep Easter. They will take the old people back to the time when you yourself were a boy. There will be for the grandson an extra cake in each oven. And grandfather and grandmother will sit and watch the prodigy, and wonder if any other family ever had such grandchildren. It will be a good thing when the evenings are short, and the old folks' eyesight is somewhat dim, if you can set up in their house for a little while one or two of these lights of childhood. For the time the aches and pains of old age will be gone, and they will feel as lithe and merry as when sixty years ago they themselves rummaged hayrick, and mow and wagon-house, hiding eggs for Easter.

CHAPTER XLII.

SINK OR SWIM.

We entered the ministry with a mortal horror of extemporaneous speaking. Each week we wrote two sermons and a lecture all out, fom the text to the amen. We did not dare to give out the notice of a prayer-meeting unless it was on paper. We were a slave to manuscript, and the chains were galling; and three months more of such work would have put us in the graveyard. We resolved on emancipation. The Sunday night was approaching when we expected to make violent rebellion against this bondage of pen and paper. We had an essay about ten minutes long on some Christian subject, which we proposed to preach as an introduction to the sermon, resolved, at the close of that brief composition, to launch out on the great sea of extemporaneousness.

It so happened that the coming Sabbath night was to be eventful in the village. The trustees of the church had been building a gasometer back of the church, and the night I speak of the building was for the first time to be lighted in the modern way. The church was, of course, crowded—not so much to hear the preacher as to see how the gas would burn. Many were unbelieving, and said that there would be an explosion, or a big fire, or that in the midst of the service the lights would go out. Several brethren disposed to hang on to old customs declared that candles and oil were the only fit material for lighting a church, and they denounced the innovation as indicative of vanity on the part of the new-comers. They used oil in the ancient temple, and it was that which ran down on Aaron's beard, and anything that was good enough for the whiskers of an old-time priest was good enough for a country meeting-house. These sticklers for the oil were present that night, hoping—and I think some of them secretly praying—that the gas might go out.

With our ten-minute manuscript we went into the pulpit, all in a tremor. Although the gas did not burn as brightly as its friends had hoped, still it was bright enough to show the people the perspiration that stood in beads on our forehead. We began our discourse, and every sentence gave us the feeling that we were one step nearer the gallows. We spoke very slowly, so as to make the ten-minute notes last fifteen minutes. During the preachment of the brief manuscript we concluded that we had never been called to the ministry. We were in a hot bath of excitement. People noticed our trepidation, and supposed it was because we were afraid the gas would go out. Alas! our fear was that it would not go out. As we came toward the close of our brief we joined the anti-gas party, and prayed that before we came to the last written line something would burst, and leave us in the darkness. Indeed, we discovered an encouraging flicker amid the burners, which gave us the hope that the brief which lay before us would be long enough for all practical purposes, and that the hour of execution might be postponed to some other night. As we came to the sentence next to the last the lights fell down to half their size, and we could just manage to see the audience as they were floating away from our vision. We said to ourselves, "Why can't these lights be obliging, and go out entirely?" The wish was gratified. As we finished the last line of our brief, and stood on the verge of rhetorical destruction, the last glimmer of light was extinguished. "It is impossible to proceed," we cried out; "receive the benediction!"

We crawled down the pulpit in a state of exhilaration; we never before saw such handsome darkness. The odor of the escaping gas was to us like "gales from Araby." Did a frightened young man ever have such fortunate deliverance? The providence was probably intended to humble the trustees, yet the scared preacher took advantage of it.

But after we got home we saw the wickedness of being in such dread. As the Lord got us out of that predicament, we resolved never again to be cornered in one similar. Forthwith the thralldom was broken, we hope never again to be felt. How demeaning that a man with a message from the Lord Almighty should be dependent upon paper-mills and gasometers! Paper is a non-conductor of gospel electricity. If a man have a five-thousand-dollar bill of goods to sell a customer, he does not go up to the purchaser and say, "I have some remarks to make to you about these goods, but just wait till I get out my manuscript." Before he got through reading the argument the customer would be in the next door, making purchases from another house.

What cowardice! Because a few critical hearers sit with lead-pencils out to mark down the inaccuracies of extemporaneousness, shall the pulpit cower? If these critics do not repent, they will go to hell, and take their lead-pencils with them. While the great congregation are ready to take the bread hot out of the oven shall the minister be crippled in his work because the village doctor or lawyer sits carping before him? To please a few learned ninnies a thousand ministers sit writing sermons on Saturday night till near the break of day, their heads hot, their feet cold, and their nerves a-twitch. Sermons born on

Saturday night are apt to have the rickets. Instead of cramping our chests over writing-desks, and being the slaves of the pen, let us attend to our physical health, that we may have more pulpit independence.

It would be a grand thing if every minister felt strong enough in body to thrash any man in his audience improperly behaving, but always kept back from such assault by the fact that it would be wrong to do so. There is a good deal of heart and head in our theology, but not enough liver and backbone. We need a more stalwart Christian character, more roast beef rare, and less calf's-foot jelly. This will make the pulpit more bold and the pew more manly.

Which thoughts came to us this week as we visited again the village church aforesaid, and preached out of the same old Bible in which, years ago, we laid the ten-minute manuscript, and we looked upon the same lights that once behaved so badly. But we found it had been snowing since the time we lived there, and heads that then were black are white now, and some of the eyes which looked up to us that memorable night when the gasometer failed us, thirteen years ago, are closed now, and for them all earthly lights have gone out for ever.

CHAPTER XLIII.

SHELLS FROM THE BEACH.

Our summer-house is a cottage at East Hampton, Long Island, overlooking the sea. Seventeen vessels in sight, schooners, clippers, hermaphrodite brigs, steamers, great craft and small. Wonder where they come from, and where they are going to, and who is aboard? Just enough clovertops to sweeten the briny air into the most delightful tonic. We do not know the geological history of this place, but imagine that the rest of Long Island is the discourse of which East Hampton is the peroration. There are enough bluffs to relieve the dead level, enough grass to clothe the hills, enough trees to drop the shadow, enough society to keep one from inanity, and enough quietude to soothe twelve months of perturbation. The sea hums us to sleep at night, and fills our dreams with intimations of the land where the harmony is like "the voice of many waters." In smooth weather the billows take a minor key; but when the storm gives them the pitch, they break forth with the clash and uproar of an overture that fills the heavens and makes the beach tremble. Strange that that which rolls perpetually and never rests itself should be a psalm of rest to others! With these sands of the beach we help fill the hour-glass of life. Every moment of the day there comes in over the waves a flotilla of joy and rest and health, and our piazza is the wharf where the stevedores unburden their cargo. We have sunrise with her bannered hosts in cloth of gold, and moonrise with her innumerable helmets and shields and swords and ensigns of silver, the morning and the night being the two buttresses from which are swung a bridge of cloud suspended on strands of sunbeam, all the glories of the sky passing to and fro with airy feet in silent procession.

We have wandered far and wide, but found no such place to rest in. We can live here forty-eight hours in one day, and in a night get a Rip Van Winkle sleep, waking up without finding our gun rusty or our dog dead.

No wonder that Mr. James, the first minister of this place, lived to eighty years of age, and Mr. Hunting, his successor, lived to be eighty-one years of age, and Doctor Buel, his successor, lived to be eighty-two years of age. Indeed, it seems impossible for a minister regularly settled in this place to get out of the world before his eightieth year. It has been only in cases of "stated supply," or removal from the place, that early demise has been possible. And in each of these cases of decease at fourscore it was some unnecessary imprudence on their part, or who knows but that they might be living yet? That which is good for settled pastors being good for other people, you may judge the climate here is salutary and delectable for all.

The place was settled in 1648, and that is so long ago that it will probably never be unsettled. The Puritans took possession of it first, and have always held it for the Sabbath, for the Bible and for God. Much maligned Puritans! The world will stop deriding them after a while, and the caricaturists of their stalwart religion will want to claim them as ancestors, but it will be too late then; for since these latter-day folks lie about the Puritans now, we will not believe them when they want to get into the illustrious genealogical line.

East Hampton has always been a place of good morals. One of the earliest Puritan regulations of this place was that licensed liquor-sellers should not sell to the young, and that half a pint only should be given to four men—an amount so small that most drinkers would consider it only a tantalization. A woman here, in those days, was sentenced "to pay a fine of fifteen dollars, or to stand one hour with a cleft stick upon her tongue, for saying that her husband had brought her to a place where there was neither gospel nor magistracy." She deserved punishment of some kind, but they ought to have let her off with a fine, for no woman's tongue ought to be interfered with. When in olden time a Yankee peddler with the measles went to church here on the Sabbath for the purpose of selling his knick-knacks, his behavior was considered so perfidious that before the peddler left town the next morning the young men gave him a free ride upon what seems to us an uncomfortable and insufficient vehicle, namely, a rail, and then dropped him into the duck-pond. But such conduct was not sanctioned by the better people of the place. Nothing could be more unwholesome for a man with the measles than a plunge in a duck-pond, and so the peddler recovered one thousand dollars damage. So you see that every form of misdemeanor was sternly put down. Think of the high state of morals and religion which induced this people, at an early day, at a political town-meeting, to adopt this decree: "We do sociate and conjoin ourselves and successors to be one town or corporation, and do for ourselves and our successors, and such as shall be adjoined to us at any time hereafter, enter into combination and confederation together to maintain and preserve the purity of the gospel of our Lord Jesus Christ which we now possess."

The pledge of that day has been fully kept; and for sobriety, industry, abhorrence of evil and adherence to an unmixed gospel, we know not the equal of this place.

That document of two centuries ago reads strangely behind the times, but it will be some hundreds of years yet before other communities come up to the point where that document stops. All our laws and institutions are yet to be Christianized. The Puritans took possession of this land in the name of Christ, and it belongs to Him; and if people do not like that religion, let them go somewhere else. They can find many lands where there is no Christian religion to bother them. Let them emigrate to Greenland, and we will provide them with mittens, or to the South Sea Islands, and we will send them ice-coolers. This land is for Christ. Our Legislatures and Congresses shall yet pass laws as radically evangelical as the venerable document above referred to. East Hampton, instead of being two hundred years behind, is two hundred years ahead.

Glorious place to summer! Darwin and Stuart, Mill and Huxley and Renan have not been through here yet. May they miss the train the day they start for this place! With an Atlantic Ocean in which to wash, and a great-hearted, practical, sympathetic gospel to take care of all the future, who could not be happy in East Hampton?

The strong sea-breeze ruffles the sheet upon which we write, and the "white caps" are tossing up as if in greeting to Him who walks the pavements of emerald and opal:

> "Waft, waft, ye winds, His story,
>   And you, ye waters, roll,
> Till, like a sea of glory,
>   It spreads from pole to pole."

CHAPTER XLIV.

CATCHING THE BAY MARE.

It may be a lack of education on our part, but we confess to a dislike for horse-races. We never attended but three; the first in our boyhood, the second at a country fair, where we were deceived as to what would transpire, the third last Sabbath morning. We see our friends flush with indignation at this last admission; but let them wait a moment before they launch their verdict.

Our horse was in the pasture-field. It was almost time to start for church, and we needed the animal harnessed. The boy came in saying it was impossible to catch the bay mare, and calling for our assistance. We had on our best clothes, and did not feel like exposing ourself to rough usage; but we vaulted the fence with pail of water in hand, expecting to try the effect of rewards rather than punishments. The horse came out generously to meet us. We said to the boy, "She is very tame. Strange you cannot catch her." She came near enough to cautiously smell the pail, when she suddenly changed her mind, and with one wild snort dashed off to the other end of the field.

Whether she was not thirsty, or was critical of the manner of presentation, or had apprehensions of our motive, or was seized with desire for exercise in the open air, she gave us no chance to guess. We resolved upon more caution of advance and gentler voice, and so laboriously approached her; for though a pail of water is light for a little way, it gets heavy after you have gone a considerable distance, though its contents be half spilled away.

This time we succeeded in getting her nose inserted into the bright beverage. We called her by pet names, addressing her as "Poor Dolly!" not wishing to suggest any pauperism by that term, but only sympathy for the sorrows of the brute creation, and told her that she was the finest horse that ever was. It seemed to take well, Flattery always does—with horses.

We felt that the time had come for us to produce the rope halter, which with our left hand we had all the while kept secreted behind our back. We put it over her neck, when the beast wheeled, and we seized her by the point where the copy-books say we ought to take Time, namely, the forelock. But we had poor luck. We ceased all caressing tone, and changed the subjunctive mood for the imperative. There never was a greater divergence of sentiment than at that instant between us and the bay mare. She pulled one way, we pulled the other. Turning her back upon us, she ejaculated into the air two shining horseshoes, both the shape of the letter O, the one interjection in contempt for the ministry, and the other in contempt for the press.

But catch the horse we must, for we were bound to be at church, though just then we did not feel at all devotional. We resolved, therefore, with the boy, to run her down; so, by the way of making an animated start, we slung the pail at the horse's head, and put out on a Sunday morning horse-race. Every time she stood at the other end of the field waiting for us to come up. She trotted, galloped and careered about us, with an occasional neigh cheerfully given to encourage us in the pursuit. We were getting more unprepared in body, mind and soul for the sanctuary. Meanwhile, quite a household audience lined the fence; the children and visitors shouting like excited Romans in an amphitheatre at a contest with wild beasts, and it was uncertain whether the audience was in sympathy with us or the bay mare.

At this unhappy juncture, she who some years ago took us for "better or for worse" came to the rescue, finding us in the latter condition. She advanced to the field with a wash-basin full of water, offering that as sole inducement, and gave one call, when the horse went out to meet her, and under a hand, not half as strong as ours, gripping the mane, the refractory beast was led to the manger.

Standing with our feet in the damp grass and our new clothes wet to a sop, we learned then and there how much depends on the way you do a thing. The proposition we made to the bay mare was far better than that offered by our companion; but ours failed and hers succeeded. Not the first nor the last time that a wash-basin has beaten a pail. So some of us go all through life clumsily coaxing and awkwardly pursuing things which we want to halter and control. We strain every nerve, only to find ourselves befooled and left far behind, while some Christian man or woman comes into the field, and by easy art captures that which evaded us.

We heard a good sermon that day, but it was no more impressive than the besweated lesson of the pasture-field, which taught us that no more depends upon the thing you do than upon the way you do it. The difference between the clean swath of that harvester in front of our house and the ragged work of his neighbor is in the way he swings the scythe, and not in the scythe itself. There are ten men with one talent apiece who do more good than the one man with ten talents. A basin properly lifted may accomplish more than a pail unskillfully swung. A minister for an hour in his sermon attempts to chase down those brutish in their habits, attempting to fetch them under the harness of Christian restraint, and perhaps miserably fails, when some gentle hand of sisterly or motherly affection laid upon the wayward one brings him safely in.

There is a knack in doing things. If all those who plough in State and Church had known how to hold the handles, and turn a straight furrow, and stop the team at the end of the field, the world would long ago have been ploughed into an Eden. What many people want is gumption—a word as yet undefined; but if you do not know what it means, it is very certain you do not possess the quality it describes. We all need to study Christian tact. The boys in the Baskinridge school-house laughed at William L. Dayton's impediment of speech, but that did not hinder him from afterward making court-room and senate-chamber thrill under the spell of his words.

In our early home there was a vicious cat that would invade the milk-pans, and we, the boys, chased her with hoes and rakes, always hitting the place where she had been just before, till one day father came out with a plain stick of oven-wood, and with one little clip back of the ear put an end to all of her nine lives. You see everything depends upon the style of the stroke, and not upon the elaborateness of the weapon. The most valuable things you try to take will behave like the bay mare; but what you cannot overcome by coarse persuasion, or reach at full run, you can catch with apostolic guile. Learn the first-rate art of doing secular or Christian work, and then it matters not whether your weapon be a basin or a pail.

CHAPTER XLV.

OUR FIRST AND LAST CIGAR.

The time had come in our boyhood which we thought demanded of us a capacity to smoke. The old people of the household could abide neither the sight nor the smell of the Virginia weed. When ministers came there, not by positive injunction but by a sort of instinct as to what would be safest, they whiffed their pipe on the back steps. If the house could not stand sanctified smoke, you may know how little chance there was for adolescent cigar-puffing.

By some rare good fortune which put in our hands three cents, we found access to a tobacco store. As the lid of the long, narrow, fragrant box opened, and for the first time we own a cigar, our feelings of elation, manliness, superiority and anticipation can scarcely be imagined, save by those who have had the same sensation. Our first ride on horseback, though we fell off before we got to the barn, and our first pair of new boots (real squeakers) we had thought could never be surpassed in interest; but when we put the cigar to our lips, and stuck the lucifer match to the end of the weed, and commenced to pull with an energy that brought every facial muscle to its utmost tension, our satisfaction with this world was so great, our temptation was never to want to leave it.

The cigar did not burn well. It required an amount of suction that tasked our determination to the utmost. You see that our worldly means had limited us to a quality that cost only three cents. But we had been taught that nothing great was accomplished without effort, and so we puffed away. Indeed, we had heard our older brothers in their Latin lessons say, Omnia vincet labor; which translated means, If you want to make anything go, you must scratch for it.

With these sentiments we passed down the village street and out toward our country home. Our head did not feel exactly right, and the street began to rock from side to side, so that it was uncertain to us which side of the street we were on. So we crossed over, but found ourself on the same side that we were on before we crossed over. Indeed, we imagined that we were on both sides at the same time, and several fast teams driving between. We met another boy, who asked us why we looked so pale, and we told him we did not look pale, but that he was pale himself.

We sat down under the bridge and began to reflect on the prospect of early decease, and on the uncertainty of all earthly expectations. We had determined to smoke the cigar all up and thus get the worth of our money, but were obliged to throw three-fourths of it away, yet knew just where we threw it, in case we felt better the next day.

Getting home, the old people were frightened, and demanded that we state what kept us so late and what was the matter with us. Not feeling that we were called to go into particulars, and not wishing to increase our parents' apprehension that we were going to turn out badly, we summed up the case with the statement that we felt miserable at the pit of the stomach. We had mustard plasters administered, and careful watching for some hours, when we fell asleep and forgot our disappointment and humiliation in being obliged to throw away three-fourths of our first cigar. Being naturally reticent, we have never mentioned it until this time.

But how about our last cigar? It was three o'clock Sabbath morning in our Western home. We had smoked three or four cigars since tea. At that time we wrote our sermons and took another cigar with each new head of discourse. We thought we were getting the inspiration from above, but were getting much of it from beneath. Our hand trembled along the line; and strung up to the last tension of nerves, we finished our work and started from the room. A book standing on the table fell over; and although it was not a large book, its fall sounded to our excited system like the crack of a pistol. As we went down the stairs their creaking made our hair stand on end. As we flung ourselves on a sleepless pillow we resolved, God helping, that we had smoked our last cigar, and committed our last sin of night-study.

We kept our promise. With the same resolution went overboard coffee and tea. That night we were born into a new physical, mental and moral life. Perhaps it may be better for some to smoke, and study nights, and take exciting temperance beverages; but we are persuaded that if thousands of people who now go moping, and nervous, and half exhausted through life, down with "sick headaches" and rasped by irritabilities, would try a good large dose of abstinence, they would thank God for this paragraph of personal experience, and make the world the same bright place we find it—a place so attractive that nothing short of heaven would be good enough to exchange for it.

The first cigar made us desperately sick; the throwing away of our last made us gloriously well. For us the croaking of the midnight owl hath ceased, and the time of the singing of birds has come.

CHAPTER XLVI.

MOVE, MOVING, MOVED.

The first of May is to many the beginning of the year. From that are dated the breakages, the social startings, the ups and downs, of domestic life. One-half New York is moving into smaller houses, the other half into larger. The past year's success or failure decides which way the horses of the furniture-wagon shall turn their heads.

Days before, the work of packing commenced. It is astonishing how many boxes and barrels are required to contain all your wares. You come upon a thousand things that you had forgotten, too good to throw away and too poor to keep: old faded carpet-bags that would rouse the mirth of the town if you dared to carry them into the street; straw hats out of the fashion; beavers that you ought to have given away while they might have been useful; odd gloves, shoes, coats and slips of carpet that have been the nest of rats, and a thousand things that you laid away because you some day might want them, but never will.

For the last few days in the old house the accommodations approach the intolerable. Everything is packed up. The dinner comes to you on shattered crockery which is about to be thrown away, and the knives are only painful reminiscences of what they once were. The teapot that we used before we got our "new set" comes on time to remind us how common we once were. You can upset the coffee without soiling the tablecloth, for there is none. The salt and sugar come to you in cups looking so much alike that you find out for the first time how coffee tastes when salted, or fish when it is sweetened. There is no place to sit down, and you have no time to do so if you found one. The bedsteads are down, and you roll into the corner at night, a self-elected pauper, and all the night long have a quarrel with your pillow, which persists in getting out of bed, and your foot wanders out into the air, feeling for greater length of cover. If the children cry in the night, you will not find the matches nor the lamp nor anything else save a trunk just in time to fall over it, getting up with confused notions as to which is the way to bed, unless there be some friendly voice to hail you through the darkness.

The first of May dawns. The carts come. It threatens rain, but not a drop until you get your best rosewood chairs out of doors, and your bedding on the top of the wagon. Be out at twelve o'clock you must, for another family are on your heels, and Thermopylæ was a very tame pass compared with the excitement which rises when two families meet in the same hall—these moving out and those moving in. They swear, unless they have positive principles to prohibit. A mere theory on the subject of swearing will be no hindrance. Long-established propriety of speech, buttressed up by the most stalwart determination is the only safety. Men who talk right all the rest of the year sometimes let slip on the first of May. We know a member of the church who uses no violence of speech except on moving day, and then he frequently cries out: "By the great United States!"

All day long the house is full of racket: "Look out how you scratch that table!" "There! you have dropped the leg out of that piano!" "There goes the looking-glass!" "Ouch! you have smashed my finger!" "Didn't you see you were pushing me against the wall?" "Get out of our way! It's one o'clock, and your things are not half moved! Carmen! take hold and tumble these things into the street!" Our carmen and theirs get into a fight. Our servants on our side, their servants on theirs. We, opposed to anything but peace, try to quiet the strife, yet, if they must go on, feel we would like to have our men triumph. Like England during our late war, we remain neutral, yet have our preferences as to which shall beat. Now dash comes the rain, and the water cools off the heat of the combatants. The carmen must drive fast, so as to get the things out of the wet, but slow, so as not to rub the furniture.

As our last load starts we go in to take a farewell look at the old place. In that parlor we have been gay with our friends many a time, and as we glance round the room we seem to see the great group of their faces. The best furniture we ever had in our parlor was a circle of well-wishers. Here is the bedroom where we slept off the world's cares, and got up glad as the lark when the morning sky beckons it upward. Many a time this room has been full of sleep from doorsill to ceiling. We always did feel grandly after we had put an eight-hour nap between us and life's perplexities. We are accustomed to divide our time into two parts: the first to be devoted to hard, blistering, consuming work, and the rest to be given to the most jubilant fun; and sleep comes under the last head.

We step into the nursery for a last look. The crib is gone, and the doll babies and the blockhouses, but the echoes have not yet stopped galloping; May's laugh, and Edith's glee, and Frank's shout, as he urged the hobby-horse to its utmost speed, both heels struck into the flanks, till out of his glass eye the horse seemed to say:

"Do that again, and I will throw you to the other side of the trundle-bed!" Farewell, old house! It did not suit us exactly, but thank God for the good times we had in it!

Moving-day is almost gone. It is almost night. Tumble everything into the new house. Put up the bedsteads. But who has the wrench, and who the screws? Packed up, are they? In what box? It may be any one of the half dozen. Ah! now I know in which box you will find it; in the last one you open! Hungry, are you? No time to talk of food till the crockery is unpacked. True enough, here they come. That last jolt of the cart finished the teacups. The jolt before that fractured some of the plates, and Bridget now drops the rest of them. The Paradise of crockery-merchants is moving-day. I think, from the results which I see, that they must about the first of May spend most of their time in praying for success in business.

Seated on the boxes, you take tea, and then down with the carpets. They must be stretched, and pieced, and pulled, and matched. The whole family are on their knees at the work, and red in the face, and before the tacks are driven all the fingers have been hammered once and are taking a second bruising. Nothing is where you expected to find it. Where is the hammer? Where are the tacks? Where the hatchet? Where the screw-driver? Where the nails? Where the window-shades? Where is the slat to that old bedstead? Where are the rollers to that stand? The sweet-oil has been emptied into the blackberry-jam. The pickles and the plums have gone out together a-swimming. The lard and the butter have united as skillfully as though a grocer had mixed them. The children who thought it would be grand sport to move are satiated, and one-half the city of New York at the close of

May-day go to bed worn out, sick and disgusted. It is a social earthquake that annually shakes the city.

It may be that very soon some of our rich relatives will, at their demise, "will" us each one a house, so that we shall be permanently fixed. We should be sorry to have them quit the world under any circumstances; but if, determined to go anyhow, they should leave us a house, the void would not be so large, especially if it were a house, well furnished and having all the modern improvements. We would be thankful for any good advice they might leave us, but should more highly appreciate a house.

May all the victims of moving-day find their new home attractive! If they have gone into a smaller house, let them congratulate themselves at the thought that it takes less time to keep a small house clean than a big one. May they have plenty of Spaulding's glue with which to repair breakages! May the carpets fit better than they expected, and the family that moved out have taken all their cockroaches and bedbugs with them!

And, better than all—and this time in sober earnest—by the time that moving-day comes again, may they have made enough money to buy a house from which they will never have to move until the House of many mansions be ready to receive them!

CHAPTER XLVII.
ADVANTAGE OF SMALL LIBRARIES.

We never see a valuable book without wanting it. The most of us have been struck through with a passion for books. Town, city and state libraries to us are an enchantment. We hear of a private library of ten thousand volumes, and think what a heaven the owner must be living in. But the probability is that the man who has five hundred volumes is better off than the man who has five thousand. The large private libraries in uniform editions, and unbroken sets, and Russia covers, are, for the most part, the idlers of the day; while the small libraries, with broken-backed books, and turned-down leaves, and lead-pencil scribbles in the margin, are doing the chief work for the world and the Church.

For the most part, the owners of large collections have their chief anxiety about the binding and the type. Take down the whole set of Walter Scott's novels, and find that only one of them has been read through. There are Motley's histories on that shelf; but get into conversation about the Prince of Orange, and see that Motley has not been read. I never was more hungry than once while walking in a Charleston mill amid whole harvests of rice. One handful of that grain in a pudding would have been worth more to me than a thousand tierces uncooked. Great libraries are of but little value if unread, and amid great profusion of books the temptation is to read but little. If a man take up a book, and feel he will never have a chance to see it again, he says: "I must read it now or never," and before the day is past has devoured it. The owner of the large library says: "I have it on my shelf, and any time can refer to it."

What we can have any time we never have. I found a group of men living at the foot of Whiteface Mountain who had never been to the top, while I had come hundreds of miles to ascend it. They could go any time so easily. It is often the case that those who have plain copies of history are better acquainted with the past than those who have most highly adorned editions of Bancroft, Prescott, Josephus and Herodotus. It ought not so to be, you say. I cannot help that; so it is.

Books are sometimes too elegantly bound to be read. The gilt, the tinge, the ivory, the clasps, seem to say: "Hands off!" The thing that most surprised me in Thomas Carlyle's library was the fewness of the books. They had all seen service. None of them had paraded in holiday dress. They were worn and battered. He had flung them at the ages.

More beautiful than any other adornments are the costly books of a princely library; but let not the man of small library stand looking into the garnished alcoves wishing for these unused volumes. The workman who dines on roast beef and new Irish potatoes will be healthier and stronger than he who begins with "mock-turtle," and goes up through the lane of a luxuriant table till he comes to almond-nuts. I put the man of one hundred books, mastered, against the man of one thousand books of which he has only a smattering.

On lecturing routes I have sometimes been turned into costly private libraries to spend the day; and I reveled in the indexes, and scrutinized the lids, and set them back in as straight a row as when I found them, yet learned little. But on my way home in the cars I took out of my satchel a book that had cost me only one dollar and a half, and afterward found that it had changed the course of my life and helped decide my eternal destiny.

We get many letters from clergymen asking advice about reading, and deploring their lack of books. I warrant they all have books enough to shake earth and heaven with, if the books were rightly used. A man who owns a Bible has, to begin with, a library as long as from here to heaven. The dullest preachers I know of have splendid libraries. They own everything that has been written on a miracle, and yet when you hear them preach, if you did not get sound asleep, that would be a miracle. They have all that Calvin and other learned men wrote about election, and while you hear them you feel that you have been elected to be bored. They have been months and years turning over the heavy tomes on the divine attributes, trying to understand God, while some plain Christian, with a New Testament in his hand, goes into the next alley, and sees in the face of an invalid woman peace and light and comfort and joy which teach him in one hour what God is.

There are two kinds of dullness—learned dullness and ignorant dullness. We think the latter preferable, for it is apt to be more spicy. You cannot measure the length of a man's brain, nor the width of his heart, nor the extent of his usefulness by the size of his library.

Life is so short you cannot know everything. There are but few things we need to know, but let us know them well. People who know everything do nothing. You cannot read all that comes out. Every book read without digestion is so much dyspepsia. Sixteen apple-dumplings at one meal are not healthy.

In our age, when hundreds of books are launched

every day from the press, do not be ashamed to confess ignorance of the majority of the volumes printed. If you have no artistic appreciation, spend neither your dollars nor your time on John Ruskin. Do not say that you are fond of Shakespeare if you are not interested in him, and after a year's study would not know Romeo from John Falstaff. There is an amazing amount of lying about Shakespeare.

Use to the utmost what books you have, and do not waste your time in longing after a great library. You wish you could live in the city and have access to some great collection of books. Be not deceived. The book of the library which you want will be out the day you want it. I longed to live in town that I might be in proximity to great libraries. Have lived in town thirteen years, and never found in the public library the book I asked for but once; and getting that home, I discovered it was not the one I wanted. Besides, it is the book that you own that most profits, not that one which you take from "The Athenæum" for a few days.

Excepting in rare cases, you might as well send to the foundling hospital and borrow a baby as to borrow a book with the idea of its being any great satisfaction. We like a baby in our cradle, but prefer that one which belongs to the household. We like a book, but want to feel it is ours. We never yet got any advantage from a borrowed book. We hope those never reaped any profit from the books they borrowed from us, but never returned. We must have the right to turn down the leaf, and underscore the favorite passage, and write an observation in the margin in such poor chirography that no one else can read it and we ourselves are sometimes confounded.

All success to great libraries, and skillful bookbindery, and exquisite typography, and fine-tinted plate paper, and beveled boards, and gilt edges, and Turkey morocco! but we are determined that frescoed alcoves shall not lord it over common shelves, and Russia binding shall not overrule sheepskin, and that "full calf" shall not look down on pasteboard. We war not against great libraries. We only plead for the better use of small ones.

CHAPTER XLVIII.

REFORMATION IN LETTER-WRITING.

We congratulate the country on the revolution in epistolary correspondence. Through postal cards we not only come to economy in stamps, and paper, and ink, and envelopes, but to education in brevity. As soon as men and women get facility in composition they are tempted to prolixity. Hence some of us formed the habit of beginning to read a letter on the second page, because we knew that the writer would not get a-going before that; and then we were apt to stop a page or two before the close, knowing that the remaining portions would be taken in putting down the brakes.

The postal card is a national deliverance. Without the conventional "I take my pen in hand," or other rigmarole—which being translated means, "I am not quite ready to begin just now, but will very soon"—the writer states directly, and in ten or twenty words, all his business.

While no one can possibly have keener appreciation than we of letters of sympathy, encouragement and good cheer, there is a vast amount of letter-writing that amounts to nothing. Some of them we carry in our pockets, and read over and over again, until they are worn out with handling. But we average about twenty begging letters a day. They are always long, the first page taken up in congratulations upon "big heart," "wide influence," "Christian sympathies," and so on, winding up with a solicitation for five dollars, more or less. We always know from the amount of lather put on that we are going to be shaved. The postal card will soon invade even that verbosity, and the correspondent will simply say, "Poor—very—children ten—chills and fever myself—no quinine—desperate—your money or your life-Bartholomew Wiggins, Dismal Swamp, Ia."

The advantage of such a thing is that if you do not answer such a letter no offence is taken, it is so short and costs only a cent; whereas, if the author had taken a great sheet of letter paper, filled it with compliments and graceful solicitations, folded it, and run the gummed edge along the lips at the risk of being poisoned, and stuck on a stamp (after tedious examination of it to see whether or not it had been used before, or had only been mauled in your vest pocket), the offence would have been mortal, and you would have been pronounced mean and unfit for the ministry.

Postal cards are likewise a relief to that large class of persons who by sealed envelope are roused to inquisitiveness. As such a closed letter lies on the mantel-piece unopened, they wonder whom it is from, and what is in it, and they hold it up between them and the light to see what are the indications, and stand close by and look over your shoulder while you read it, and decipher from your looks whether it is a love-letter or a dun. The postal card is immediate relief to them, for they can read for themselves, and can pick up information on various subjects free of charge.

But, after all, the great advantage of this new postal arrangement is economy in the consumption of time. It will practically add several years to a man's life, and will keep us a thousand times, at the beginning of our letters, from saying "Dear Sir" to those who are not at all dear, and will save us from surrendering ourselves with a "Yours, truly," to those to whom we will never belong. We hail the advent of the postal-card system.

CHAPTER XLIX.

ROYAL MARRIAGES.

There has lately been such a jingle of bells in St. Petersburg and London that we have heard them quite across the sea. The queen's son has married the daughter of the Russian emperor. We are glad of it. It is always well to have people marry who are on the same level. The famous affiancing in New York of a coachman with the daughter of the millionaire who employed him did not turn out well. It was bad for her, but worse for the coachman. Eagle and ox are both well in their places, but let them not marry. The ox would be dizzy in the eyrie, and the eagle ill at home in the barnyard. When the children of two royal homes are united, there ought be no begrudging of powder for the cannonading, or of candles for the illumination. All joy to the Duke of Edinburgh and his fortunate duchess.

But let not our friends across the sea imagine that we have no royal marriages here in this western wilderness. Whenever two hearts come together pledged to make each other happy, binding all their hopes and fears and anticipations in one sheaf, calling on God to bless and angels to witness, though no organ may sound the wedding-march, and no bells may chime, and no Dean of Westminster travel a thousand miles to pronounce the ceremony,—that is a royal marriage.

When two young people start out on life together with nothing but a determination to succeed, avoiding the invasion of each other's idiosyncrasies, not carrying the candle near the gunpowder, sympathetic with each other's employment, willing to live on small means till they get large facilities, paying as they go, taking life here as a discipline, with four eyes watching its perils, and with four hands fighting its battles, whatever others may say or do,—that is a royal marriage. It is so set down in the heavenly archives, and the orange blossoms shall wither on neither side the grave.

We deplore the fact that because of the fearful extravagances of modern society many of our best people conclude that they cannot possibly afford to marry.

We are getting a fearful crop of old bachelors. They swarm around us. They go through life lop-sided. Half dressed, they sit round cold mornings, all a-shiver, sewing on buttons and darning socks, and then go down to a long boarding-house table which is bounded on the north and south and east and west by the Great Sahara Desert. We do not pity them at all. May all their buttons be off to-morrow morning! Why do they not set up a plain home of their own and come into the ark two and two?

The supporting of a wife is looked upon as a great horror. Why, dear friends, with right and healthy notions of time and eternity it is very easy to support a wife if she be of the kind worth supporting. If she be educated into false notions of refinement and have "young ladies' institutes" piled on her head till she be imbecile, you will never be able to support her. Everything depends on whether you take for your wife a woman or a doll-baby. Our opinion is that three-fourths the successful men of the day owe much of their prosperity to the wife's help. The load of life is so heavy it takes a team of two to draw it. The ship wants not only a captain, but a first mate. Society to-day, trans-Atlantic and cis-Atlantic, very much needs more royal marriages.

CHAPTER L.

THREE VISITS.

Yesterday was Saturday to you, but it was Sunday to me. In other words, it was a day of rest. We cannot always be working. If you drive along in a deep rut, and then try to turn off, you are very apt to break the shafts. A skillful driver is careful not to get into a deep rut. You cannot always be keeping on in the same way. We must have times of leisure and recreation.

A great deal of Christian work amounts to nothing, from the fact that it is not prefaced and appendixed by recreation. Better take hold of a hammer and give one strong stroke and lay it down than to be all the time so fagged out that we cannot move the hammer.

Well, yesterday being a day of rest to me, I made three visits in New York.

The first was to the Tombs—an institution seemingly full now, a man or woman or boy at every wicket. A great congregation of burglars, thieves, pickpockets and murderers. For the most part, they are the clumsy villains of society; the nimble, spry ones get out of the way, and are not caught. There are those who are agile as well as depraved in that dark place. Stokes, representing the aristocracy of crime; Foster, the democracy of sin; and Rozensweig, the brute. Each cell a commentary upon the Scripture passage, "The way of the transgressor is hard."

I was amazed to see that the youth are in the majority in that building. I said to the turnkey: "What a pity it is that that bright fellow is in here!" "Oh," he says, "these bright fellows keep us busy." I talked some with the boys, and they laughed; but there was a catch in the guffaw, as though the laughter on its way had stumbled over a groan. It was not a deep laugh and a laugh all over, as boys generally do when they are merry. These boys have had no chance. They have been in the school of crime all their days, and are now only taking their degree of "M. V."—master of villainy.

God hasten the time when our Sabbath-schools, instead of being flower-pots for a few choice children, shall gather up the perishing rabble outside, like Ralph Wells' school in New York, and Father Hawley's school in Hartford, and John Wanamaker's school in Philadelphia! There is not much chance in our fashionable Sunday-schools for a boy out at the elbows. Many of our schools pride themselves on being gilt-edged; and when we go out to fulfill the Saviour's command, "Feed my lambs," we look out chiefly for white fleeces. I like that school the best which, in addition to the glorious gospel, carries soap and fine-tooth combs. God save the dying children of the street! I saw a child in the Tombs four years of age, and said, "What in the world can this little child be doing here?" They told me the father had been arrested and the child had to go with him. Allegory, parable, prophecy: "Where the father goes the child goes." Father inside the grates, and son outside waiting to get in.

All through the corridors of that prison I saw Scripture passages: "I am the way of life;" "Believe in the Lord, and thou shalt be saved;" and like passages. Who placed them there? The turnkey? No. The sheriff? No. They are marks left by the city missionary and Christian philanthropist in recognition of that gospel by which the world is to be regenerated or never saved at all.

I wish they would get some other name for that—the Tombs—for it is the cleanest prison I ever saw. But the great want of that prison and of all others is sunshine. God's light is a purifier. You cannot expect reformation where you brood over a man with perpetual midnight. Oh that some Howard or Elizabeth Fry would cry through all the dungeons of the earth, "Let there be light!" I never heard of anybody being brought to God or reformed through darkness. God Himself is light, and that which is most like God is most healthful and pure.

Saddened by this awful wreck of men and morals, we came along the corridors where the wives stood weeping at the wicket-door of their husbands, and parents over their lost children. It was a very sad place. There were some men I was surprised to find there—men whom I had seen in other places, in holy places, in consecrated places.

We came out into the sunlight after that, and found ourselves very soon in the art-gallery at Twenty-third street. That was my second visit. Mr. Kensett, the great artist, recently died, and six hundred and fifty of his pictures are now on exhibition. In contrast with the dark prison scene, how beautiful the canvas! Mr. Kensett had an irresistible way of calling trees and rocks and waters into his pictures. He only beckoned and they came. Once come, he pinioned them for ever. Why, that man could paint a breeze on the water, so it almost wet your face with the spray. So restful are his pictures you feel after seeing them as though for half a day you had been sprawled under a tree in July weather, summered through and through.

Thirty of such pictures he painted each year in

one hundred and twenty days, and then died—quickly and unwarned, dropping his magician's wand, to be picked up never. I wondered if he was ready, and if the God whom he had often met amid the moss on the sea-cliffs and in the offing was the God who pardoned sin and by His grace saves painter and boor. The Lord bless the unappreciated artists; they do a glorious work for God and the world, but for the most part live in penury, and the brightest color on their palette is crimson with their own blood.

May the time hasten when the Frenchmen who put on canvas their Cupids poorly clad, and the Germans who hang up homely Dutch babies in the arms of the Virgin Mary and call them Madonnas, shall be overruled by the artists who, like Kensett, make their canvas a psalm of praise to the Lord of the winds and the waters!

I stepped across the way into the Young Men's Christian Association of New York, with its reading-rooms and library and gymnasium and bath-rooms, all means of grace—a place that proposes to charm young men from places of sin by making religion attractive. It is a palace for the Lord—the pride of New York, or ought to be; I do not believe it really is, but it ought to be. It is fifty churches with its arms of Christian usefulness stretched out toward the young men.

If a young man come in mentally worn out, it gives him dumb-bells, parallel bars and a bowling-alley with no rum at either end of it. If physically worsted, it rests him amid pictures and books and newspapers. If a young man come in wanting something for the soul, there are the Bible-classes, prayer-meetings and preaching of the gospel.

Religion wears no monk's cowl in that place, no hair shirt, no spiked sandals, but the floor and the ceiling and the lounges and the tables and the cheerful attendants seem to say: "Her ways are ways of pleasantness, and all her paths are peace."

I never saw a more beautiful scene in any public building than on one of these bright sofas, fit for any parlor in New York, where lay a weary, plain, exhausted man resting—sound asleep.

Another triumph of Christianity that building is—a Christianity that is erecting lighthouses on all the coasts, and planting its batteries on every hill-top, and spreading its banquets all the world over.

Well, with these reflections I started for Brooklyn. It was just after six o'clock, and tired New York was going home. Street cars and ferries all crowded. Going home! Some to bright places, to be lovingly greeted and warmed and fed and rested. Others to places dark and uncomely; but as I sat down in my own home I could not help thinking of the three spectacles. I had seen during the day Sin, in its shame; Art, in its beauty; Religion, in its work of love. God give repentance to the first, wider appreciation to the second, and universal conquest to the third!

CHAPTER LI.

MANAHACHTANIENKS.

We should like to tell so many of our readers as have survived the pronunciation of the above word that the Indians first called the site on which New York was built Manahachtanienks. The translation of it is, "The place where they all got drunk." Most uncomplimentary title; we are glad that it has been changed; for though New York has several thousand unlicensed grog-shops, we consider the name inappropriate, although, if intemperance continues to increase as rapidly for the next hundred years as during the last twenty years, the time will come when New York may appropriately take its old Indian nomenclature.

Old-time New York is being rapidly forgotten, and it may be well to revive some historical facts. At an expense of three thousand dollars a year men with guide-book in hand go through the pyramids of Egypt and the picture-galleries of Rome and the ruins of Pompeii, when they have never seen the strange and historical scenes at home.

We advise the people who live in Brooklyn, Jersey City and up-town New York to go on an exploration.

Go to No. 1 Broadway and remember that George Washington and Lord Cornwallis once lived there.

Go to the United States Treasury, on Wall street, and remember that in front of it used to stand a pillory and a whipping-post.

In a building that stood where the United States

Treasury stands, General Washington was installed as President. In the open balcony he stood with silver buckles and powdered hair, in dress of dark silk velvet. (People in those days dressed more than we moderns. Think of James Buchanan or General Grant inaugurated with hair and shoes fixed up like that!)

Go to the corner of Pearl and Broad streets, and remember that was the scene of Washington's farewell to the officers with whom he had been so long associated.

Go to Canal street, and remember it was so called because it once was literally a canal.

The electric telegraph was born in the steeple of the old Dutch Church, now the New York post-office—that is, Benjamin Franklin made there his first experiments in electricity. When the other denominations charge the Dutch Church with being slow, they do not know that the world got its lightning out of one of its church steeples.

Washington Irving was born in William street, halfway between John and Fulton. "Knickerbocker" was considered very saucy; but if any man ever had a right to say mirthful things about New York, it was Washington Irving, who was born there. At the corner of Varick and Charlton streets was a house in which Washington, John Adams and Aaron Burr resided.

George Whitfield preached at the corner of Beekman and Nassau streets.

But why particularize, when there is not a block or a house on the great thoroughfare which has not been the scene of a tragedy, a fortune ruined, a reputation sacrificed, an agony suffered or a soul lost?

CHAPTER LII.

A DIP IN THE SEA.

Shakespeare has been fiercely mauled by the critics for confusion of metaphor in speaking of taking up "arms against a sea of troubles." The smart fellows say, How could a man take "arms against a sea?" In other words, it is not possible to shoot the Pacific Ocean. But what Shakespeare suggests is, this jocund morning, being done all around the coast from Florida to Newfoundland, especial regiments going out from Cape May, Long Branch, East Hampton, Newport and Nahant; ten thousand bathers, with hands thrown into the air, "taking up arms against the sea." But the old giant has only to roll over once on his bed of seaweed, and all this attacking host are flung prostrate upon the beach.

The sensation of sea-bathing is about the same everywhere. First you have the work of putting on the appropriate dress, sometimes wet and chill from the previous bathing. You get into the garments cautiously, touching them at as few points as possible, your face askew, and with a swift draft of breath through your front teeth, punctuating the final lodgment of each sleeve and fold with a spasmodic "Oh!" Then, having placed your watch where no villainous straggler may be induced to examine it to see whether he can get to the depot in time for the next train, you issue forth ingloriously, your head down in consciousness that you are cutting a sorry figure before the world. Barefoot as a mendicant, your hair disheveled in the wind, the stripes of your clothes strongly suggestive of Sing Sing, your appearance a caricature of humankind, you wander up and down the beach a creature that the land is evidently trying to shake off and the sea is unwilling to take. But you are consoled by the fact that all the rest are as mean and forlorn-looking as yourself; and so you wade in, over foot-top, unto the knee, and waist deep. The water is icy-cold, so that your teeth chatter and your frame quakes, until you make a bold dive; and in a moment you and the sea are good friends, and you are not certain whether you have surrendered to the ocean or the ocean has surrendered to you.

At this point begin the raptures of bathing. You have left the world on the beach, and are caught up in the arms of experiences that you never feel on land. If you are far enough out, the breaking wave curves over you like a roof inlaid and prismatic, bending down on the other side of you in layers of chalk and drifts of snow, and the lightning flash of the foam ends in the thunder of the falling wave. You fling aside from your arms, as worthless, amethyst and emerald and chrysoprase. Your ears are filled with the halo of sporting elements, and your eyes with all tints and tinges and double-dyes and liquid emblazonment. You leap and shout and clap your hands, and tell the billows to come on, and in excess of glee greet persons that you never saw before and never will again, and never want to, and act so wildly that others would think you demented but that they also are as fully let loose; so that if there be one imbecile there is a whole asylum of lunatics.

It is astonishing how many sounds mingle in the water: the faint squall of the affrighted child, the shrill shriek of the lady just introduced to the uproarious hilarities, the souse of the diver, the snort of the half-strangled, the clear giggle of maidens, the hoarse bellow of swamped obesity, the whine of the convalescent invalid, the yell of unmixed delight, the te-hee and squeak of the city exquisite learning how to laugh out loud, the splash of the brine, the cachinnation of a band of harmless savages, the stun of the surge on your right ear, the hiss of the surf, the saturnalia of the elements; while overpowering all other sounds are the orchestral harmonies of the sea, which roll on through the ages, all shells, all winds, all caverns, all billows heard in "the oratorio of the creation."

But while bathing, the ludicrous will often break through the grand. Swept hither and thither, you find, moving in reel and cotillon, saraband and rigadoon and hornpipe, Quakers and Presbyterians who are down on the dance. Your sparse clothing feels the stress of the waves, and you think what an awful thing it would be if the girdle should burst or a button break, and you should have, out of respect to the feelings of others, to go up the beach sidewise or backward or on your hands and knees.

Close beside you, in the surf, is a judge of the Court of Appeals, with a garment on that looks like his grandmother's night-gown just lifted from the wash-tub and not yet wrung out. On the other side is a maiden with a twenty-five-cent straw hat on a head that ordinarily sports a hundred dollars' worth of millinery. Yonder is a doctor of divinity with his head in the sand and his feet beating the air, traveling heavenward, while his right hand clutches his wife's foot, as much as to say, "My feet are useless in this emergency; give me the benefit of yours."

Now a stronger wave, for which none are ready, dashes in, and with it tumble ashore, in one great wreck of humanity, small craft and large, stout hulk and swift clipper, helm first, topsail down, forestay-sail in tatters, keel up, everything gone to pieces in the swash of the surges.

Oh, the glee of sea-bathing! It rouses the apathetic. It upsets the supercilious and pragmatical. It is balsamic for mental wounds. It is a tonic for those who need strength, and an anodyne for those who require soothing, and a febrifuge for those who want their blood cooled; a filling up for minds pumped dry, a breviary for the superstitious with endless matins and vespers, and to the Christian an apocalyptic vision where the morning sun gilds the waters, and there is spread before him "a sea of glass mingled with fire." "Thy way, O God, is in the sea, and thy path in the great waters!"

CHAPTER LIII.

HARD SHELL CONSIDERATIONS.

The plumage of the robin redbreast, the mottled sides of the Saranac trout, the upholstery of a spider's web, the waist of the wasp fashionably small without tight lacing, the lustrous eye of the gazelle, the ganglia of the star-fish, have been discoursed upon; but it is left to us, fagged out from a long ramble, to sit down on a log and celebrate the admirable qualities of a turtle. We refer not to the curious architecture of its house—ribbed, plated, jointed, carapace and plastron divinely fashioned—but to its instincts, worthy almost of being called mental and moral qualities.

The tortoise is wiser than many people we wot of, in the fact that he knows when to keep his head in his shell. No sooner did we just now appear on the edge of the wood than this animal of the order Testudinata modestly withdrew. He knew he was no match for us. But how many of the human race are in the habit of projecting their heads into things for which they have no fittedness! They thrust themselves into discussions where they are almost sure to get trod on. They will dispute about vertebræ with Cuvier, or metaphysics with William Hamilton, or paintings with Ruskin, or medicine with Doctor Rush, and attempt to sting Professor Jaeger to death with his own insects. The first and last important lesson for such persons to learn is, like this animal at our foot, to shut up their shell. If they could see how, in the case of this roadside tortoise, at our appearance the carapace suddenly came down on the plastron, or, in other words, how the upper bone snapped against the lower bone, they might become as wise as this reptile.

We admire also the turtle's capacity of being at home everywhere. He carries with him his parlor, nursery, kitchen, bed-chamber and bathroom. Would that we all had an equal faculty of domestication! In such a beautiful world, and with so many comfortable surroundings, we ought to feel at home in any place we are called to be. While we cannot, like the tortoise, carry our house on our back, we are better off than he, for by the right culture of a contented spirit we may make the sky itself the mottled shell of our residence, and the horizon all around us shall be the place where the carapace shuts down on the plastron.

We admire still more the tortoise's determination to right itself. By way of experiment, turn it upside down, and then go off a piece to see it regain its position. Now, there is nothing when put upon its back which has such little prospect of getting to its feet again as this animal. It has no hands to push with and nothing against which to brace its feet, and one would think that a turtle once upside down would be upside down for ever. But put on its back, it keeps on scrabbling till it is right side up. We would like to pick up this animal from the dust and put it down on Broadway, if men passing by would learn from it never to stop exertion, even when overthrown. You cannot by commercial disasters be more thoroughly flat on your back than five minutes ago was this poor thing; but see it yonder nimbly making for the bushes. Vanderbilt or Jay Gould may treat you as we did the tortoise a few moments ago. But do not lie still, discouraged. Make an effort to get up. Throw your feet out, first in one direction and then in another. Scrabble!

We find from this day's roadside observation that the turtle uses its head before it does its feet: in other words, it looks around before it moves. You never catch a turtle doing anything without previous careful inspection. We would, all of us, do better if we always looked before we leaped. It is easier to get into trouble than to get out. Better have goods weighed before we buy them. Better know where a road comes out before we start on 'it. We caught one hundred flies in our sitting-room yesterday because they sacrificed all their caution to a love of molasses. Better use your brain before you do your hands and feet. Before starting, the turtle always sticks its head out of its shell.

But tortoises die. They sometimes last two hundred years. We read that one of them outlived seven bishops. They have a quiet life and no wear and tear upon their nervous system. Yet they, after a while, notwithstanding all their slow travel, reach the end of their journey. For the last time they draw their head inside their shell and shut out the world for ever. But notwithstanding the useful thoughts they suggest while living, they are of still more worth when dead. We fashion their bodies into soup and their carapace into combs for the hair, and tinged drops for the ear, and bracelets for the wrist. One of Delmonico's soup tureens is waiting for the hero we celebrate, and Tiffany for his eight plates of bone. Will we be as useful after we are dead? Some men are thrown aside like a turtle-shell crushed by a cart-wheel; but others, by deeds done or words spoken, are useful long after they quit life, their example an encouragement, their memory a banquet. He who helps build an asylum or gives healthful and cultured starting to a young man may twenty years after his decease be doing more for the world than during his residence upon it. Stephen Girard and George Peabody are of more use to the race than when Philadelphia and London saw them.

But we must get up off this log, for the ants are crawling over us, and the bull-frogs croak as though the night were coming on. The evening star hangs its lantern at the door of the night to light the tired day to rest. The wild roses in the thicket are breathing vespers at an altar cushioned with moss, while the fire-flies are kindling their dim lamps in the cathedral of the woods. The evening dew on strings of fern is counting its beads in prayer. The "Whip-poor-will" takes up its notes of complaint, making us wonder on our way home what "Will" it was that in boyhood maltreated the ancestors of this species of birds, whether William Wordsworth, or William Cowper, or William Shakspeare, so that the feathered descendants keep through all the forests, year after year, demanding for the cruel perpetrator a sound threshing, forgetting the Bryant that praised them and the Tennyson that petted them and the Jean Ingelow who throws them crumbs, in their anxiety to have some one whip poor Will.

CHAPTER LIV.

WISEMAN, HEAVYASBRICKS AND QUIZZLE.

We had muffins that night. Indeed, we always had either muffins or waffles when Governor Wiseman was at tea. The reason for this choice of food was that a muffin or a waffle seemed just suited to the size of Wiseman's paragraphs of conversation. In other words, a muffin lasted him about as long as any one subject of discourse; and when the muffin was done, the subject was done.

We never knew why he was called governor, for he certainly never ruled over any State, but perhaps it was his wise look that got him the name. He never laughed; had his round spectacles far down on the end of his nose, so that he could see as far into his plate as any man that ever sat at our tea-table. When he talked, the conversation was all on his side. He considered himself oracular on most subjects. You had but to ask him a question, and without lifting his head, his eye vibrating from fork to muffin, he would go on till he had said all he knew on that theme. We did not invite him to our house more than once in about three months, for too much of a good thing is a bad thing.

At the same sitting we always had our young friend Fred Quizzle. He did not know much, but he was mighty in asking questions. So when we had Governor Wiseman, the well, we had Quizzle, the pump.

Fred was long and thin and jerky, and you never knew just where he would put his foot. Indeed, he was not certain himself. He was thoroughly illogical, and the question he asked would sometimes seem quite foreign to the subject being discoursed upon. His legs were crooked and reminded you of interrogation points, and his arms were interrogations, and his neck was an interrogation, while his eyes had a very inquisitive look.

Fred Quizzle did not talk until over two years of age, notwithstanding all his parents' exertions toward getting him to say "papa" and "mamma." After his parents had made up their minds that he would never talk at all, he one day rose from his block houses, looked into his father's eyes, and cried out, "How?" as if inquiring in what manner he had found his way into this world. His parent, outraged at the child's choice of an adverb for his first expression instead of a noun masculine or a noun feminine indicative of filial affection, proceeded to chastise the youngster, when Fred Quizzle cried out for his second, "Why?" as though inquiring the cause of such hasty punishment.

This early propensity for asking questions grew on him till at twenty-three years of age he was a prodigy in this respect. So when we had Governor Wiseman we also had Fred Quizzle, the former to discourse, the latter to start him and keep him going.

Doctor Heavyasbricks was generally present at the same interview. We took the doctor as a sort of sedative. After a season of hard work and nervous excitement, Doctor Heavyasbricks had a quieting influence upon us. There was no lightning in his disposition. He was a great laugher, but never at any recent merriment. It took a long while for him to understand a joke. Indeed, if it were subtle or elaborate, he never understood it. But give the doctor, when in good health, a plain pun or repartee, and let him have a day or two to think over it, and he would come in with uproarious merriment that well-nigh would choke him to death, if the paroxysm happened to take him with his mouth full of muffins.

When at our table, the time not positively occupied in mastication he employed in looking first at Quizzle, the interlocutor, and then at Governor Wiseman, the responding oracle.

Quizzle.—How have you, Governor Wiseman, kept yourself in such robust health so long a time?

Wiseman.—By never trifling with it, sir. I never eat muffins too hot. This one, you see, has had some time to cool. Besides, when I am at all disordered, I immediately send for the doctor.

There are books proposing that we all become our own medical attendant. Whenever we are seized with any sort of physical disorder, we are to take down some volume in homeopathy, allopathy, hydropathy, and running our finger along the index, alight upon the malady that may be afflicting us. We shall find in the same page the name of the disease and the remedy. Thus: chapped hands—glycerine; cold—squills; lumbago—mustard-plasters; nervous excitement—valerian; sleeplessness—Dover's powders.

This may be very well for slight ailments, but we have attended more funerals of people who were their own doctor than obsequies of any other sort. In your inexperience you will be apt to get the wrong remedy. Look out for the agriculturist who farms by book, neglecting the counsel of his long-experienced neighbors. He will have poor turnips and starveling wheat, and kill his fields with undue apportionments of guano and bonedust. Look out just as much for the patient who in the worship of some "pathy" blindly adheres to a favorite hygienic volume, rejecting in important cases medical admonition.

In ordinary cases the best doctor you can have is mother or grandmother, who has piloted through the rocks of infantile disease a whole family. She has salve for almost everything, and knows how to bind a wound or cool an inflammation. But if mother be dead or you are afflicted with a maternal ancestor that never knew anything practical, and never ill, better in severe cases have the doctor right away. You say that it is expensive to do that, while a book on the treatment of diseases will cost you only a dollar and a half. I reply that in the end it is very expensive for an inexperienced man to be his own doctor; for in addition to the price of the book there are the undertaker's expenses.

Some of the younger persons at the table laughed at the closing sentence of Wiseman, when Doctor Heavyasbricks looked up, put down his knife and said: "My young friends, what are you laughing at? I see no cause of merriment in the phrase 'undertaker's expenses.' It seems to me to be a sad business. When I think of the scenes amid which an undertaker moves, I feel more like tears than hilarity."

Quizzle.—If you are opposed, Governor Wiseman, to one's being his own doctor, what do you think of every man's being his own lawyer?

Wiseman.—I think just as badly of that.

Books setting forth forms for deeds, mortgages, notes, and contracts, are no doubt valuable. It should be a part of every young man's education to know something of these. We cannot for the small business transactions of life be hunting up the "attorney-at-law" or the village squire. But economy in the transfer of property or in the making of wills is sometimes a permanent disaster. There are so many quirks in the law, so many hiding-places for scamps, so many modes of twisting phraseology, so many decisions, precedents and rulings, so many John Does who have brought suits against Richard Roes, that you had better in all important business matters seek out an honest lawyer.

"There are none such!" cries out Quizzle.

Why, where have you lived? There are as many honest men in the legal profession as in any other, and rogues more than enough in all professions. Many a farmer, going down to attend court in the county-seat, takes a load of produce to the market, carefully putting the specked apples at the bottom of the barrel, and hiding among the fresh ones the egg which some discouraged hen after five weeks of "setting" had abandoned, and having secured the sale of his produce and lost his suit in the "Court of Common Pleas," has come home denouncing the scoundrelism of attorneys.

You shall find plenty of honest lawyers if you really need them; and in matters involving large interests you had better employ them.

Especially avoid the mistake of making your own "last will and testament" unless you have great legal skillfulness. Better leave no will at all than one inefficiently constructed. The "Orphans' Court" could tell many a tragedy of property distributed adverse to the intention of the testator. You save twenty to a hundred dollars from your counsel by writing your own will, and your heirs pay ten thousand dollars to lawyers in disputes over it. Perhaps those whom you have wished especially to favor will get the least of your estate, and a relative against whom you always had especial dislike will get the most, and your charities will be apportioned differently from what you anticipated—a hundred dollars to the Bible Society, and three thousand to the "hook and ladder company."

Quizzle.—Do you not think, governor (to go back to the subject from which we wandered), that your good spirits have had much to do with your good health?

Wiseman.—No doubt. I see no reason why, because I am advancing in years, I should become melancholy.

One of the heartiest things I have seen of late is the letter of Rev. Dr. Dowling as he retires from active work in the ministry. He hands over his work to the younger brethren without sigh, or groan, or regret. He sees the sun is quite far down in the west, and he feels like hanging up his scythe in the first apple tree he comes to. Our opinion is that he has made a little mistake in the time of day, and that while he thinks it is about half-past five in the afternoon, it is only about three. I guess his watch is out of order, and that he has been led to think it later than it really is. But when we remember how much good he has done, we will not begrudge him his rest either here or hereafter.

At any rate, taking the doctor's cheerful valedictory for a text, I might preach a little bit of a sermon on the best way of getting old. Do not be fretted because you have to come to spectacles. While glasses look premature on a young man's nose, they are an adornment on an octogenarian's face. Besides that, when your eyesight is poor, you miss seeing a great many unpleasant things that youngsters are obliged to look at.

Do not be worried because your ear is becoming dull. In that way you escape being bored with many of the foolish things that are said. If the gates of sound keep out some of the music, they also keep out much of the discord. If the hair be getting thin, it takes less time to comb it, and then it is not all the time falling down over your eyes; or if it be getting white, I think that color is quite as respectable as any other: that is the color of the snow, and of the blossoms, and of the clouds, and of angelic habiliments.

Do not worry because the time comes on when you must go into the next world. It is only a better room, with finer pictures, brighter society and sweeter music. Robert McCheyne, and John Knox, and Harriet Newell, and Mrs. Hemans, and John Milton, and Martin Luther will be good enough company for the most of us. The cornshocks standing in the fields to-day will not sigh dismally when the huskers leap over the fence, and throwing their arms around the stack, swing it to the ground. It is only to take the golden ear from the husk. Death to the aged Christian is only husking-time, and then the load goes in from the frosts to the garner.

My congratulations to those who are nearly done with the nuisances of this world. Give your staff to your little grandson to ride horse on. You are going to be young again, and you will have no need of crutches. May the clouds around the setting sun be golden, and such as to lead the "weather-wise" to prophesy a clear morning!

Quizzle.—But, Governor Wiseman, does it not give you a little uneasiness in this day of so much talk about cremation as to what will become of your body after you leave this sphere?

At this point Doctor Heavyasbricks wiped his spectacles, as though he could not see well, and interrupted the conversation by saying, "Cremation! Cremation! What's that?" Sitting at the head of the table, I explained that it was the reduction of the deceased human body through fire into ashes to be preserved in an urn. "Ah! ah!" said Doctor Heavyasbricks, "I had the idea, from the sound of that word 'cremation,' it must be something connected with cream. I will take a little more of that delicious bovine liquid in my tea, if you please," said the doctor as he passed his cup toward the urn, adding, to the lady of the house, "I hope that urn you have your hand on has nothing to do with cremation." This explanation having been made, Governor Wiseman proceeded to answer the question of Quizzle:

No; I have no uneasiness about my body after I have left it. The idea you speak of will never be carried out. I know that the papers are ardently discussing whether or not it will be best to burn the bodies of the dead, instead of burying them. Scientific journals contend that our cemeteries are the means of unhealthy exhalations, and that cremation is the only safe way of disposing of the departed. Some have advocated the chemical reduction of the physical system.

I have, as yet, been unable to throw myself into a mood sufficiently scientific to appreciate this proposal. It seems to me partly horrible and partly ludicrous. I think that the dead populations of the world are really the most quiet and unharmful. They make no war upon us, and we need make no war upon them. I am very certain that all the damage we shall ever do this world, will be while we are animate. It is not the dead people that are hard to manage, but the living. Some whistle to keep their courage up while going along by graveyards; I whistle while moving among the wide awake. Before attempting this barbaric disposal of the human form as a sanitary improvement, it would be better to clear the streets and "commons" of our cities of their pestiferous surroundings. Try your cremation on the dogs and cats with extinct animation.

We think Greenwood is healthier than Broadway, and Laurel Hill than Chestnut street, Père la Chaise than Champs Elysées. Urns, with ashes scientifically prepared, may look very well in Madras or Pekin, but not in a Christian country. Not having been able to shake off the Bible notions about Christian burial, we adhere to the mode that was observed when devout men carried Stephen to his burial. Better not come around here with your chemical apparatus for the reduction of the human body. I give fair warning that if your philosopher attempts such a process on my bones, and I am of the same way of thinking as now, he will be sorry for it.

But I have no fear that I shall thus be desecrated by my surviving friends. I have more fear of epitaphs. I do not wonder that people have sometimes dictated the inscription on their own tombstones when I see what inappropriate lines are chiseled on many a slab. There needs to be a reformation in epitaphiology.

People often ask me for appropriate inscriptions for the graves of their dead. They tell the virtues of the father, or wife, or child, and want me to put in compressed shape all that catalogue of excellences.

Of course I fail in the attempt. The story of a lifetime cannot be chiseled by the stone-cutter on the side of a marble slab. But it is not a rare thing to go a few months after by the sacred spot and find that the bereft friends, unable to get from others an epitaph sufficiently eulogistic, have put their own brain and heart to work and composed a rhyme. Now, the most unfit sphere on earth for an inexperienced mind to exercise the poetic faculty is in epitaphiology. It does very well in copy-books, but it is most unfair to blot the resting-place of the dead with unskilled poetic scribble. It seems to me that the owners of cemeteries and graveyards should keep in their own hand the right to refuse inappropriate and ludicrous epitaph.

Nine-tenths of those who think they can write respectable poetry are mistaken. I do not say that poesy has passed from the earth, but it does seem as if the fountain Hippocrene had been drained off to run a saw-mill. It is safe to say that most of the home-made poetry of graveyards is an offence to God and man.

One would have thought that the New Hampshire village would have risen in mob to prevent the inscription that was really placed on one of its tombstones descriptive of a man who had lost his life at the foot of a vicious mare on the way to brook:

"As this man was leading her to drink
She kick'd and kill'd him quicker'n a wink."

One would have thought that even conservative New Jersey would have been in rebellion at a child's epitaph which in a village of that State reads thus:

"She was not smart, she was not fair,
  But hearts with grief for her are swellin';
All empty stands her little chair:
  She died of eatin' watermelon."

Let not such discretions be allowed in hallowed places. Let not poetizers practice on the tombstone. My uniform advice to all those who want acceptable and suggestive epitaph is, Take a passage of Scripture. That will never wear out. From generation to generation it will bring down upon all visitors a holy hush; and if before that stone has crumbled the day comes for waking up of all the graveyard sleepers, the very words chiseled on the marble may be the ones that shall ring from the trumpet of the archangel.

While the governor was buttering another muffin, and, according to the dietetic principle a little while ago announced, allowing it sufficiently to cool off, he continued the subject already opened by saying: I keep well by allowing hardly anything to trouble me, and by looking on the bright side of everything. One half of the people fret themselves to death.

Four months ago the air was full of evil prophecies. If a man believed one half he saw in the newspapers, he must have felt that this world was a failure, not paying more than ten cents on a dollar. To one good prophet like Isaiah or Ezekiel we had a thousand Balaams, each mounted on his appropriate nag.

First came the fearful announcement that in consequence of the financial depression we would have bread-riots innumerable and great slaughter. But where have been your riots? There was here and there a swinging of shillalahs, and a few broken heads which would probably have got broken anyhow; but the men who made the disturbance were found to be lounging vagabonds who never worked even when they had a chance.

Prophecy was also made that there would be a general starvation. We do not believe that in the United States there have been twenty sober people famished in the last year. Aware of the unusual stress upon the poor, the hand of charity has been more active and full than ever; and though many have been denied their accustomed luxuries, there has been bread for all.

Weather prophets also promised us a winter of unusual severity. They knew it from the amount of investment the squirrels had made in winter stock, and from the superabundance of wool on the sheep's back, and the lavishness of the dog's hair. Are the liars ready to confess their fault? The boys have found but little chance to use their skates, and I think the sheep-shearing of the flocks on celestial pasture-fields must have been omitted, judging from the small amount of snowy fleece that has fallen through the air. I have not had on my big mittens but once or twice, and my long-ago frost-bitten left ear has not demanded an extra pinching. To make up for the lack of fuel on the hearth, the great brass handiron of the sun has been kept unusually bright and hot. And yesterday we heard the horn of the south wind telling that the flowery bands of spring are on the way up from Florida.

The necessity for retrenchment has blessed the whole land. Many of us have learned how to make a thousand dollars do what fifteen hundred dollars—

Quizzle broke in at the first opportunity and said, "No doubt, governor, it is easy for you to be placid, for everything has gone well with you since you started life, whereas my mother died when I was little, and I was kicked and cuffed about by a step-mother whose name I cannot bear to hear."

Ha! ha! said Governor Wiseman. It is the old story of step-mothers. I don't believe they are any worse than other people, taking the average. I have often wondered why it is that the novels and romances always make the step-mother turn out so very badly. She always dresses too much and bangs the children. The authors, if writing out of their own experience, must have had a very hard time.

In society it has become a proverb: "Cruel as a step-mother." I am disposed, however, to think that, while there may be marked exceptions, step-mothers are the most self-sacrificing beings in all the world. They come into the family scrutinized by the household and the relatives of the one who used to occupy the motherly position. Neighborly busybodies meet the children on the street and sigh over them and ask them how their new mother treats them. The wardrobe of the youngsters comes under the severe inspection of outsiders.

The child, having been taught that the lady of the household is "nothing but a step-mother," screams at the least chastisement, knowing that the neighbors' window is up and this will be a good way of making publication. That is called cruelty which is only a most reasonable, moderate and Christian spanking. What a job she has in navigating a whole nursery of somebody else's children through mumps, measles, whooping-cough and chicken-pox! One of the things that I rejoice over in life is that it is impossible that I ever become a step-mother. In many cases she has the largest possible toil for the least reward.

Blessed be the Lord who setteth the solitary in families that there are glorious exceptions! The new mother comes to the new home, and the children gather the first day around her as the natural protector. They never know the difference between the first and second mother. They seem like two verses of the same hymn, two days of the summer, two strokes of the same bell, two blessings from the same God.

She is watchful all night long over the sick little one, bathing the brow and banishing the scare of the feverish dream. After a while those children will rise up to do her honor; and when her work is done, she will go up to get the large reward that awaits a faithful, great-hearted Christian step-mother in the land where the neighbors all mind their own business.

CHAPTER LV.

A LAYER OF WAFFLES.

Several months had passed along since we had enjoyed the society of Governor Wiseman, Doctor Heavyasbricks and Fred Quizzle. At our especial call they had come again.

The evening air was redolent with waffles baked in irons that had given them the square imprint which has come down through the ages as the only orthodox pattern.

No sooner had our friends seated themselves at the tea-table than—

Quizzle began: I see, Governor Wiseman, that the races have just come off in England. What do you think of horse-racing?

Wiseman.—That has become a very important question for every moralist to answer. I see that last week England took carriage and horses and went out to Epsom Downs to see the Derby races. The race was won by Sir George Frederick; that is the name of the successful horse. All the particulars come by telegraph. There is much now being done for the turf in this country as well as in England, and these horses are improved year by year. I wonder if the race of men who frequent these entertainments are as much improved as the horses? I like horses very much, but I like men better. So far as we can judge, the horses are getting the best part of these exercises, for they never bet, and always come home sober. If the horses continue to come up as much as they have, and our sporting friends continue to go down in the same ratio, by an inevitable law of progression we shall after a while have two men going round the course neck and neck, while Dexter and

Sir George Frederick are on the judges' stand deciding which man is the winner.

Quizzle.—But do you not, Governor Wiseman, believe in out-door sports and recreations?

Yes, said the governor, but it ought to be something that helps a man as well as the brute. I prefer those recreations that are good both for a man's body and soul. We want our entire nature developed.

Two thousand people the other day waited at the depot in Albany for the arrival of the remains of the great pugilist, Heenan. Then they covered the coffin with immortelles. No wonder they felt badly. The poor fellow's work was done. He had broken the last nose. He had knocked out the last tooth. He had bunged up the last eye. He had at last himself thrown up the sponge. The dead hero belonged to the aristocracy of hard-hitters. If I remember rightly, he drew the first blood in the conflict with one who afterward became one of the rulers of the nation—the Honorable John Morrissey, member of Congress of the United States and chief gambler at Saratoga.

There is just now an attempt at the glorification of muscle. The man who can row the swiftest, or strike a ball the farthest, or drop the strongest wrestler is coming to be of more importance. Strong muscle is a grand thing to have, but everything depends on how you use it. If Heenan had become a Christian, he would have made a capital professor in Polemic Theology. If the Harvard or Yale students shall come in from the boat-race and apply his athletic strength to rowing the world out of the breakers, we say "All hail!" to him. The more physical force a man has, the better; but if Samson finds nothing more useful to do than carrying of gate-posts, his strong muscle is only a nuisance.

By all means let us culture physical energy. Let there be more gymnasiums in our colleges and theological seminaries. Let the student know how to wield oar and bat, and in good boyish wrestle see who is the strongest. The health of mental and spiritual work often depends on physical health. If I were not opposed to betting, I would lay a wager that I can tell from the book column in any of the newspapers or magazines of the land the condition of each critic's liver and spleen at the time of his writing.

A very prominent literary man apologized to me the other day for his merciless attack on one of my books, saying that he felt miserable that morning and must pitch into something; and my book being the first one on the table, he pitched into that. Our health decides our style of work. If this world is to be taken for God, we want more sanctified muscle. The man who comes to his Christian work having had sound sleep the night before, and the result of roast beef rare in his organism, can do almost anything. Luther was not obliged to nurse his appetite with any plantation bitters, but was ready for the coarsest diet, even the "Diet of Worms."

But while I advocate all sports, and exercises, and modes of life that improve the physical organism, I have no respect for bone, and nerve, and muscle in the abstract. Health is a fine harp, but I want to know what tune you are going to play on it. I have not one daisy to put on the grave of a dead pugilist or mere boat-racer, but all the garlands I can twist for the tomb of the man who serves God, though he be as physically weak as Richard Baxter, whose ailments were almost as many as his books, and they numbered forty.

At this last sentence the company at the table, forgetful of the presence of Doctor Heavyasbricks, showed some disposition at good humor, when the doctor's brows lifted in surprise, and he observed that he thought a man with forty ailments was a painful spectacle, and ought to be calculated to depress a tea-table rather than exhilarate it.

"But, Governor Wiseman," said Quizzle, "do you not think that it is possible to combine physical, mental and spiritual recreations?"

Oh yes, replied the governor; I like this new mode of mingling religion with summer pleasures. Soon the Methodists will be shaking out their tents and packing their lunch-baskets and buying their railroad and steamboat tickets for the camp-meeting grounds. Martha's Vineyard, Round Lake, Ocean Grove and Sea Cliff will soon mingle psalms and prayers with the voice of surf and forest. Rev. Doctor J. H. Vincent, the silver trumpet of Sabbath-schoolism, is marshaling a meeting for the banks of Chautauqua Lake which will probably be the grandest religious picnic ever held since the five thousand sat down on the grass and had a surplus of provision to take home to those who were too stupid to go. From the arrangement being made for that meeting in August, I judge there will be so much consecrated enthusiasm that there may be danger that some morning, as the sun strikes gloriously through the ascending mist of Chautauqua Lake, our friends may all go up in a chariot of fire, leaving our Sunday-schools in a bereft condition. If they do go up in that way, may their mantle or their straw hat fall this way!

Why not have all our churches and denominations take a summer airing? The breath of the pine woods or a wrestle with the waters would put an end to everything like morbid religion.

One reason why the apostles had such healthy theology is that they went a-fishing. We would like to see the day when we will have Presbyterian camp-meetings, and Episcopalian camp-meetings, and Baptist camp-meetings, and Congregational camp-meetings, or, what would be still better, when, forgetful of all minor distinctions, we could have a church universal camp-meeting. I would like to help plant the tent-pole for such a convocation.

Quizzle.—Do you not think, governor, that there are inexpensive modes of recreation which are quite as good as those that absorb large means?

Yes, said the governor; we need to cut the coat according to our cloth. When I see that the Prince of Wales is three hundred thousand dollars in debt, notwithstanding his enormous income, I am forcibly reminded that it is not the amount of money a man gets that makes him well off, but the margin between the income and the outgo. The young man who while he makes a dollar spends a dollar and one cent is on the sure road either to bankruptcy or the penitentiary.

Next to the evil of living beyond one's means is that of spending all one's income. There are multitudes who are sailing so near shore that a slight wind in the wrong direction founders them. They get on well while the times are usual and the wages promptly paid; but a panic or a short period of sickness, and they drop helpless. Many a father has gone with his family in a fine carriage drawn by a spanking team till he came up to his grave; then he lay down, and his children have got out of the carriage, and not only been compelled to walk, but to go barefoot. Against parsimony and niggardliness I proclaim war; but with the same sentence I condemn those who make a grand splash while they live, leaving their families in destitution when they die

Quizzle.—Where, governor, do you expect to recreate this coming summer?

Wiseman.—Have not yet made up my mind. The question is coming up in all our households as to the best mode of vacation. We shall all need rest. The first thing to do is to measure the length of your purse; you cannot make a short purse reach around Saratoga and the White Mountains. There may be as much health, good cheer and recuperation in a country farmhouse where the cows come up every night and yield milk without any chalk in it.

What the people of our cities need is quiet. What the people of the country need is sightseeing. Let the mountains come to New York and New York go to the mountains. The nearest I ever get to heaven in this world is lying flat down on my back under a tree, looking up through the branches, five miles off from a post-office or a telegraph station. But this would be torture to others.

Independent of what others do or say, let us in the selection of summer recreations study our own temperament and finances. It does not pay to spend so much money in July and August that you have to go pinched and half mad the rest of the year. The healthiest recreations do not cost much. In boyhood, with a string and a crooked pin attached to it, I fished up more fun from the mill-pond than last summer with a five-dollar apparatus I caught among the Franconia Mountains.

There is a great area of enjoyment within the circumference of one dollar if you only know how to make the circuit. More depends upon ourselves than upon the affluence of our surroundings. If you are compelled to stay home all summer, you may be as happy as though you went away. The enjoyment of the first of July, when I go off, is surpassed by nothing but the first of September, when I come home.

There being a slight pause in the conversation, Doctor Heavyasbricks woke gradually up and began to move his lips and to show strong symptoms of intention to ask for himself a question. He said: I have been attending the anniversaries in New York, and find that they are about dead. Wiseman, can you tell me what killed them?

Governor Wiseman replied: It is a great pity that the anniversaries are dead. They once lived a robust life, but began some fifteen years ago to languish, and have finally expired. To the appropriate question, What killed them? I answer, Peregrination was one of the causes. There never has been any such place for the anniversaries as the Broadway Tabernacle. It was large and social and central. When that place was torn down, the anniversaries began their travels. Going some morning out of the warm sunshine into some cathedral-looking place, they got the chills, and under the dark stained glass everything looked blue. In the afternoon they would enter some great square hall where everything was formal.

It is almost impossible to have a genial and successful meeting in a square hall. When in former days the country pastor said to his congregation, "Meet me at the New York anniversaries," they all knew where to go; but after the old Broadway Tabernacle went down, the aforesaid congregation might have looked in five or six places and not found their minister. The New York anniversaries died on the street between the old Tabernacle and St. Paul's Methodist Cathedral.

Prolix reports also helped to kill the patient. Nothing which was not in its nature immortal could have survived these. The secretary would read till he got out of wind, and would then say that the remainder of the report would be found in the printed copies in the pews. The speakers following had the burden of galvanizing an exhausted meeting, and the Christian man who attended the anniversary on retiring that evening had the nightmare in the shape of a portly secretary sitting astride his chest reading from a huge scroll of documents.

Diluted Christian oratory also helped to kill the anniversaries. The men whom we heard in our boyhood on the Broadway platform believed in a whole Bible, and felt that if the gospel did not save the world nothing ever would; consequently, they spoke in blood-red earnestness and made the place quake with their enthusiasm. There came afterward a weak-kneed stock of ministers who thought that part of the Bible was true, if they were not very much mistaken, and that, on the whole, religion was a good thing for most people, certainly if they had weak constitutions, and that man could be easily saved if we could get the phrenologist to fix up his head, and the gymnasium to develop his muscle, and the minister to coax him out of his indiscretions. Well, the anniversaries could not live on pap and confectionery, and so they died for lack of strong meat.

But the day of resurrection will come. Mark that! The tide of Bible evangelism will come up again. We may be dead, but our children will see it. New York will be thronged with men and women who will come up once a year to count the sheaves of harvest, and in some great building thronged from the platform to the vestibule an aroused Christian audience will applaud the news, just received by telegraph, of a nation born in a day, and sing with more power than when Thomas Hastings used to act as precentor:

"The year of jubilee has come;
Return, ye ransom'd sinners, home."

Quizzle.—You speak, governor, of the ruinous effect of prolixity in religious service. How long ought a public service continue?

Wiseman.—There is much discussion in the papers as to how long or short sermons and prayers ought to be. Some say a discourse ought to last thirty minutes, and others forty, and others an hour, and prayers should be three minutes long, or five, or fifteen. You might as well discuss how long a frock-coat ought to be, or how many ounces of food a man ought to eat. In the one case, everything depends upon the man's size; in the other, everything on the capacity of his stomach. A sermon or a prayer ought to go on as long as it is of any profit. If it is doing no good, the sermon is half an hour too long, though it take only thirty minutes. If the audience cough, or fidget, or shuffle their feet, you had better stop praying. There is no excuse for a man's talking or praying too long if he have good eyesight and hearing.

But suppose a man have his sermon written and before him. You say he must go through with it? Oh no. Let him skip a few leaves. Better sacrifice three or four sheets of sermon-paper than sacrifice the interest of your hearers. But it is a silly thing for a man in a prayer-meeting or pulpit to stop merely because a certain number of minutes have expired while the interest is deepening—absurd as a hunter on the track of a roebuck, and within two minutes of bringing down its antlers, stopping because his wife said that at six o'clock precisely he must be home to supper. Keep on hunting till your ammunition gives out.

Still, we must all admit that the danger is on the side of prolixity. The most interesting prayers we ever hear are by new converts, who say everything they have to say and break down in one minute. There are men who, from the way they begin their supplications, indicate a long siege. They first pray you into a good frame, and then pray you out. They take literally what Paul meant to be figurative: "Pray without ceasing."

Quizzle.—I see there was no lack of interest when the brewers' convention met the other day in Boston, and that in their longest session the attention did not flag.

Wiseman.—Yes; I see that speeches were made on the beneficial use of fermented liquors. The announcement was made that during the year 8,910,823 barrels of the precious stuff had been manufactured. I suppose that while the convention was there Boston must have smelt like one great ale-pitcher. The delegates were invited to visit the suburbs of the city. Strange that nobody thought of inviting them to visit the cemeteries and graveyards, especially the potter's field, where thousands of their victims are buried. Perhaps you are in sympathy with these brewers, and say that if people would take beer instead of alcohol drunkenness would cease. But for the vast majority who drink, beer is only introductory to something stronger. It is only one carriage in the same funeral. Do not spell it b-e-e-r, but spell it b-i-e-r. May the lightnings of heaven strike and consume all the breweries from river Penobscot to the Golden Horn!

Quizzle.—I see, governor, that you were last week in Washington. How do things look there?

Wiseman.—Very well. The general appearance of our national capital never changes. It is always just as far from the Senate-chamber to the White House; indeed, so far that many of our great men have never been able to travel it. There are the usual number of petitioners for governmental patronage hanging around the hotels and the congressional lobbies. They are willing to take almost anything they can get, from minister to Spain to village postmaster. They come in with the same kind of carpet-bags, look stupid and anxious for several days, and having borrowed money enough from the member from their district to pay their fare, take the cars for home, denouncing the administration and the ungratefulness of republics.

I think that the two houses of Congress are the best and most capable of any almost ever assembled. Of course there is a dearth of great men. Only here and there a Senator or Representative you ever before heard of. Indeed, the nuisances of our national council in other days were the great men who took, in making great speeches, the time that ought to have been spent in attending to business. We all know that it was eight or ten "honorable" bloats of the last thirty years who made our chief international troubles.

Our Congress is made up mostly of practical every-day men. They have no speeches to make, and no past political reputation to nurse, and no national fame to achieve. I like the new crop of statesmen better than the old, although it is a shorter crop. They do not drink so much rum, and not so large a proportion of them will die of delirium tremens. They may not have such resounding names as some of their predecessors, but I prefer a Congress of ordinary men to a group of Senators and Representatives overawed and led about by five or six overgrown, political Brobdingnagians.

While in Washington we had a startling occurrence. A young man in high society shot another young man, who fell dead instantly.

I wonder that there is not more havoc with human life in this day, when it is getting so popular to carry firearms. Most of our young men, and many of our boys, do not feel themselves in tune unless they have a pistol accompaniment. Men are locked up or fined if found with daggers or slung-shot upon their persons, but revolvers go free. There is not half so much danger from knife as pistol. The former may let the victim escape minus a good large slice, but the latter is apt to drop him dead. On the frontiers, or engaged in police duty, firearms may be necessary; but in the ordinary walk of life pistols are, to say the least, a superfluity. Better empty your pockets of these dangerous weapons, and see that your sons do not carry them. In all the ordinary walks of life an honest countenance and orderly behavior are sufficient defence. You had better stop going into society where you must always be ready to shoot somebody.

But do not think, my dear Fred, that I am opposed to everything because I have this evening spoken against so many different things. I cannot take the part of those who pride themselves in hurling a stout No against everything.

A friend called my attention to the fact that Sanballat wanted to hold consultation with Nehemiah in the plain of O-no. That is the place where more people stay, to-day, than in any other. They are always protesting, throwing doubt on grand undertakings; and while you are in the mountain of O-yes, they spend their time on the plain of O-no. In the harness of society they are breeching-straps, good for nothing but to hold back.

You propose to call a minister. All the indications are that he is the right man. Nine-tenths of the congregation are united in his favor. The matter is put to vote. The vast majority say "Ay!" the handful of opponents responded "O no!"

You propose to build a new church. About the site, the choice of architect, the upholstery, the plumbing and the day of dedication there is almost a unanimity. You hope that the crooked sticks will all lie still, and that the congregation will move in solid phalanx. But not so. Sanballat sends for Nehemiah, proposing to meet him in the plain of O-no.

Some men were born backward, and have been going that way ever since. Opposition to everything has become chronic. The only way they feel comfortable is when harnessed with the face toward the whiffletree and their back to the end of the shafts. They may set down their name in the hotel register as living in Boston, Chicago, Savannah or Brooklyn, but they really have been spending all their lives on the plain of O-no. There let them be buried with their face toward the west, for in that way they will lie more comfortably, as other people are buried with their face to the east. Do not impose upon them by putting them in the majority. O-no!

We rejoice that there seems more liberality among good men, and that they have made up their minds to let each one work in his own way. The scalping-knives are being dulled.

The cheerfulness and good humor which have this year characterized our church courts is remarkable and in strong contrast with the old-time ecclesiastical fights which shook synods and conferences. Religious controversies always have been the most bitter of all controversies; and when ministers do fight, they fight like vengeance. Once a church court visiting a place would not only spend much of their own time in sharp contention, but would leave the religious community to continue the quarrel after adjournment. Now they have a time of good cheer while in convention, and leave only one dispute behind them among the families, and that arising from the fact that each one claims it had the best ministers and elders at their house. Contention is a child of the darkness, peace the daughter of the light. The only help for a cow's hollow horn is a gimlet-hole bored through it, and the best way to cure religious combatants is to let more gospel light through their antlers.

As we sat at the head of the table interested in all that was going on, and saw Governor Wiseman with his honorable name, and Quizzle and Heavyasbricks with their unattractive titles, we thought of the affliction of an awkward or ill-omened name.

When there are so many pleasant names by which children may be called, what right has a parent to place on his child's head a disadvantage at the start? Worse than the gauntlet of measles and whooping-cough and mumps which the little ones have to run is this parental outrage.

What a struggle in life that child will have who has been baptized Jedekiah or Mehitabel! If a child is "called after" some one living, let that one be past mid-life and of such temperament that there shall be no danger of his becoming an absconder and a cheat. As far as possible let the name given be short, so that in the course of a lifetime there be not too many weeks or months taken up in the mere act of signature. The burdens of life are heavy enough without putting upon any one the extra weight of too much nomenclature. It is a sad thing when an infant has two bachelor uncles, both rich and with outrageous names, for the baby will have to take both titles, and that is enough to make a case of infant mortality.

Quizzle.—You seem to me, governor, to be more sprightly at every interview.

Well, that is so, but I do not know how long it will last; stout people like myself often go the quickest.

There is a constant sympathy expressed by robust people for those of slight physical constitution. I think the sympathy ought to turn in the opposite direction. It is the delicate people who escape the most fearful disorders, and in three cases out of four live the longest. These gigantic structures are almost always reckless of health. They say, "Nothing hurts me," and so they stand in draughts, and go out into the night air to cool off, and eat crabs at midnight, and doff their flannels in April, and carelessly get their feet wet.

But the delicate people are shy of peril. They know that disease has been fishing for them for twenty years, and they keep away from the hook. No trout can be caught if he sees the shadow of the sportsman on the brook. These people whom everybody expects to die, live on most tenaciously.

I know of a young lady who evidently married a very wealthy man of eighty-five years on the ground he was very delicate, and with reference to her one-third. But the aged invalid is so careful of his health, and the young wife so reckless of hers, that it is now uncertain whether she will inherit his store-houses or he inherit her wedding-rings.

Health and longevity depend more upon caution and intelligent management of one's self than upon original physical outfit. Paul's advice to the sheriff is appropriate to people in all occupations: "Do thyself no harm!"

Besides that, said the governor, I have moved and settled in very comfortable quarters since I was at this table before. The house I have moved in is not a better house, but somehow I feel more contented.

Most of our households are quieted after the great annual upsetting. The last carpet is tacked down. The strings that were scattered along the floor have been rolled up in a ball. We begin to know the turns in the stairway. Things are settling down, and we shall soon feel at home in our new residence. If it is a better house than we had, do not let us be too proud of the doorplate, nor worship too ardently the fine cornice, nor have any idea that superb surroundings are going to make us any happier than we were in the old house.

Set not your affections on luxurious upholstery and spacious drawing-room. Be grateful and be humble.

If the house is not as large nor in as good neighborhood as the one you formerly occupied, make the best of it. It is astonishing what a good time you may have in a small room. Your present neighbors are just as kind as those you left, if you only knew them. Do not go around your house sticking up your nose at the small pantry, and the ugly mantel-pieces, and the low ceiling. It is a better place than your divine Master occupied, and to say the least you are no better than He. If you are a Christian, you are on your way to a King's mansion, and you are now only stopping a little in the porter's lodge at the gate. Go down in the dark lanes of the city and see how much poorer off many of your fellow-citizens are. If the heart be right, the home will be right.

CHAPTER LVI.

FRIDAY EVENING.

Our friend Churchill was a great man for religious meetings. As he shoved back from our tea-table he said, "I must be off to church."

Then he yawned as though he expected to have a dull time, and asked me why it was that religious meetings were often so very insipid and that many people went to them merely as a matter of duty. Without waiting for me to give my opinion, he said he thought that there was a sombre hue given to such meetings that was killing and in a sort of soliloquy continued:

There is one thing Satan does well. He is good at stating the discouraging side. He knows how to fish for obstacles, and every time brings up his net full. Do not let us help him in his work. If you have anything to say in prayer-meeting that is disheartening, may you forget your speech! Tell us something on the bright side.

I know a Christian man who did something outrageously wrong. Some one said to me: "Why do you not expose him?" I replied: "That is the devil's work and it will be thoroughly done. If there is anything good about him, we would rather speak of that."

Give us no sermons or newspaper articles that are depressing. We know all that before you start; amid the greatest disheartenments there are hopeful things that may be said. While the Mediterranean corn-ship was going to smash, Paul told the crew to "Be of good cheer." We like apple trees because, though they are not handsome, they have bright blossoms and good fruit, but we despise weeping willows because they never do anything but cry.

On a dark day do not go around closing the window-shutters. The world is dark enough without your making it more so. Is there anybody in the room who has a match? Please then strike it. There is only one kind of champagne that we temperance folks can take, and that is encouraging remark. It is a stimulus, and what makes it better than all other kinds of champagne is it leaves no headache.

I said to him, I think religious meetings have been improved in the last few years. One of the grandest results of the Fulton street prayer-meeting is the fact that all the devotional services of the country have been revolutionized. The tap of the bell of that historical prayer-meeting has shortened the prayers and exhortations of the church universal.

But since it has become the custom to throw open the meetings for remark and exhortation, there has been a jubilee among the religious bores who wander around pestering the churches. We have two or three outsiders who come about once in six weeks into our prayer-meeting; and if they can get a chance to speak, they damage all the interest. They talk long and loud in proportion as they have nothing to say. They empty on us several bushels of "ohs" and "ahs." But they seldom get a chance, for we never throw the meeting open when we see they are there. We make such a close hedge of hymns and prayers that they cannot break into the garden.

One of them we are free of because, one night, seeing him wiggle-waggle in his seat as if about to rise, we sent an elder to him to say that his remarks were not acceptable. The elder blushed and halted a little when we gave him the mission, but setting his teeth together he started for the offensive brother, leaned over the back of the pew and discharged the duty. We have never seen that brother since, but once in the street, and then he was looking the other way.

By what right such men go about in ecclesiastical vagabondism to spoil the peace of devotional meetings it is impossible to tell. Either that nuisance must be abated or we must cease to "throw open" our prayer-meetings for exhortation.

A few words about the uses of a week-night service. Many Christians do not appreciate it; indeed, it is a great waste of time, unless there be some positive advantage gained.

The French nation at one time tried having a Sabbath only once in ten days. The intelligent Christian finds he needs a Sabbath every three or four days, and so builds a brief one on the shore of a week-day in the shape of an extra religious service. He gets grace on Sabbath to bridge the chasm of worldliness between that and the next Sabbath, but finds the arch of the bridge very great, and so runs up a pier midway to help sustain the pressure.

There are one hundred and sixty-eight hours in a week, and but two hours of public religious service on Sabbath. What chance have two hours in a battle with one hundred and sixty-eight?

A week-night meeting allows church membership utterance. A minister cannot know how to preach unless in a conference meeting he finds the religious state of the people. He must feel the pulse before giving the medicine, otherwise he will not know whether it ought to be an anodyne or a stimulant. Every Christian ought to have something to say. Every man is a walking eternity. The plainest man has Omnipotence to defend him, Omniscience to watch him, infinite Goodness to provide for him. The tamest religious experience has in it poems, tragedies, histories, Iliads, Paradise Lost and Paradise Regained. Ought not such a one have something to say?

If you were ever in the army you know what it is to see an officer on horseback dash swiftly past carrying a dispatch. You wondered as he went what the news was. Was the army to advance, or was an enemy coming?

So every Christian carries a dispatch from God to the world. Let him ride swiftly to deliver it. The army is to advance and the enemy is coming. Go out and fulfill your mission. You may have had a letter committed to your care, and after some days you find it in one of your pockets, you forgot to deliver it. Great was your chagrin when you found that it pertained to some sickness or trouble. God gives every man a letter of warning or invitation to carry, and what will be your chagrin in the judgment to find that you have forgotten it!

A week-night meeting widens the pulpit till all the people can stand on it. Such a service tests one's piety. No credit for going to church on Sabbath. Places of amusement are all closed, and there is no money to be made. But week-nights every kind of temptation and opportunity spreads before a man, and if he goes to the praying circle he must give up these things. The man who goes to the weekly service regularly through moonlight and pitch darkness, through good walking and slush ankle-deep, will in the book of judgment find it set down to his credit. He will have a better seat in heaven than the man who went only when the walking was good, and the weather comfortable, and the services attractive, and his health perfect. That service which costs nothing God accounts as nothing.

A week-night service thrusts religion in the secularities of the week. It is as much as to say, "This is God's Wednesday, or God's Thursday, or God's Friday, or God's week." You would not give much for a property the possession of which you could have only one-seventh of the time, and God does not want that man whose services he can have only on Sabbath. If you paid full wages to a man and found out that six-sevenths of the time he was serving a rival house, you would be indignant; and the man who takes God's goodness and gives six-sevenths of his time to the world, the flesh and the devil is an abomination to the Lord. The whole week ought to be a temple of seven rooms dedicated to God. You may, if you will, make one room the holy of holies, but let all the temple be consecrate.

The week-night service gives additional opportunity of religious culture, and we find it so difficult to do right and be right that we cannot afford to miss any opportunity. Such a service is a lunch between the Sabbath meals, and if we do not take it we get weak and faint. A truth coming to us then ought to be especially effective.

If you are on a railroad train, and stop at the depot, and a boy comes in with a telegram, all the passengers lean forward and wonder if it is for them. It may be news from home. It must be urgent or it would not be brought there. Now, if while we are rushing on in the whirl of everyday excitement, a message of God meets us, it must be an urgent and important message. If God speaks to us in a meeting mid-week, it is because there is something that needs to be said before next Sunday.

Sabbath Evening Tea-Table.

CHAPTER LVII.

THE SABBATH EVENING TEA-TABLE.

When this evening comes we do not have any less on our table because it is a sacred day, but a little more. On other evenings we have in our dining-hall three of the gas-burners lighted, but on Sabbath evening we have four. We try to have the conversation cheerfully religious.

After the children are sleepy we do not keep them up to recite the "Larger Catechism." During summer vacation, when we have no evening service to attend at church, we sometimes have a few chapters of a Christian book read or a column of a Christian newspaper, or if any one has an essay on any religious theme, we hear that.

We tarry long after the tea has got cold. We do not care if the things are not cleared off till next morning. If any one has a perplexing passage of Scripture to explain, we gather all the lights possible on that subject. We send up stairs for concordance and Bible dictionary. It may be ten o'clock at night before the group is dispersed from the Sabbath evening tea-table.

Some of the chapters following may be considered as conversations condensed or as paragraphs read. You will sometimes ascribe them to the host, at other times to the hostess, at other times to the strangers within the gates.

Old Dominie Scattergood often came in on Sabbath evenings. He was too old to preach, and so had much leisure. Now, an old minister is a great joy to us, especially if life has put sugar rather than vinegar in his disposition. Dominie Scattergood had in his face and temper the smiles of all the weddings he had ever solemnized, and in his handshaking all the hearty congratulations that had ever been offered him.

His hair was as white as any snow-bank through which he had waded to meet his appointments. He sympathized with every one, could swing from mood to mood very easily, and found the bridge between laughter and tears a short one and soon crossed. He was like an orchard in October after some of the frosts, the fruit so ripe and mellow that the least breeze would fill the laps of the children. He ate scarcely anything at the tea-table, for you do not want to put much fuel in an engine when it has nearly reached the depot. Old Dominie Scattergood gave his entire time to religious discourse when he sat with us at the close of the Lord's day.

How calm and bright and restful the light that falls on the Sabbath evening tea-table! Blessed be its memories for ever and ever! and Jessie, and De Witt, and May, and Edith, and Frank, and the baby, and all the visitors, old and young, thick-haired and bald-headed, say Amen!

CHAPTER LVIII.

THE WARM HEART OF CHRIST.

The first night that old Dominie Scattergood sat at our tea-table, we asked him whether he could make his religion work in the insignificant affairs of life, or whether he was accustomed to apply his religion on a larger scale. The Dominie turned upon us like a day-dawn, and addressed us as follows:

There is no warmer Bible phrase than this: "Touched with the feeling of our infirmities." The Divine nature is so vast, and the human so small, that we are apt to think that they do not touch each other at any point. We might have ever so many mishaps, the government at Washington would not hear of them, and there are multitudes in Britain whose troubles Victoria never knows; but there is a throne against which strike our most insignificant perplexities. What touches us, touches Christ. What annoys us, annoys Christ. What robs us, robs Christ. He is the great nerve-centre to which thrill all sensations which touch us who are his members.

He is touched with our physical infirmities. I do not mean that he merely sympathizes with a patient in collapse of cholera, or in the delirium of a yellow fever, or in the anguish of a broken back, or in all those annoyances that come from a disordered nervous condition. In our excited American life sound nerves are a rarity. Human sympathy in the case I mention amounts to nothing. Your friends laugh at you and say you have "the blues," or "the high strikes," or "the dumps," or "the fidgets." But Christ never laughs at the whims, the notions, the conceits, the weaknesses, of the nervously disordered. Christ probably suffered in something like this way, for He had lack of sleep, lack of rest, lack of right food, lack of shelter, and His temperament was finely strung.

Chronic complaints, the rheumatism, the neuralgia, the dyspepsia, after a while cease to excite human sympathy, but with Christ they never become an old story. He is as sympathetic as when you felt the first twinge of inflamed muscle or the first pang of indigestion. When you cannot sleep, Christ keeps awake with you. All the pains you ever had in your head are not equal to the pains Christ had in His head. All the acute suffering you ever had in your feet is not equal to the acute suffering Christ had in His feet. By His own hand He fashioned your every bone, strung every nerve, grew every eyelash, set every tooth in its socket, and your every physical disorder is patent to Him, and touches His sympathies.

He is also touched with the infirmities of our prayers. Nothing bothers the Christian more than the imperfections of his prayers. His getting down on his knees seems to be the signal for his thoughts to fly every whither. While praying about one thing he is thinking about another. Could you ever keep your mind ten minutes on one supplication? I never could. While you are praying, your store comes in, your kitchen comes in, your losses and gains come in. The minister spreads his hands for prayer, and you put your head on the back of the pew in front, and travel round the world in five minutes.

A brother rises in prayer-meeting to lead in supplication. After he has begun, the door slams, and you peep through your fingers to see who is coming in. You say to yourself, "What a finely expressed prayer, or what a blundering specimen! But how long he keeps on! Wish he would stop! He prays for the world's conversion. I wonder how much he gives toward it? There! I don't think I turned the gas down in the parlor! Wonder if Bridget has got home yet? Wonder if they have thought to take that cake out of the oven? Oh what a fool I was to put my name on the back of that note! Ought to have sold those goods for cash and not on credit!'' And so you go on tumbling over one thing after another until the gentleman closes his prayer with Amen! and you lift up your head, saying, "There! I haven't prayed one bit. I am not a Christian!" Yes, you are, if you have resisted the tendency. Christ knows how much you have resisted, and how thoroughly we are disordered of sin, and He will pick out the one earnest petition from the rubbish and answer it. To the very depth of His nature He sympathizes with the infirmity of our prayers.

He is touched with the infirmity of our temper.

There are some who, notwithstanding all that is said or done to them can smile back. But many of you are so constructed that if a man insults you, you either knock him down or wish you could. While with all resolution and prayer you resist this, remember that Christ knows how much you have been lied about, and misrepresented, and trod on. He knows that though you said something that was hot, you kept back something that was ten times hotter. He takes into account your explosive temperament. He knows that it requires more skill to drive a fiery span than a tame roadster. He knows how hard you have put down the "brakes" and is touched with the feeling of your infirmity.

Christ also sympathizes with our poor efforts at doing good.

Our work does not seem to amount to much. We teach a class, or distribute a bundle of tracts, or preach a sermon, and we say, "Oh, if I had done it some other way!" Christ will make no record of our bungling way, if we did the best we could. He will make record of our intention and the earnestness of our attempt. We cannot get the attention of our class, or we break down in our exhortation, or our sermon falls dead, and we go home disgusted, and sorry we tried to speak, and feel Christ is afar off. Why, He is nearer than if we had succeeded, for He knows that we need sympathy, and is touched with our infirmity.

It is comforting to know that it is not the learned and the great and the eloquent that Christ seems to stand closest by. The "Swamp-angel" was a big gun, and made a stunning noise, but it burst before it accomplished anything, while many an humble rifle helped decide the contest. Christ made salve out of spittle to cure a blind man, and the humblest instrumentality may, under God, cure the blindness of the soul. Blessed be God for the comfort of His gospel!

CHAPTER LIX.

SACRIFICING EVERYTHING.

Ourselves.—Dominie Scattergood, why did Christ tell the man inquiring about his soul to sell all he had and give everything to the poor? Is it necessary for one to impoverish himself in order to be a Christian?

The Dominie.—You mistake the purport of Christ's remark. He was not here teaching the importance of benevolence, but the duty of self-conquest. That young man had an all absorbing love of wealth. Money was his god, and Christ is not willing to occupy the throne conjointly with any other deity. This was a case for what the doctors call heroic treatment. If a physician meet a case of unimportant sickness, he prescribes a mild curative, but sometimes he comes to a room where the case is almost desperate; ordinary medicine would not touch it. It is "kill or cure," and he treats accordingly. This young man that Christ was medicating was such a case. There did not seem much prospect, and He gives him this powerful dose, "Sell all that thou hast and give to the poor!"

It does not follow that we must all do the same, any more than because belladonna or arsenic is administered in one case of illness we should therefore all go to taking belladonna or arsenic. Because one man in the hospital must have his arm amputated all the patients need not expect amputation. The silliest thing that business-men could do would be to give all their property away and turn their families into the street. The most Christian thing for you to do is to invest your money in the best way possible, and out of your business, industriously carried on, to contribute the largest possible percentage to the kingdom of God.

Still, we must admire the manner in which the Great Physician took the diagnosis of this man's case and grappled it. We all need heroic spiritual treatment. We do not get well of sin because we do not realize what a dire disease it is, and that we cannot cure it with a spiritual panacea, a gentle antidote, a few grains of spiritual morphine, a mild moral corrective or a few drops of peppermint on white sugar.

We want our pride killed, and we read an essay on that sweet grace of humility, and we go on as proud as ever. The pleasant lozenge does not do the work. Rather let us set ourselves to do that for Christ which is most oppugnant to our natural feelings. You do not take part in prayer-meeting because you cannot pray like Edward Payson, or exhort like John Summerfield. If you want to crush your pride, get up anyhow, though your knees knock together, and your tongue catches fast, and you see some godless hearer in prayer-meeting laughing as though she would burst.

Deal with your avarice in the same heroic style. Having heard the charitable cause presented, at the first right impulse thrust your hand in your pocket where the money is, and pull it out though it half kills you. Pull till it comes. Put it on the plate with an emphasis, and turn your face away before you are tempted to take it back again. All your sweet contemplation about benevolence will not touch your case. Heroic treatment or nothing!

In the same way destroy the vindictiveness of your nature. Treatises on Christian brotherhood are not what you need. Select the man most disagreeable to you, and the one who has said the hardest things about you. Go up and shake hands with him, and ask him how his family is, and how his soul prospers. All your enmities will fly like a flock of quails at the bang of a rifle.

We treat our sins too politely. We ought to call them by their right names. Hatred to our neighbor should not be called hard thoughts, but murder: "whoso hateth his brother is a murderer!" Sin is abominable. It has tusks and claws, and venom in its bite, and death in its stroke. Mild treatment will not do. It is loathsome, filthy and disgusting. If we bid a dog in gentle words to go out of the house, he will lie down under the table. It wants a sharp voice and a determined manner to make him clear out, and so sin is a vile cur that cannot be ejected by any conservative policy. It must be kicked out!

Alas for the young man of the text! He refused Christ's word and went away to die, and there are now those who cannot submit to Christ's command, and after fooling their time away with moral elixirs suddenly relapse and perish. They might have been cured, but would not take the medicine.

CHAPTER LX.

THE YOUNGSTERS HAVE LEFT.

The children after quitting the tea-table were too noisy for Sabbath night, and some things were said at the table critical of their behavior, when old Dominie Scattergood dawned upon the subject and said:

We expect too much of our children when they become Christians. Do not let us measure their qualifications by our own bushel. We ought not to look for a gravity and deep appreciation of eternal things such as we find in grown persons. We have seen old sheep in the pasture-field look anxious and troubled because the lambs would frisk.

No doubt the children that were lifted by their mothers in Christ's arms, and got His blessing, five minutes after He set them down were as full of romp as before they came to Him. The boy that because he has become a Christian is disgusted with ball-playing, the little girl who because she has given her heart to God has lost her interest in her waxen-doll, are morbid and unhealthy. You ought not to set the life of a vivacious child to the tune of Old Hundred.

When the little ones come before you and apply for church membership, do not puzzle them with big words, and expect large "experiences." It is now in the church as when the disciples of old told the mothers not to bother Christ with their babes. As in some households the grown people eat first, and the children have to wait till the second table, so there are persons who talk as though God would have the grown people first sit down at His banquet; and if there is anything over the little ones may come in for a share.

No, no! If the supply at the Lord's table were limited, He would let the children come in first and the older ones go without, as a punishment for not having come in while they themselves were children. If the wind is from the northeast, and the air is full of frost and snow, and part of the flock must be left out on the mountains, let it be the old sheep, for they can stand it better than the lambs. O Shepherd of Israel, crowd them all in before the coming of the tempest!

Myself.—Dominie Scattergood, what do you think of this discussion in the papers on the subject of liturgies?

Scattergood.—I know there has been much talk of late about liturgies in the churches, and whether or not audiences should take audible part in religious service. While others are discussing that point, let me say that all the service of the Church ought to be responsive if not with audible "Amen," and unanimous "Good Lord, deliver us," then with hearty outburst of soul.

Let not the prayer of him that conducts public service go up solitary and alone, but accompanied by the heartfelt ejaculation of all the auditory. We sit down on a soft cushion, in a pew by architectural skill arranged to fit the shape of our back, and are tempted to fall into unprofitable reveries. Let the effort be on the part of every minister to make the prayer and the Scripture-reading and the giving out of the hymn so emphatic that the audience cannot help but respond with all the soul.

Let the minister, before going into the pulpit, look over the whole field and recall what are the styles of bereavement in the congregation— whether they be widowhood, orphanage or childlessness; what are the kinds of temporal loss his people may recently have suffered—whether in health, in reputation or estate; and then get both his shoulders under these troubles, and in his prayer give one earnest and tremendous lift, and there will be no dullness, no indifference, no lack of multitudinous response.

The reason that congregations have their heads bobbing about in prayer-time is because the officiating clergyman is apt to petition in the abstract. He who calls the troubles of his people by their right names, and tenderly lays hold of the cancers of the souls before him, will not lack in getting immediate heartfelt, if not audible, response.

While we have not as much interest in the agitated question of liturgies as would make us say ten words about it, we are interested more than we can tell in the question, How shall the officiating ministers, in all the churches, give so much point, and adaptedness, and vigor and blood-red earnestness of soul to their public devotions as shall make all the people in church feel that it is the struggle for their immortal life in which the pastor is engaged? Whether it be in tones that strike the ear, or with a spiritual emphasis heard only in the silent corridor of the heart, let all the people say Amen!

Myself.—What do you think, Dominie, about all this talk about sensationalism in the pulpit?

Scattergood.—As far as I can understand, it seems to be a war between stagnation and sensationalism, and I dislike both.

I do not know which word is the worst. It is the national habit in literature and religion to call that sensationalism which we ourselves cannot do. If an author write a book that will not sell, he is apt to charge the books of the day which do succeed as being sensational. There are a great many men who, in the world and the Church, are dead failures, who spend their time in letting the public know that they are not sensationalists. The fact is that they never made any stir while living, nor will they in dying, save as they rob the undertaker of his fees, they not leaving enough to pay their dismission expenses.

I hate sensationalism in the pulpit so far as that word means the preaching of everything but the gospel, but the simple fact is that whenever and wherever faith and repentance and heaven and hell are proclaimed with emphasis there will be a sensation. The people in our great cities are hungry for the old gospel of Christ. If our young men in the ministry want large audiences, let them quit philosophizing, and hair-splitting, and botanizing, and without gloves take hold of men's sins and troubles, and there will be no lack of hearers. Stagnation is worse than sensationalism.

I have always noticed that just in proportion as a man cannot get along himself he is fearful of some one else making an excitement. Last week a mud-turtle down by the brook opened its shell and discoursed to a horse that was coming down to drink. The mud-turtle said to the horse: "Just as I get sound asleep you are sure to come past and wake me up. We always used to have a good quiet time down here in the swamp till you got in the habit of thumping along this way. I am conservative and like to keep in my shell. I have been pastor of thirteen other mud-turtles, and we always had peace until you came, and next week at our semi-annual meeting of mud-turtles we shall either have you voted a nuisance or will talk it over in private, eight or ten of us, which will probably be the more prudent way." Then the mud-turtle's shell went shut with a snap, at which the horse kicked up his heels as he turned to go up to the barn to be harnessed to a load of corn that was ready for the market.

Let us all wake up and go to work. There are in the private membership of our churches and in the ministry a great many men who are dead, but have never had the common decency to get buried. With the harvest white and "lodging" for lack of a sickle, instead of lying under the trees criticising the sweating reapers who are at work, let us throw off our own coat and go out to see how good a swathe we can cut.

Myself.—You seem, Dominie Scattergood, though you have been preaching a great while, to be very healthy and to have a sound throat.

Scattergood.—Yes; I don't know any reason why ministers should not be as well as other persons. I have never had the ministers' sore throat, but have avoided it by the observance of two or three rules which I commend to you of less experience. The drug stores are full of troches, lozenges and compounds for speakers and singers. All these medicines have an important mission, but how much better would it be to avoid the ills than to spend one's time in trying to cure them!

1. Speak naturally. Let not incompetent elocutionists or the barbarisms of custom give you tones or enunciations at war with those that God implanted. Study the vocal instrument and then play the best tune on it possible, but do not try to make a flute sound like a trumpet, or a bagpipe do the work of a violin.

2. Remember that the throat and lungs were no more intended to speak with than the whole body. If the vocal organs get red hot during a religious service, while the rest of the body does not sympathize with them, there will be inflammation, irritation and decay. But if the man shall, by appreciation of some great theme of time and eternity, go into it with all his body and soul,

there will be an equalization of the whole physical organism, and bronchitis will not know whether to attack the speaker in his throat, right knee or left ankle, and while it is deciding at what point to make assault the speaker will go scot-free. The man who besieges an audience only with his throat attempts to take a castle with one gun, but he who comes at them with head, eyes, hand, heart, feet, unlimbers against it a whole park of artillery. Then Sebastopol is sure to be taken.

Myself.—I notice, Dominie, that your handwriting is not as good as your health. Your letter in reply to my invitation to be here was so indistinct that I could not tell whether it was an acceptance or a declinature.

Scattergood.—Well, I have not taken much care of my autograph. I know that the attempt has been made to reduce handwriting to a science. Many persons have been busy in gathering the signatures of celebrated men and women. A Scotchman, by the name of Watson, has paid seventy-five thousand dollars for rare autographs. Rev. Dr. Sprague, of Albany, has a collection marvelous for interest.

After we read an interesting book we want to see the author's face and his autograph. But there is almost always a surprise or disappointment felt when for the first time we come upon the handwriting of persons of whom we have heard or read much. We often find that the bold, dashing nature sometimes wields a trembling pen, and that some man eminent for weakness has a defiant penmanship that looks as if he wrote with a splinter of thunderbolt.

I admit that there are instances in which the character of the man decides the style of his penmanship. Lord Byron's autograph was as reckless as its author. George Washington's signature was a reflection of his dignity. The handwriting of Samuel Rogers was as smooth as his own nature. Robespierre's fierce-looking autograph seems to have been written with the dagger of a French revolution.

On the contrary, one's handwriting is often the antipodes of his character. An unreasonable schoolmaster has often, by false instruction, cramped or ruined the pupil's chirography for ever. If people only knew how a brutal pedagogue in the academy used to pull my ears while learning to write, I should not be so often censured for my own miserable scribble. I defy any boy to learn successfully to make "hooks and trammels" in his copy-book, or ever after learn to trace a graceful calligraphy, if he had "old Talyor" bawling over him. I hope never to meet that man this side of heaven, lest my memory of the long-ago past be too much for the sense of ministerial propriety.

There are great varieties of circumstances that influence and decide the autograph. I have no faith in the science of chirography. I could, from a pack of letters in one pigeon-hole, put to rout the whole theory. I have come to the conclusion that he who judges of a man's character by his penmanship makes a very poor guess. The boldest specimen of chirography I ever received was from a man whose wife keeps him in perpetual tremor, he surrendering every time she looks toward the broomstick.

Myself.—What do you think, Dominie, of the fact that laymen have begun to preach? and what is your opinion of the work they are doing in Scotland?

For the first time in many a day the old Dominie grew sarcastic, and said:

What are we coming to? Get out your fire-engines. There is a conflagration. What work

Messrs. Moody, Sankey, Phillips, Bliss, Jacobs, Burnell, Durant and fifty other laymen are doing! Wherever they go they have large concourses of people, and powerful revivals of religion follow. Had we not better appoint a meeting of conference or presbytery to overhaul these men who are saving souls without license? No! What we want is ten thousand men just like them, coming up from among the people, with no professional garb, and hearts hot with religious fervor, and bound by no conventionalities or stereotyped notions about the way things ought to be done.

I have a sly suspicion that the layman who has for seven years given the most of his time to the study of the truth is better prepared to preach the gospel than a man who has given that length of time in theological seminaries to the study of what other people say about the Bible. In other words, we like water just dipped from the spring, though handed in a gourd, rather than water that has been standing a week in a silver pitcher.

After Calvin has twisted us one way, and Arminius has twisted us another, and we get our head full of the old Andover and New Haven theological fights, and the difference between Ante-Nicene Trinitarianism and Post-Nicene Trinitarianism, it is a luxury to meet some evangelist who can tell us in our common mother-tongue of Him who came to seek and to save that which was lost.

I say let our learned institutions push theological education to its highest excellency, preparing men for spheres which none but the cultured and scholarly are fit for, but somehow let us beat the drum and gather a battalion of lay-workers. We have enough wise men to tell us about fishes, about birds, about rocks, about stars—enough Leyden jars, enough telescopes, enough electric batteries; but we have not more than one man where we ought to have a hundred to tell the story of Christ and the soul.

Some cry out, "It is dangerous to have laymen take such prominent positions in the Church." Dangerous to what? Our dignity, our prerogatives, our clerical rights? It is the same old story. If we have a mill on the stream, we do not want some one else to build a mill on the same stream. It will take the water off our wheel. But, blessed be God! the river of salvation is deep and strong enough to grind corn for all nations.

If a pulpit is so weak that the wave of religious zeal on the part of the laity submerges it, then let it go under. We cannot expect all other shipping to forsake the sea lest they run down our craft. We want more watchmen on the wall, more sentinels at the gate, more recruits for the field. Forward the whole Christian laity! Throw up no barrier to their advancement. Do not hang the Church until dead by the neck with "red-tape."

I laughed outright, though I ought to have cried, when I read in one of our papers a statement of the work of Moody and Sankey in Edinburgh, which statement closed with the luscious remark that "Probably the Lord is blessing their work." I never saw a word put in more awkward and forced and pitiable predicament than that word probably. While heaven and earth and hell have recognized the stupendous work now going on in Scotland under God and through the instrumentality of these American evangelists, a correspondent thinks that probably something has happened.

Oh how hard it is to acknowledge that men are doing good if they do not work in our way and by our methods! One's heart must have got awfully twisted and near being damned who can look on a great outpouring of the Holy Ghost and have any use for probabilities. The tendency is even among Christians to depreciate that which goes on independent of themselves and in a way oppugnant to their personal taste. People do not like those who do a thing which they themselves have not been able to accomplish.

The first cry is, "The people converted are the lower population, and not the educated." We wonder if five hundred souls brought to Christ from the "Cowgate" and "Coalhole," and made kings and priests unto God, and at last seated on thrones so high they will not be able to reach down with their foot to the crown of an earthly monarch, is not worth some consideration?

Then the cry is, "They will not hold out." Time only will show that. They are doing all they can. You cannot expect them to hold out ten years in six weeks. The most faithful Christians we have ever known were brought in through revivals, and the meanest, stingiest, dullest, hardest-to-get-on-with Christians have joined when the church was dead.

When a candidate for admission comes before session in revival times, I ask him only seven or eight questions; but when he comes during a cold state of religion, I ask him twenty questions, and get the elders to ask him as many more. In other words, I have more faith in conversions under special religious influence than under ordinary.

The best luck I ever had in fishing was when I dropped the net in the bay and brought up at one haul twenty bluefish, with only three or four moss-bunkers, and the poorest luck I ever had was when, after standing two hours in the soggy meadow with one hook on the line, I felt I had a bite, and began to pull, more and more persuaded of the great size of the captive, until I flung to the shore a snapping-turtle. As a gospel fisherman I would rather run the risk of a large haul than of a solitary angling. I can soon sort out and throw overboard the few moss-bunkers.

Oh for great awakenings all over Christendom!

We have had a drought so long we can stand a freshet. Let the Hudson and the Thames and the Susquehanna rise and overflow the lowlands, and the earth be full of the knowledge of God as the waters fill the seas. That time is hastening, probably!

CHAPTER LXI.

FAMILY PRAYERS.

Take first the statement that unless our children are saved in early life they probably never will be. They who go over the twentieth year without Christ are apt to go all the way without Him. Grace, like flower-seed, needs to be sown in spring. The first fifteen years of life, and often the first six, decide the eternal destiny.

The first thing to do with a lamb is to put it in the arms of the Great Shepherd. Of course we must observe natural laws. Give a child excessive meat diet, and it will grow up sensual, and catechism three times a day, and sixty grains in each dose, won't prevent it. Talk much in your child's presence about the fashions, and it will be fond of dress, notwithstanding all your lectures on humility. Fill your house with gossip, and your children will tattle. Culture them as much as you will, but give them plenty of money to spend, and they will go to destruction.

But while we are to use common sense in every direction respecting a child, the first thing is to strive for its conversion, and there is nothing more potent than family prayers. No child ever gets over having heard parents pray for him. I had many sound threshings when I was a boy (not as many as I ought to have had, for I was the last child and my parents let me off), but the most memorable scene in my childhood was father and mother at morning and evening prayers. I cannot forget it, for I used often to be squirming around on the floor and looking at them while they were praying. Your son may go to the ends of the earth, and run through the whole catalogue of transgression, but he will remember the family altar, and it will be a check, and a call, and perhaps his redemption.

Family prayers are often of no use. Perhaps they are too hurried. We have so much before us of the day's work that we must hustle the children together. We get half through the chapter before the family are seated. We read as if we were reading for a wager. We drop on our knees, are in the second or third sentence before they all get down. It is an express train, with amen for the first depot. We rush for the hat and overcoat, and are on the way to the store, leaving the impression that family prayers are a necessary nuisance, and we had better not have had any gathering of the family at all. Better have given them a kiss all around; it would have taken less time and would have been more acceptable to God and them.

Family prayers often fail in adaptedness. Do not read for the morning lesson a genealogical chapter, or about Samson setting the foxes' tails on fire, or the prophecy about the horses, black and red, and speckled, unless you explain why they were speckled. For all the good your children get from such reading, you might as well have read a Chinese almanac. Rather give the story of Jesus, and the children climbing into his arms, or the lad with the loaves and fishes, or the Sea of Galilee dropping to sleep under Christ's lullaby.

Stop and ask questions. Make the exercise so interesting that little Johnny will stop playing with his shoe-strings, and Jenny will quit rubbing the cat's fur the wrong way. Let the prayer be pointed and made up of small words, and no wise information to the Lord about things He knows without your telling Him. Let the children feel they are prayed for. Have a hymn if any of you can sing. Let the season be spirited, appropriate and gladly solemn.

Family prayer also fails when the whole day is not in harmony with it. A family prayer, to be worth anything, ought to be twenty-four hours long. It ought to give the pitch to all the day's work and behavior. The day when we get thoroughly mad upsets the morning devotion. The life must be in the same key with the devotion.

Family prayer is infinitely important. If you are a parent, and are not a professor of religion, and do not feel able to compose a prayer, get some one of the many books that have been written, put it down before you, and read prayers for the household. God has said that He will "pour out His fury upon the family that call not upon His name."

Prayer for our children will be answered. My grandmother was a praying woman. My father's name was David. One day, he and other members of the family started for a gay party. Grandmother said: "Go, David, and enjoy yourself; but all the time you and your brothers and sisters are there, I will be praying for you." They went, but did not have a very good time, knowing that their mother was praying for them.

The next morning, grandmother heard loud weeping in the room below. She went down and found her daughter crying violently. What was the matter? She was in anxiety about her soul— an anxiety that found no relief short of the cross. Word came that David was at the barn in great agony. Grandmother went and found him on the barn floor, praying for the life of his soul.

The news spread to the neighboring houses, and other parents became anxious about their children, and the influence spread to the village of Somerville, and there was a great turning unto

God; and over two hundred souls, in one day, stood up in the village church to profess faith in Christ. And it all started from my grandmother's prayer for her sons and daughters. May God turn the hearts of the fathers to the children, and the hearts of the children to their fathers, lest He come and smite the earth with a curse!

CHAPTER LXII.

CALL TO SAILORS.

One of the children asked us at the tea-table if we had ever preached at sea. We answered, No! but we talked one Sabbath, mid-Atlantic, to the officers, crew and passengers of the steamship "China." By the way, I have it as it was taken down at the time and afterward appeared in a newspaper, and here is the extract:

No persons bound from New York to Liverpool ever had more cause for thanksgiving to God than we. The sea so smooth, the ship so staunch, the companionship so agreeable, all the circumstances so favorable. O Thou who holdest the winds in Thy fist, blessed be Thy glorious name for ever!

Englishmen, Costa Ricans, Germans, Spaniards, Japanese, Irishmen, Americans—gathered, never to meet again till the throne of judgment is lifted—let us join hands to-day around the cross of Jesus and calculate our prospect for eternity. A few moments ago we all had our sea-glasses up watching the vessel that went by. "What is her name?" we all asked, and "Whither is she bound?"

We pass each other on the ocean of life to-day. We only catch a glimpse of each other. The question is, "Whither are we bound? For harbor of light or realm of darkness?" As we decide these questions, we decide everything.

No man gets to heaven by accident. If we arrive there, it will be because we turn the helm, set the sail, watch the compass and stand on the "lookout" with reference to that destination. There are many ways of being lost—only one way of being saved; Jesus Christ is the way. He comes across the sea to-day, His feet on the glass of the wave, as on Galilee, His arm as strong, His voice as soothing, His heart as warm. Whosoever will may have His comfort, His pardon, His heaven.

Officers and crew of this ship, have you not often felt the need of divine help? In the hour of storm and shipwreck, far away from your homes, have you not called for heavenly rescue? The God who then heard thy prayer will hear thee now. Risk not your soul in the great future without compass, or chart, or anchor, or helmsman. You will soon have furled your last sail, and run up the last ratline, and weathered the last gale, and made the last voyage. What next? Where then will be your home, who your companions, what your occupation?

Let us all thank God for this Sabbath which has come to us on the sea. How beautifully it bridges the Atlantic! It hovers above every barque and brig and steamer. It speaks of a Jesus risen, a grave conquered, a heaven open. It is the same old Sabbath that blessed our early days. It is tropical in its luxuriance, but all its leaves are prayers, and all its blossoms praise. Sabbath on the sea! How solemn! How suggestive! Let all its hours, on deck, in cabin, in forecastle, be sacred.

Some of the old tunes that these sailors heard in boyhood times would sound well to-day floating among the rigging. Try "Jesus, lover of my soul," or "Come, ye sinners, poor and needy," or "There is a fountain filled with blood." As soon as they try those old hymns, the memory of loved ones would come back again, and the familiar group of their childhood would gather, and father would be there, and mother who gave them such good advice when they came to sea, and sisters and brothers long since scattered and gone.

Some of you have been pursued by benedictions for many years. I care not how many knots an hour you may glide along, the prayers once offered up for your welfare still keep up with you. I care not on what shore you land, those benedictions stand there to greet you. They will capture you yet for heaven. The prodigal after a while gets tired of the swine-herd and starts for home, and the father comes out to greet him, and the old homestead rings with clapping cymbals, and quick feet, and the clatter of a banquet. If the God of thy childhood days should accost thee with forgiving mercy, this ship would be a Bethel, and your hammock to-night would be the foot of the ladder down which the angels of God's love would come trooping.

Now, may the blessing of God come down upon officers and crew and passengers! Whatever our partings, our losses, our mistakes, our disasters in life, let none of us miss heaven. On that shore may we land amid the welcome of those who have gone before. They have long been waiting our arrival, and are now ready to conduct us to the foot of the throne. Look, all ye voyagers for eternity! Land ahead! Weeping may endure for a night, but joy cometh in the morning.

What Paul said to the crew and passengers on the corn-ship of the Mediterranean is appropriate here: "Now I exhort you to be of good cheer!" God fit us for the day when the archangel, with one foot on the sea and the other on the land, shall swear by Him that liveth for ever and ever that time shall be no longer!

CHAPTER LXIII.

JEHOSHAPHAT'S SHIPPING.

Your attention is called to a Bible incident that you may not have noticed. Jehoshaphat was unfortunate with his shipping. He was about to start another vessel. The wicked men of Ahaziah wanted to go aboard that vessel as sailors. Jehoshaphat refused to allow them to go, for the reason that he did not want his own men to mingle with those vicious people.

In other words, he knew what you and I know very well, that it is never safe to go in the same boat with the wicked. But there are various applications of that idea. We too often forget it, and are not as wise as Jehoshaphat was when he refused to allow his men to be in companionship in the same boat with the wicked men of Ahaziah.

The principle I stated is appropriate to the formation, in the first place, of all domestic alliances. I have often known women who married men for the purpose of reforming them from dissipated habits. I never knew one successful in the undertaking. Instead of the woman lifting the man up, the man drags her down. This is inevitably the case. The greatest risk that one ever undertakes is attempting the voyage of life in a boat in which the wicked sail; this remark being most appropriate to the young persons who are in my presence. It is never safe to sail with the sons of Ahaziah. The aged men around me will bear out the statement that I have made. There is no exception to it.

The principle is just as true in regard to all business alliances. I know it is often the case that men have not the choice of their worldly associations, but there are instances where they may make their choice, and in that case I wish them to understand that it is never safe to go in the same boat with the vicious. No man can afford to stand in associations where Christ is maligned and scoffed at, or the things of eternity caricatured. Instead of your Christianizing them, they will heathenize you. While you propose to lift them up, they will drag you down. It is a sad thing when a man is obliged to stand in a business circle where men are deriding the religion of the Lord Jesus Christ. For instance, rather than to be associated in business circles with Frothinghamite infidelity, give me a first-class Mohammedan, or an unconverted Chinese, or an unmixed Hottentot. There is no danger that they will draw me down to their religion.

If, therefore, you have a choice when you go out in the world as to whether you will be associated in business circles with men who love God, or those who are hostile to the Christian religion, you might better sacrifice some of your financial interests and go among the people of God than risk the interests of your immortal soul.

Jehoshaphat knew it was unsafe for his men to go in one boat with the men of Ahaziah, and you cannot afford to have business associations with those who despise God, and heed not His commandments. I admit the fact that a great many men are forced into associations they despise, and there are business circles in which we are compelled to go which we do not like, but if you have a choice, see that you make an intelligent and safe one.

This principle is just as true in regard to social connections. Let no young man or woman go in a social circle where the influences are vicious or hostile to the Christian religion. You will begin by reproving their faults, and end by copying them. Sin is contagious. You go among those who are profane, and you will be profane. You go among those who use impure language, and you will use impure language. Go among those who are given to strong drink, and you will inevitably become an inebriate. There is no exception to the rule. A man is no better than the company he continually keeps.

It is always best to keep ourselves under Christian influences. It is not possible, if you mingle in associations that are positively Christian, not to be made better men or women. The Christian people with whom you associate may not be always talking their religion, but there is something in the moral atmosphere that will be life to your soul. You choose out for your most intimate associates eight or ten Christian people. You mingle in that association; you take their counsel; you are guided by their example, and you live a useful life, and die a happy death, and go to a blessed eternity. There is no possibility of mistaking it; there is not an exception in all the universe or ages—not one.

For this reason I wish that Christians engage in more religious conversation. I do not really think that Christian talk is of so high a type as it used to be. Some of you can look back to your very early days and remember how the neighbors used to come in and talk by the hour about Christ and heaven and their hopes of the eternal world. There has a great deal of that gone out of fashion.

I suppose that if ten or fifteen of us should happen to come into a circle to spend the evening, we would talk about the late presidential election, or the recent flurry in Wall street, and about five hundred other things, and perhaps we would not talk any about Jesus Christ and our hopes of heaven. That is not Christianity; that is heathenism. Indeed, I have sometimes been amazed to find Christian people actually lacking in subjects of conversation, while the two persons knew each of the other that he was a Christian.

You take two Christian people of this modern day and place them in the same room (I suppose the two men may have no worldly subjects in common). What are they talking about? There being no worldly subject common to them, they are in great stress for a subject, and after a long pause Mr. A remarks: "It is a pleasant evening."

Again there is a long pause. These two men, both redeemed by the blood of the Lord Jesus Christ, heaven above them, hell beneath them, eternity before them, the glorious history of the Church of Jesus Christ behind them, certainly after a while they will converse on the subject of religion. A few minutes have passed and Mr. B remarks: "Fine autumn we are having."

Again there is a profound quiet. Now, you suppose that their religious feelings have really been dammed back for a little while; the men have been postponing the things of God and eternity that they may approach the subject with more deliberation, and you wonder what useful thing Mr. B will say to Mr. A in conversation.

It is the third time, and perhaps it is the last that these two Christian men will ever meet until they come face to face before the throne of God. They know it. The third attempt is now made. Mr. A says to Mr. B: "Feels like snow!"

My opinion is, it must have felt more like ice. Oh, how little real, practical religious conversation there is in this day! I would to God that we might get back to the old-time Christianity, when men and women came into associations, and felt, "Here I must use all the influence I can for Christ upon that soul, and get all the good I can.

This may be the last opportunity I shall have in this world of interviewing that immortal spirit."

But there are Christian associations where men and women do talk out their religion; and my advice to you is to seek out all those things, and remember that just in proportion as you seek such society will you be elevated and blessed. After all, the gospel boat is the only safe boat to sail in. The ships of Jehoshaphat went all to pieces at Eziongeber.

Come aboard this gospel craft, made in the drydock of heaven and launched nineteen hundred years ago in Bethlehem amid the shouting of the angels. Christ is the captain, and the children of God are the crew. The cargo is made up of the hopes and joys of all the ransomed. It is a ship bound heavenward, and all the batteries of God will boom a greeting as we sail in and drop anchor in the still waters. Come aboard that ship; it is a safe craft! The fare is cheap! It is a certain harbor!

The men of Ahaziah were forbidden to come aboard the ships of Jehoshaphat, but all the world is invited to board this gospel craft. The vessel of Jehoshaphat went to pieces, but this craft shall drop anchor within the harbor, and mountains shall depart, and hills shall be removed, and seas shall dry up, and time itself shall perish, but the mercy of the Lord is from everlasting to everlasting upon them that fear Him.

CHAPTER LXIV.

ALL ABOUT MERCY.

Benedict XIII. decreed that when the German Catholics met each other, they should always give the following salutation, the one first speaking saying, "Praised be Jesus Christ," the other responding, "For ever, amen," a salutation fit for Protestants whenever they come together.

The word "mercy" is used in the Bible two hundred and fourteen times; it seems to be the favorite word of all the Scriptures. Sometimes it glances feebly upon us like dew in the starlight; then with bolder hand it seems to build an arched bridge from one storm-cloud of trouble to another; and then again it trickles like a fountain upon the thirst of the traveler.

The finest roads I ever saw are in Switzerland. They are built by the government, and at very short intervals you come across water pouring out of the rocks. The government provides cups for men and troughs for the animals to drink out of. And our King has so arranged it that on the highway we are traveling toward heaven, ever and anon there shall dash upon us the clear, sweet water that flows from the eternal Rock. I propose to tell you some things about God's mercy.

First, think of His pardoning mercy. The gospel finds us shipwrecked; the wave beneath ready to swallow us, the storm above pelting us, our good works foundered, there is no such thing as getting ashore unhelped. The gospel finds us incarcerated; of all those who have been in thick dungeon darkness, not one soul ever escaped by his own power. If a soul is delivered at all, it is because some one on the outside shall shove the bolt and swing open the door, and let the prisoner come out free.

The sin of the soul is not, as some would seem to think, just a little dust on the knee or elbow that you can strike off in a moment and without any especial damage to you. Sin has utterly discomfited us; it has ransacked our entire nature; it has ruined us so completely that no human power can ever reconstruct us; but through the darkness of our prison gloom and through the storm there comes a voice from heaven, saying, "I will abundantly pardon."

Then think of His restraining mercy. I do not believe that it is possible for any man to tell his capacity for crime until he has been tested. There have been men who denounced all kinds of frauds, who scorned all mean transactions, who would have had you believe that it was impossible for them ever to be tempted to dishonesty, and yet they may be owning to-day the chief part of the stock in the Credit Mobilier.

There are men who once said they never could be tempted to intemperance. They had no mercy on the drunkard. They despised any man who became a victim of strong drink. Time passed on, and now they are the victims of the bottle, so far gone in their dissipation that it is almost impossible that they ever should be rescued.

So there have been those who were very hard on all kinds of impurity, and who scoffed at unchastity, and who said that it was impossible that they should ever be led astray; but to-night they are in the house whose gates are the gates of hell! It is a very dangerous thing for a man to make a boast and say, "Such and such a sin I never could be tempted to commit."

There are ten thousand hands of mercy holding us up; there are ten thousand hands of mercy holding us back, or we would long ago have gone over the precipice, and instead of sitting to-night in a Christian sanctuary, amid the respected and the good, our song would have been that of the drunkard, or we would be "hail fellows well met" with the renegade and the profligate. Oh, the restraining mercy of God! Have you never celebrated it? Have you never rejoiced in it?

Think also of His guiding mercy. You have sometimes been on a journey, and come to where there were three roads—one ahead of you, one to the right and one to the left. It was a lonely place, and you had no one of whom to ask advice. You took the left-hand road, thinking that was the right one, but before night you found out your mistake, and yet your horse was too exhausted and you were too tired to retrace your steps, and the mistake you made was an irretrievable mistake.

You come on in life, many a time, and find there are three or four or fifty roads, and which one of the fifty to take you do not know. Let me say that there are forty-nine chances out of fifty that you will take the wrong one, unless God directs you, since it is a great deal easier to do that which is wrong than that which is right, our nature being corrupt and depraved.

Blessed be God, we have a directory! As a man lost on the mountains takes out his map and sees the right road marked down, and makes up his mind what to do, so the Lord, in His gospel map, has said: "This is the way, walk ye in it." Blessed be God for His guiding mercy!

Think also of the comforting mercy of God. In the days when men lived five or six or seven hundred years, I suppose that troubles and misfortunes came to them at very great intervals. Life did not go so fast. There were not so many vicissitudes; there was not so much jostling. I suppose that now a man in forty years will have as many vexations and annoyances and hardships and trials and temptations as those antediluvians had in four hundred years.

No one escapes. If you are not wounded in this side, you must be wounded in that. There are foes all around about you. There is no one who has come up to this moment without having been cleft of misfortunes, without having been disappointed and vexed and outraged and trampled on.

The world comes and tries to solace us, but I think the most impotent thing on earth is human comfort when there is no gospel mixed with it. It is a sham and an insult to a wounded spirit—all the comfort that this world can offer a man; but in his time of darkness and perplexity and bereavement and persecution and affliction, Christ comes to him with the solace of His Spirit, and He says: "Oh, thou tempted one, thou shalt not be tempted above that thou art able." He tells the invalid, "There is a land where the inhabitants never say, 'I am sick.'" He says to the assaulted one, "You are no better than I am; they maltreated me, and the servant ought not to expect to have it easier than his Lord."

He comes to the bereaved one and says: "I am the resurrection and the life; he that believeth in me, though he were dead, yet shall he live." And if the trouble be intricate, if there be so many prongs to it, so many horns to it, so many hoofs to it, that he cannot take any of the other promises and comforts of God's word to his soul, he can take that other promise made for a man in the last emergency and when everything else fails: "All things work together for good to those that love God." Oh, have you never sung of the comforting mercy of God?

Think also of His enthroning mercy. Notwithstanding there are so many comforts in Christ's gospel, I do not think that we could stand the assault and rebuff of the world for ever. We all were so weary of the last war. It seemed as if those four years were as long as any fifteen or twenty years of our life. But how could we endure one hundred years, or five hundred years, or a thousand years, of earthly assault? Methinks the spirit would wear down under the constant chafing and the assault of the world.

Blessed be God, this story of grief and trouble and perplexity will come to an end! There are twelve gates to heaven, and they are all gates of mercy. There are paths coming into all those gates, and they are all paths of mercy. There are bells that ring in the eternal towers, and they are all chimes of mercy. There are mansions prepared for us in this good land when we have done with the toils of earth, and all those mansions are mansions of mercy. Can you not now strike upon your soul, saying, "Bless the Lord, O my soul, for thy pardoning mercy, for thy restraining mercy, for thy guiding mercy, for thy comforting mercy, for thy enthroning mercy!"

CHAPTER LXV.

UNDER THE CAMEL'S SADDLE.

Rachel had been affianced to Jacob, and one day while her father, Laban, was away from home she eloped with Jacob. Laban returned home and expressed great sorrow that he had not been there when his daughter went away, saying that he would have allowed her to go, and that she might have been accompanied with a harp and the dance and with many beautiful presents.

Laban started for Rachel and Jacob. He was very anxious to recover the gods that had been stolen from his household. He supposed that Rachel had taken them, as she really had. He came up in the course of a few days to the party and demanded the gods that had been taken from his house. Jacob knew nothing about the felony, but Rachel was secreting these household gods.

Laban came into the tent where she was, and asked for them. She sat upon a saddle of a camel, the saddle having been laid down at the side of the tent, and under this camel's saddle were the images. Rachel pretended to be sick, and said she could not rise. Her father, Laban, supposed that she told the truth, and looked everywhere but under the camel's saddle, where really the lost images were. He failed in the search, and went back home without them.

It was a strange thing for Laban to do. He pretended to be a worshiper of the true God. What did he want of those images? Ah, the fact was, that though he worshiped God, he worshiped with only half a heart, and he sometimes, I suppose, repented of the fact that he worshiped him at all, and really had a hankering after those old gods which in his earliest days he had worshiped. And now we find him in Rachel's tent looking for them.

Do not let us, however, be too severely critical of Laban. He is only the representative of thousands of Christian men and women, who, once having espoused the worship of God, go back to their idols. When a man professes faith in Christ on communion-day, with the sacramental cup in his hand, he swears allegiance to the Lord God Almighty, and says, "Let all my idols perish!" but how many of us have forsaken our fealty to God, and have gone back to our old idols!

There are many who sacrifice their soul's interests in the idolatry of wealth. There was a time when you saw the folly of trying with money to satisfy the longing of your soul. You said, when you saw men going down into the dust and tussle of life, "Whatever god I worship, it won't be a golden calf." You saw men plunge into the life of a spendthrift, or go down into the life of a miser, like one of old smothered to death in his own money-chest, and you thought, "I shall be very careful never to be caught in these traps in which so many men have fallen, to their souls' eternal discomfiture."

But you went down into the world; you felt the force of temptation; you saw men all around you making money very fast, some of them sacrificing all their Christian principle; you felt the fascination come upon your own soul, and before you knew it, you were with Laban going down to hunt in Rachel's tent for your lost idols.

On one of our pieces of money you find the head of a goddess, a poor inscription for an American coin; far better the inscription that the old Jews put upon the shekel, a pot of manna and an almond rod, alluding to the mercy and deliverance of God in their behalf in other days. But how seldom it is that money is consecrated to Christ! Instead of the man owning the money, the money owns the man. It is evident, especially to those with whom they do business every day, that they have an idol, or that, having once forsaken the idol, they are now in search of it, far away from the house of God, in Rachel's tent looking for the lost images.

One of the mighty men of India said to his servants: "Go not near the cave in such a ravine." The servants talked the matter over, and said: "There must be gold there, or certainly this mighty man would not warn us against going." They went, expecting to find a pile of gold; they rolled away the stone from the door of the cave, when a tiger sprang out upon them and devoured them.

Many a man in the search of gold has been craunched in the jaws of destruction. Going out far away from the God whom they originally worshiped, they are seeking in the tent of Rachel, Laban's lost images.

There are a great many Christians in this day renewing the idolatry of human opinion. There was a time when they woke up to the folly of listening to what men said to them. They soliloquized in this way: "I have a God to worship, and I am responsible only to Him. I must go straight on and do my whole duty, whether the world likes it or don't like it;" and they turned a deaf ear to the fascinations of public applause. After a while they did something very popular. They had the popular ear and the popular heart. Men approved them, and poured gentle words of flattery into their ear, and before they realized it they went into the search of that which they had given up, and were, with Laban, hunting in Rachel's tent for the lost images.

Between eleven and twelve o'clock one June night, Gibbon, the great historian, finished his history. Seated in a summer garden, he says that as he wrote the last line of that wonderful work he felt great satisfaction. He closed the manuscript, walked out into the moonlight in the garden, and then, he said, he felt an indescribable melancholy come upon his soul at the thought that so soon he must leave all the fame that he would acquire by that manuscript.

The applause of this world is a very mean god to worship. It is a Dagon that falls upon its worshipers and crushes them to death. Alas for those who, fascinated by human applause, give up the service of the Lord God and go with Laban to hunt in Rachel's tent for the lost images!

There are many Christians being sacrificed to appetite. There was a time when they said: "I will not surrender to evil appetites." For a while they seemed to break away from all the allurements by which they were surrounded, but sometimes they felt that they were living upon a severe regimen. They said: "After all, I will go back to my old bondage;" and they fell away from the house of God, and fell away from respectability, and fell away for ever.

One of the kings in olden times, the legend says, consented that the devil might kiss him on both shoulders, but no sooner were the kisses imprinted upon the shoulders than serpents grew forth and began to devour him, and as the king tried to tear off the serpents he found he was tearing his own life out. And there are men who are all enfolded in adders of evil appetite and passion that no human power can ever crush; and unless the grace of God seizes hold of them, these adders will become "the worm that never dies." Alas for those who, once having broken away from the mastery of evil appetites and passion, go back to the sins that they once renounced, and, with Laban in Rachel's tent, go to hunt for the lost images!

There are a great many also sacrificed by indolence. In the hour of their conversion they looked off upon the world, and said: "Oh how much work to be done, how many harvests to be gathered, how many battles to be fought, how many tears to be wiped away, and how many wounds to be bound up!" and they looked with positive surprise upon those who could sit idle in the kingdom of God while there was so much work to do. After a while they found their efforts were unappreciated, that some of their best work in behalf of Christ was caricatured and they were laughed at, and they began to relax their effort, and the question was no more, "What can I do for Christ?" but "How can I take my ease? where can I find my rest?" Are there not some of you who in the hour of your consecration started out nobly, bravely and enthusiastically for the Saviour's kingdom who have fallen back into ease of body and ease of soul, less anxious about the salvation of men than you once were, and are actually this moment in Rachel's tent hunting up the lost images?

Oh, why go down hunting for our old idols? We have found out they are insufficient for the soul. Eyes have they, but they see not; ears have they, but they hear not; and hands have they, but they handle not. There is only one God to worship, and He sits in the heavens.

How do I know that there is only one God? I know it just as the boy knew it when his teacher asked him how many Gods there are. He said, "There is but one."

"How do you know that?" inquired the teacher.

The boy replied, "There is only room for one, for He fills the heavens and the earth."

Come into the worship of that God. He is a

wise God. He can plan out all the affairs of your life. He can mark out all the steps that you ought to take. He will put the sorrows in the right place, and the victories in the right place, and the defeats in the right place; and coming to the end of your life, if you have served Him faithfully, you will be compelled to say, "Just and true are thy ways; thou art, O Lord, always right."

He is a mighty God. Have Him on your side, and you need not fear earth or hell. He can ride down all your spiritual foes. He is mighty to overthrow your enemies. He is mighty to save your soul. Ay, He is a loving God. He will put the arms of His love around about your neck. He will bring you close to His heart and shelter you from the storm. In times of trouble He will put upon your soul the balm of precious promises. He will lead you all through the vale of tears trustfully and happily, and then at last take you to dwell in His presence, where there is fullness of joy, and at His right hand, where there are pleasures for evermore. Oh, compared with such a wise God, such a mighty God, such a loving God, what are all the images under the camel's saddle in the tent of Rachel?

CHAPTER LXVI.

HALF-AND-HALF CHURCHES.

There is a verse in Revelation that presents a nauseated Christ: "Because thou art lukewarm, and neither cold nor hot, I will spew thee out of my mouth."

After we have been taking a long walk on a summer day, or been on a hunting chase, a draught of cold water exhilarates. On the other hand, after standing or walking in the cold air and being chilled, hot water, mingled with some beverage, brings life and comfort to the whole body; but tepid water, neither hot nor cold, is nauseating.

Now, Christ says that a church of that temperature acts on him as an emetic: I will spew thee out of my mouth.

The church that is red hot with religious emotion, praying, singing, working, Christ having taken full possession of the membership, must be to God satisfactory.

On the other hand, a frozen church may have its uses. The minister reads elegant essays, and improves the session or the vestry in rhetorical composition. The music is artistic and improves the ear of the people, so that they can better appreciate concert and opera.

The position of such a church is profitable to the book-binder who furnishes the covers to the liturgy, and the dry-goods merchants who supply the silks, and the clothiers who furnish the broadcloth. Such a church is good for the business world, makes trade lively and increases the demand for fineries of all sorts, for a luxurious religion demands furs and coats, and gaiters to match. Christ says he gets along with a church, cold or hot.

But an unmitigated nuisance to God and man is a half-and-half church, with piety tepid. The pulpit in such a church makes more of orthodoxy than it does of Christ. It is immense on definitions. It treats of justification and sanctification as though they were two corpses to be dissected. Its sermons all have a black morocco cover, which some affectionate sister gave the pastor before he was married, to wrap his discourse in, lest it get mussed in the dust of the pulpit. Its gestures are methodical, as though the man were ever conscious that they had been decreed from all eternity, and he were afraid of interfering with the decree by his own free agency.

Such a pulpit never startles the people with the horrors of an undone eternity. No strong meat, but only pap, flour and water, mostly water. The church prayer-meeting is attended only by a few gray heads who have been in the habit of going there for twenty years, not because they expect any arousing time or rapturous experiences, but because they feel only a few will be there, and they ought to go.

The minister is sound. The membership sound. The music sound. If, standing in a city of a hundred thousand people, there are five or ten conversions in a year, everything is thought to be "encouraging." But Christ says that such a church is an emetic. "Because thou art neither cold nor hot, I will spew thee out of my mouth."

My friends, you had better warm up or freeze over. Better set the kettle outside in the atmosphere at zero, or put it on the altar of God and stir up the coals into a blaze. If we do not, God will remove us.

Christian men are not always taken to heaven as a reward, but sometimes to get them out of the way on earth. They go to join the tenth-rate saints in glory; for if such persons think they will stand with Paul, and Harlan Page, and Charlotte Elizabeth, they are much mistaken.

When God takes them up, the church here is better off. We mourn slightly to have them go, because we have got used to having them around, and at the funeral the minister says all the good things about the man that can well be thought of, because we want to make the funeral as respectable as possible. I never feel so much tempted to lie as when an inconsistent and useless Christian has died, and I want in my final remarks to make a good case out for the poor fellow. Still, it is an advantage to have such a man get out of the way. He is opposed to all new enterprises. He puts back everything he tries to help. His digestion of religious things is impaired, and his circulation is so poor that no amount of friction can arouse him.

Now, it is dangerous for any of you to stay in that condition. If you cannot be moved, God will kill you, and He will put in your place those who will do the work you are neglecting.

My friends, let all arouse! The nearness of our last account, the greatness of the work to be done, and the calls of God's word and providence, ought to stir our souls. After having been in the harvest field so long it would be a shame in the nightfall of death to go home empty-handed. Gather up a few gleanings from the field, and beat them out, that it may be found that Ruth had at least "one ephah of barley."

CHAPTER LXVII.

THORNS.

The Christian world has long been guessing what Paul's thorn in the flesh was. I have a book that in ten pages tries to show what Paul's thorn was not, and in another ten pages tries to show what it was.

Many of the theological doctors have felt Paul's pulse to see what was the matter with him. I suppose that the reason he did not tell us what it was may have been because he did not want us to know. He knew that if he stated what it was there would have been a great many people from Corinth bothering him with prescriptions as to how he might cure it.

Some say it was diseased eyes, some that it was a humped back. It may have been neuralgia. Perhaps it was gout, although his active habits and a sparse diet throw doubt on the supposition. Suffice to say it was a thorn—that is, it stuck him. It was sharp.

It was probably of not much account in the eyes of the world. It was not a trouble that could be compared to a lion or a boisterous sea. It was like a thorn that you may have in your hand or foot and no one know it. Thus we see that it becomes a type of those little nettlesome worries of life that exasperate the spirit.

Every one has a thorn sticking him. The housekeeper finds it in unfaithful domestics; or an inmate who keeps things disordered; or a house too small for convenience or too large to be kept cleanly. The professional man finds it in perpetual interruptions or calls for "more copy."

The Sabbath-school teacher finds it in inattentive scholars, or neighboring teachers that talk loud and make a great noise in giving a little instruction.

One man has a rheumatic joint which, when the wind is northeast, lifts the storm signal. Another a business partner who takes full half the profits, but does not help earn them. These trials are the more nettlesome because, like Paul's thorn, they are not to be mentioned. Men get sympathy for broken bones and mashed feet, but not for the end of sharp thorns that have been broken off in the fingers.

Let us start out with the idea that we must have annoyances. It seems to take a certain number of them to keep us humble, wakeful and prayerful. To Paul the thorn was as disciplinary as the shipwreck. If it is not one thing, it is another. If the stove does not smoke, the boiler must leak. If the pen is good, the ink must be poor. If the editorial column be able, there must be a typographical blunder. If the thorn does not pierce the knee, it must take you in the back. Life must have sharp things in it. We cannot make up our robe of Christian character without pins and needles.

We want what Paul got—grace to bear these things. Without it we become cross, censorious and irascible. We get in the habit of sticking our thorns into other people's fingers. But God helping us, we place these annoyances in the category of the "all things that work together for good." We see how much shorter these thorns are than the spikes that struck through the palms of Christ's hands; and remembering that he had on his head a whole crown of thorns, we take to ourselves the consolation that if we suffer with him on earth we shall be glorified with him in heaven.

But how could Paul positively rejoice in these infirmities? I answer that the school of Christ has three classes of scholars. In the first class we learn how to be stuck with thorns without losing our patience. In the second class we learn how to make the sting positively advantageous. In the third class of this school we learn how even to rejoice in being pierced and wounded, but that is the senior class; and when we get to that, we are near graduation into glory.

CHAPTER LXVIII.

WHO TOUCHED ME?

There is nothing more unreasonable and ungovernable than a crowd of people. Men who standing alone or in small groups are deliberate in all they do, lose their self-control when they come to stand in a crowd. You have noticed this, if you have heard a cry of fire in a large assemblage, or have seen people moving about in great excitement in some mass-meeting, shoving, jostling and pulling at each other.

But while the Lord Jesus had been performing some wonderful works, and a great mob of people were around Him, shoving this way and that way, all the jostling He received evoked from Him no response.

After a while I see a wan and wasted woman pressing through the crowd. She seems to have a very urgent errand. I can see from her countenance that she has been a great sufferer. She comes close enough to put her finger on the hem of Christ's garment, and the very moment she puts her finger on that garment, Jesus says: "Who touched me?"

I would like to talk to you of the extreme sensitiveness of Jesus. It is very often the case that those men who are mighty, have very little fineness of feeling; but notwithstanding the fact that the Lord Jesus Christ was the King of glory, having all power in heaven and on earth, so soon as this sick woman comes up and puts her finger on the hem of His garment, that moment all the feelings of His soul are aroused, and He cries out: "Who touched me?"

I remark that poverty touches Him. The Bible says that this woman had spent all her money on physicians; she had not got the worth of her money. Those physicians in Oriental lands were very incompetent for their work, and very exorbitant in their demands. You know they have a habit even to this day in those countries of making very singular charges. Sometimes they examine the capacity of the person to pay, and they take the entire estate.

At any rate, this woman spoken of in the text had spent her money on physicians, and very poor physicians at that. The Lord saw her poverty and destitution. He knew from what a miserable home she had come. He did not ask, "Who touched me?" because He did not know; He wanted to evoke that woman's response, and He wanted to point all the multitude to her particular case before her cure was effected, in order that the miraculous power might be demonstrated before all the people, and that they might be made to believe.

In this day, as then, the touch of poverty always evokes Christ's attention. If you be one who has had a hard struggle to get daily bread—if the future is all dark before you—if you are harassed and perplexed, and know not which way to turn, I want you to understand that, although in this world there may be no sympathy for you, the heart of the Lord Jesus Christ is immediately moved, and you have but to go to Him and touch Him with your little finger, and you arouse all the sympathies of His infinite nature.

I also learn that sickness touches Him. She had been an invalid for twelve years. How many sleepless nights, what loss of appetite, what nervousness, what unrest, what pain of body, the world knew not. But when she came up and put her finger on Christ's garment, all her suffering thrilled through the heart of Christ instantaneously.

When we are cast down with Asiatic cholera or yellow fever, we cry to God for pity; but in the ailments of life that continue from day to day, month to month and year to year are you in the habit of going to Christ for sympathy? Is it in some fell disaster alone that you call to God for mercy, or is it in the little aches and pains of your life that you implore Him? Don't try to carry these burdens alone. These chronic diseases are the diseases that wear out and exhaust Christian grace, and you need to get a new supply. Go to Him this night, if never before, with all your ailments of body, and say: "Lord Jesus, look upon my aches and pains. In this humble and importunate prayer I touch thee."

I remark further that the Saviour is touched with all bereavements. Perhaps there is not a single room in your house but reminds you of some one who has gone. You cannot look at a picture without thinking she admired that. You cannot see a toy but you think she played with it. You cannot sit down and put your fingers on the piano without thinking she used to handle this instrument, and everything that is beautiful in your home is suggestive of positive sadness.

Graves! graves! graves! It is the history of how many families to-night! You measure your life from tear to tear, from groan to groan, from anguish to anguish, and sometimes you feel that God has forsaken you, and you say, "Is His mercy clean gone forever, and will He be favorable no more?"

Can it be, my afflicted friends, that you have been so foolish as to try to carry the burden alone, when there is an almighty arm willing to be thrust under you? Can it be that you have traveled that desert not willing to drink of the fountains that God opened at your feet? Oh, have you not realized the truth that Jesus is sympathetic with bereavement? Did He not mourn at the grave of Lazarus, and will He not weep with all those who are mourning over the dead?

You may feel faint from your bereavements, and you may not know which way to turn, and all human solace may go for nothing; but if you would this night with your broken heart just go one step further forward, pressing through all the crowd of your perplexities, anxieties and sorrows, you might with one finger move His heart, and He would say, looking upon you with infinite comfort and compassion, "Who touched me?"

I remark that all our sins touch Him. It is generally the fact that we make a record only of those sins which are sins of the action; but where there is one sin of the action there are thousands of thought. Let us remember that God puts down in His book all the iniquitous thoughts that have ever gone through your souls. There they stand—the sins of 1820; the sins of 1825; all the sins of 1831; the sins of 1835; the sins of 1840; the sins of 1846; the sins of 1850; the sins of 1853; the sins of 1859; the sins of 1860; the sins of 1865; the sins of 1870; the sins of 1874. Oh, I can't think of it with any degree of composure. I should fly in terror did I not feel that those sins had been erased by the hand of my Lord Jesus Christ—that hand which was wounded for my transgression.

The snow falls on the Alps flake by flake, and day after day, and month after month, and after a while, at the touch of a traveler's foot, the avalanche slides down upon the villages with terrific crash and thunder. So the sins of our life accumulate and pile up, and after a while, unless we are rescued by the grace of our Lord Jesus, they will come down upon our souls in an avalanche of eternal ruin.

When we think of our sins, we are apt to think of those we have recently committed—those sins of the past day, or the past week, or the past year; those sins that have been in the far distance are all gone from our memory. You can't call a half dozen of them up in your mind. But God remembers every one of them. There is a record made of them. They will be your overthrow unless you somehow get them out of that book.

In the great day of judgment, God will call the roll, and they will all answer, "here!" "here!" "here!"

Oh, how they have wounded Jesus! Did He not come into this world to save us? Have not these sins been committed against the heart and mercy of our Lord Jesus? Sins committed against us by an enemy we can stand; but by a friend, how hard it is to bear! Have we not wounded the Lord Jesus Christ in the house of His friends?

Since we stood up in the presence of the great congregation and attested our love for Christ and said from this time we will serve the Lord, have we not all been recreant? Have we not gone astray like lost sheep, and there is no health in us? Oh, they touch Christ; they have touched Him on the tenderest spot of His heart.

Let us bemoan this treatment of our best friend. It seems to me Christ was never so lovely as He is now—the chief among ten thousand and the one altogether lovely. Why can't you come and put your trust in Him? He is an infinite Saviour. He can take all the iniquities of your life and cast them behind His back. Blessed is the man who has obtained His forgiveness, and whose sins are covered!

www.ingramcontent.com/pod-product-compliance
Lightning Source LLC
Chambersburg PA
CBHW030019240426
43672CB00007B/1017